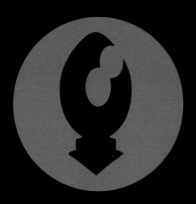

Created by
MIKE MIGNOLA

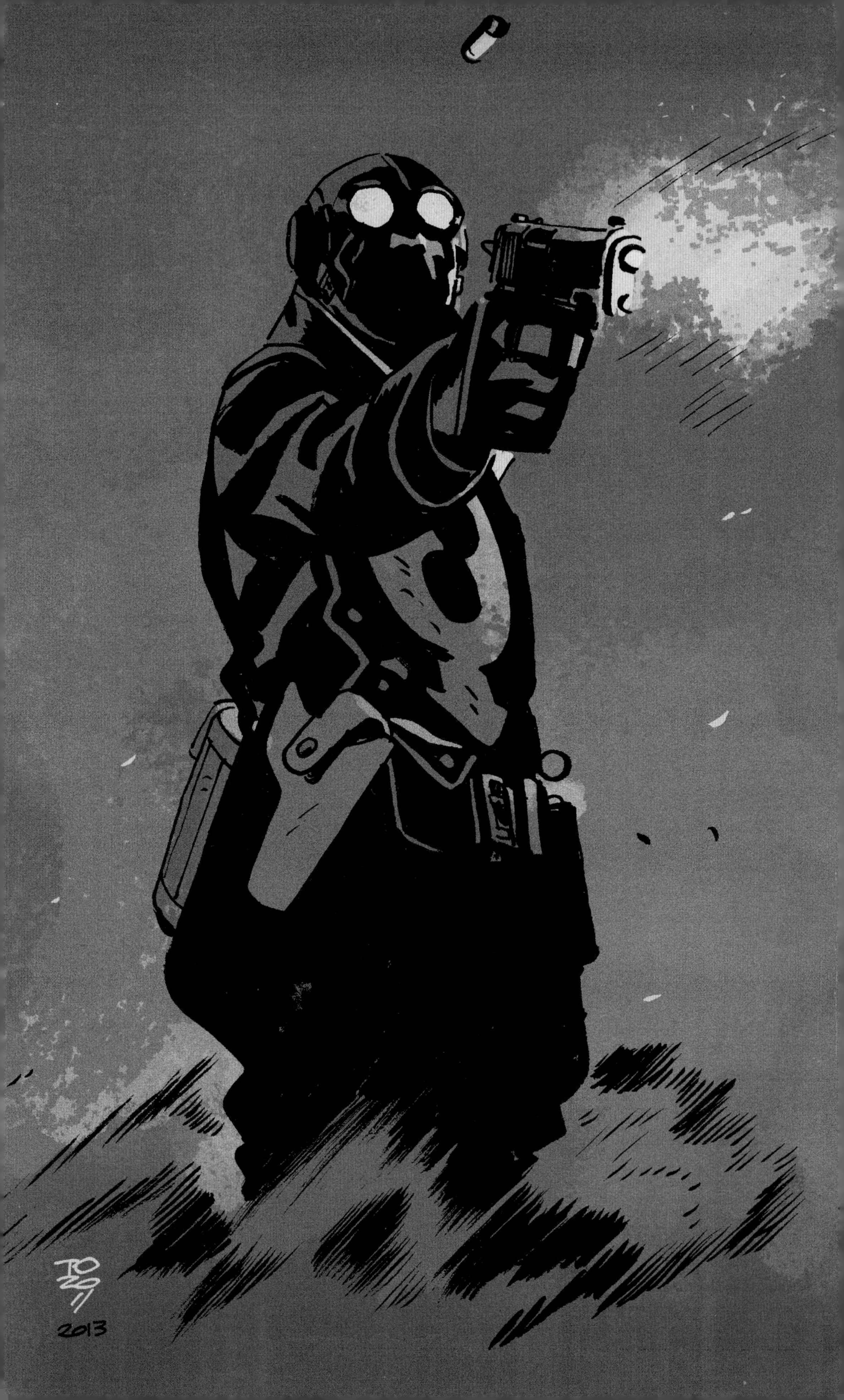
2013

LOBSTER JOHNSON™

GET THE LOBSTER

Story by
MIKE MIGNOLA *and* **JOHN ARCUDI**

Art by
TONCI ZONJIC

Colors by
DAVE STEWART

Letters by
CLEM ROBINS

Cover and Chapter Break Art by
TONCI ZONJIC

Editor *SCOTT ALLIE*

Associate Editor *DANIEL CHABON*

Assistant Editor *SHANTEL LAROCQUE*

Collection Designer *AMY ARENDTS*

Publisher *MIKE RICHARDSON*

DARK HORSE BOOKS

DarkHorse.com
Hellboy.com

Published by Dark Horse Books
A division of Dark Horse Comics, Inc.
10956 SE Main Street
Milwaukie, OR 97222

First edition: December 2014
ISBN 978-1-61655-505-4

1 3 5 7 9 10 8 6 4 2
Printed in China

This book collects *Lobster Johnson: Get the Lobster* #1–#5

CHAPTER ONE

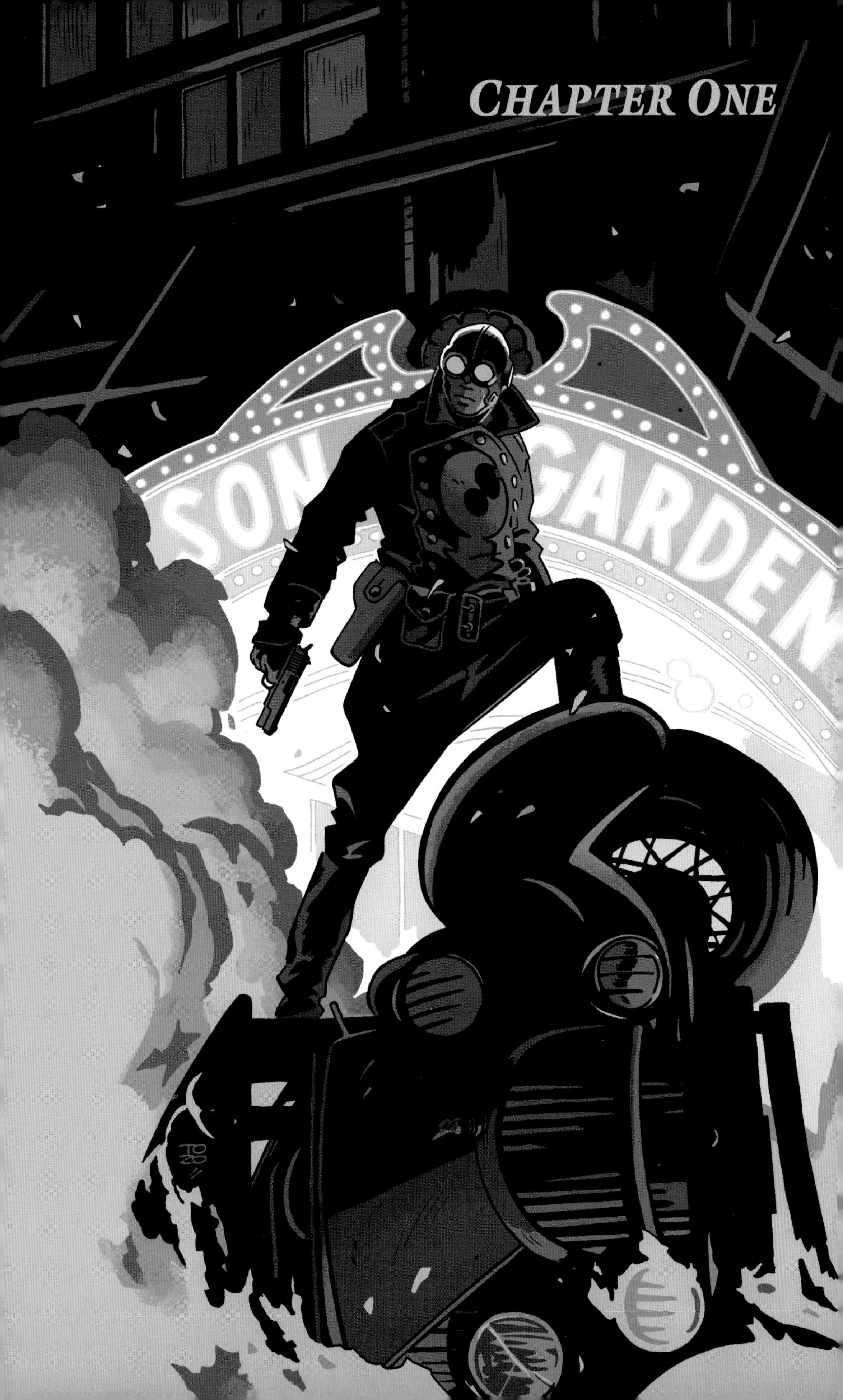
SON
GARDEN

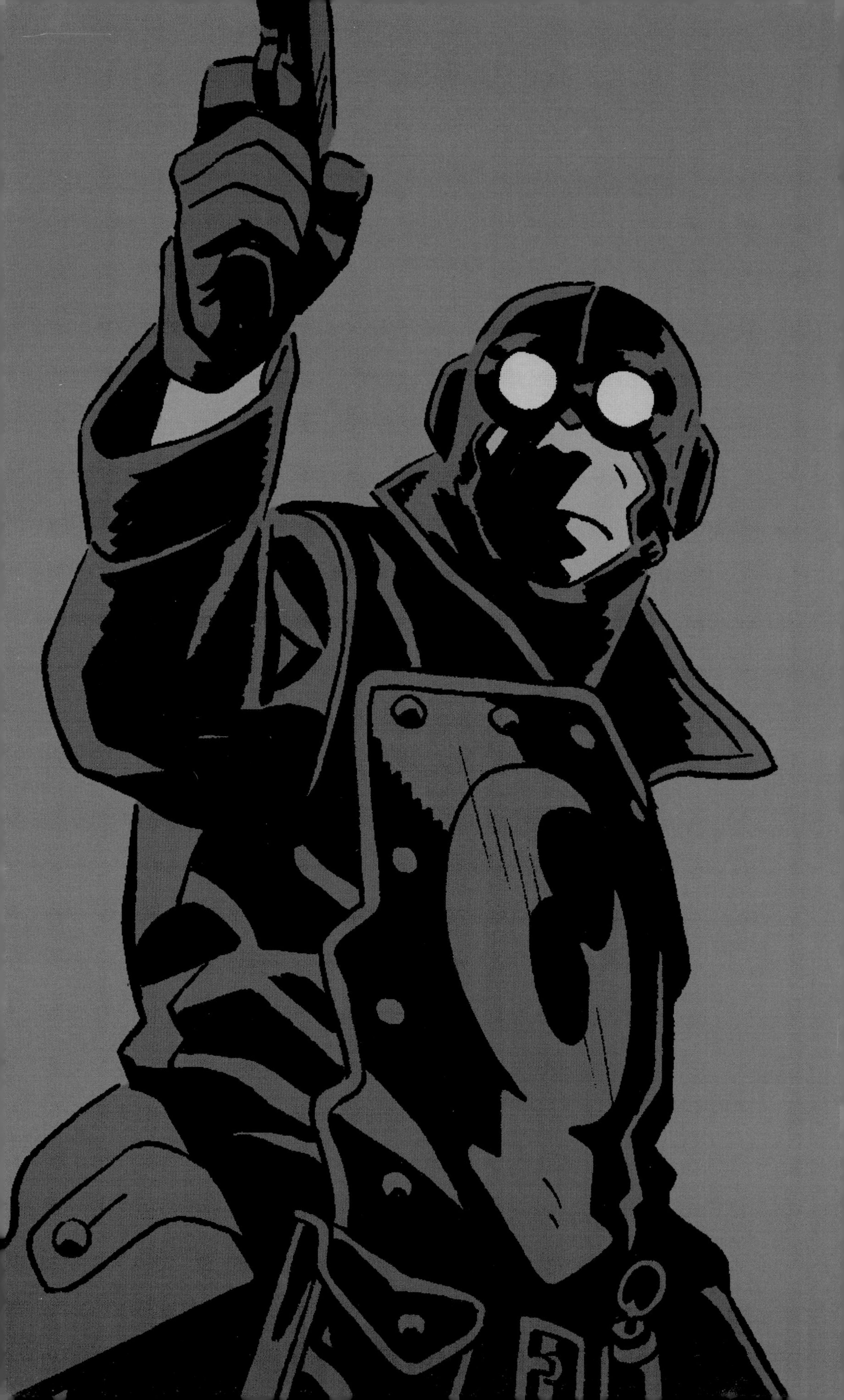

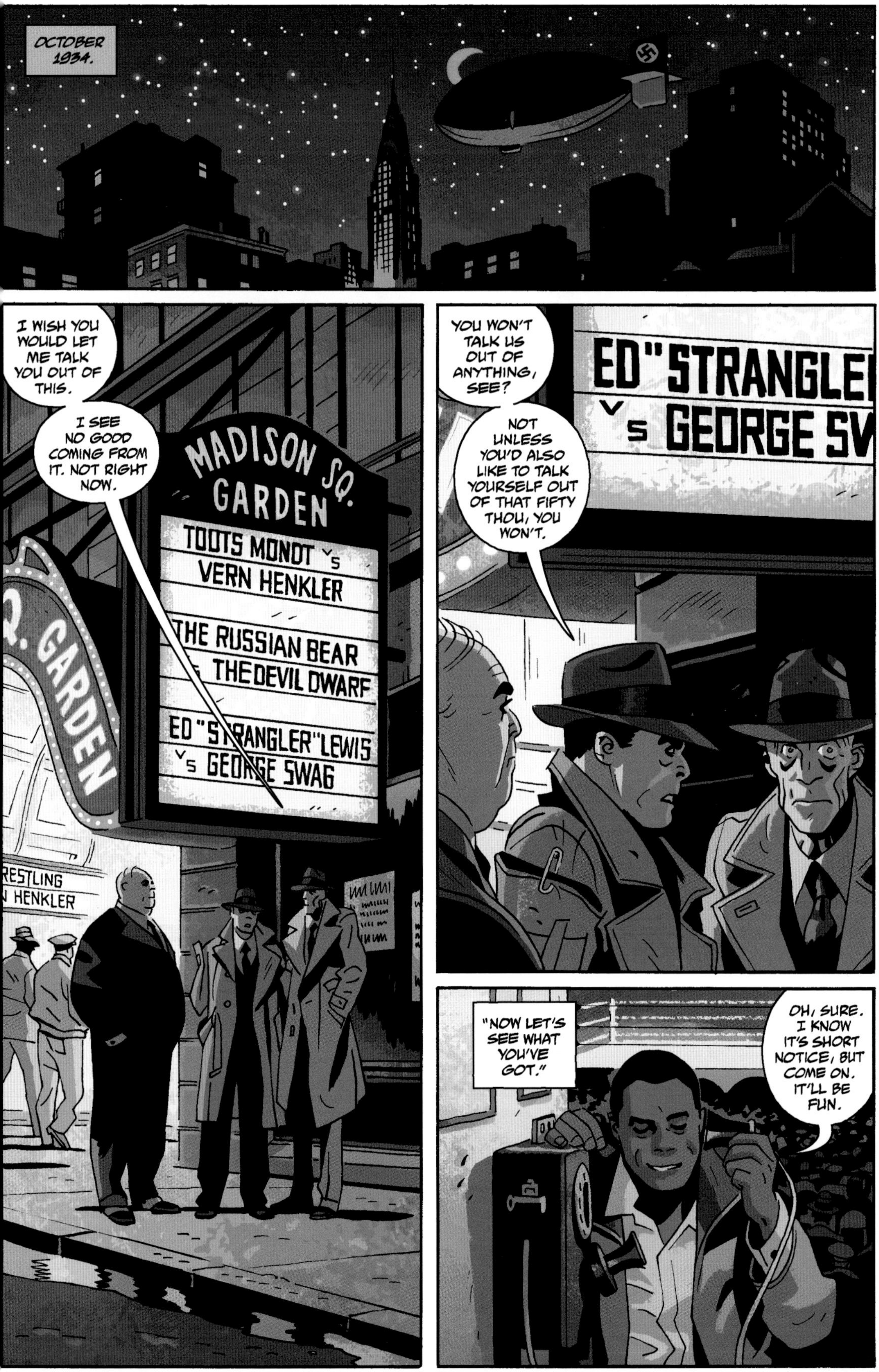

OCTOBER 1934.
I WISH YOU WOULD LET ME TALK YOU OUT OF THIS.
I SEE NO GOOD COMING FROM IT. NOT RIGHT NOW.
MADISON SQ. GARDEN
TOOTS MONDT VS VERN HENKLER
THE RUSSIAN BEAR VS THE DEVIL DWARF
ED "STRANGLER" LEWIS VS GEORGE SWAG
Q. GARDEN
RESTLING
N HENKLER
YOU WON'T TALK US OUT OF ANYTHING, SEE?
NOT UNLESS YOU'D ALSO LIKE TO TALK YOURSELF OUT OF THAT FIFTY THOU, YOU WON'T.
ED "STRANGLE
VS GEORGE SV
"NOW LET'S SEE WHAT YOU'VE GOT."
OH, SURE. I KNOW IT'S SHORT NOTICE, BUT COME ON. IT'LL BE FUN.

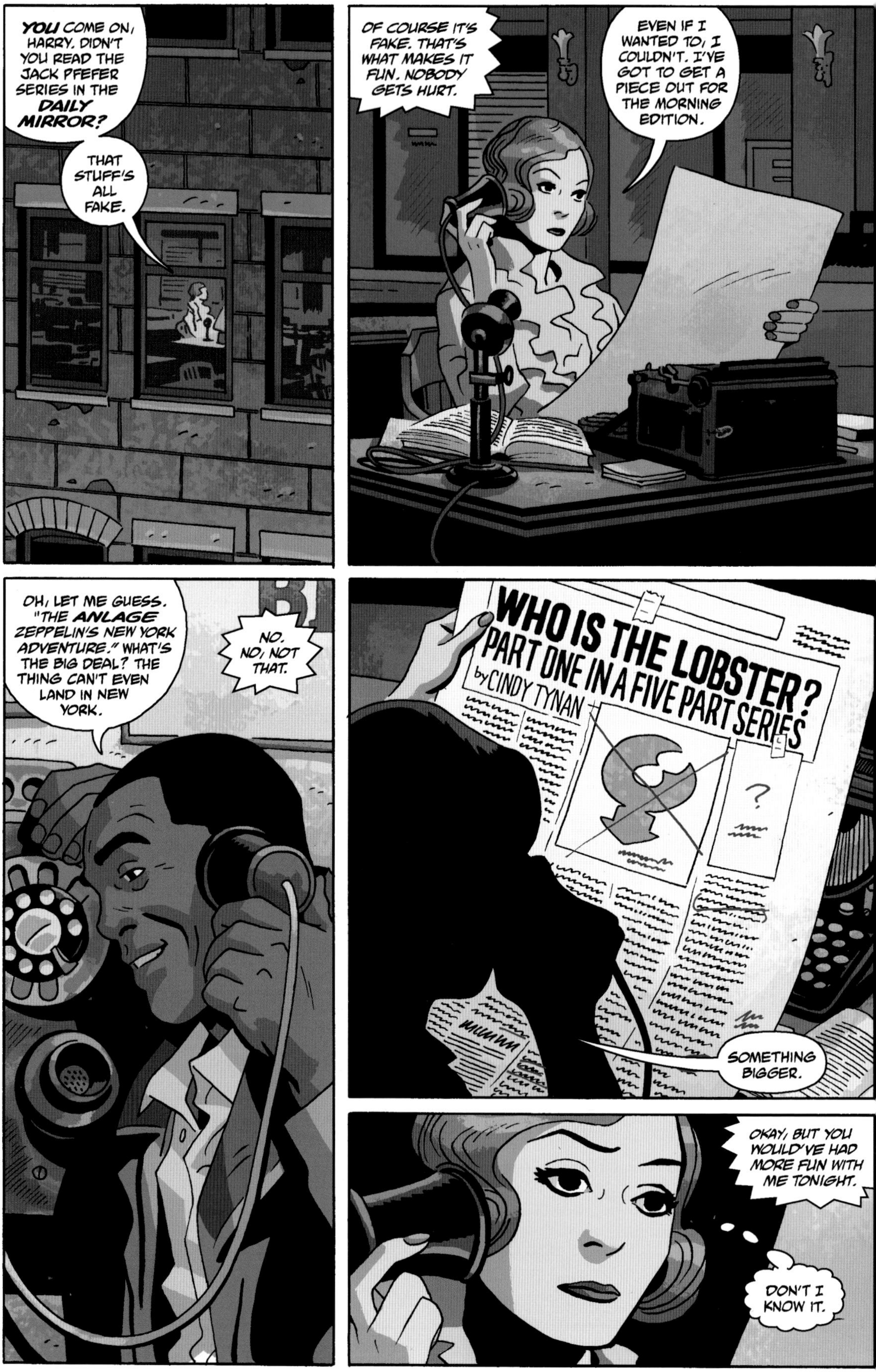

YOU COME ON, HARRY. DIDN'T YOU READ THE JACK PFEFER SERIES IN THE DAILY MIRROR?
THAT STUFF'S ALL FAKE.
OF COURSE IT'S FAKE. THAT'S WHAT MAKES IT FUN. NOBODY GETS HURT.
EVEN IF I WANTED TO, I COULDN'T. I'VE GOT TO GET A PIECE OUT FOR THE MORNING EDITION.
OH, LET ME GUESS. "THE ANLAGE ZEPPELIN'S NEW YORK ADVENTURE." WHAT'S THE BIG DEAL? THE THING CAN'T EVEN LAND IN NEW YORK.
NO. NO, NOT THAT.
WHO IS THE LOBSTER?
PART ONE IN A FIVE PART SERIES
by CINDY TYNAN
SOMETHING BIGGER.
OKAY, BUT YOU WOULD'VE HAD MORE FUN WITH ME TONIGHT.
DON'T I KNOW IT.

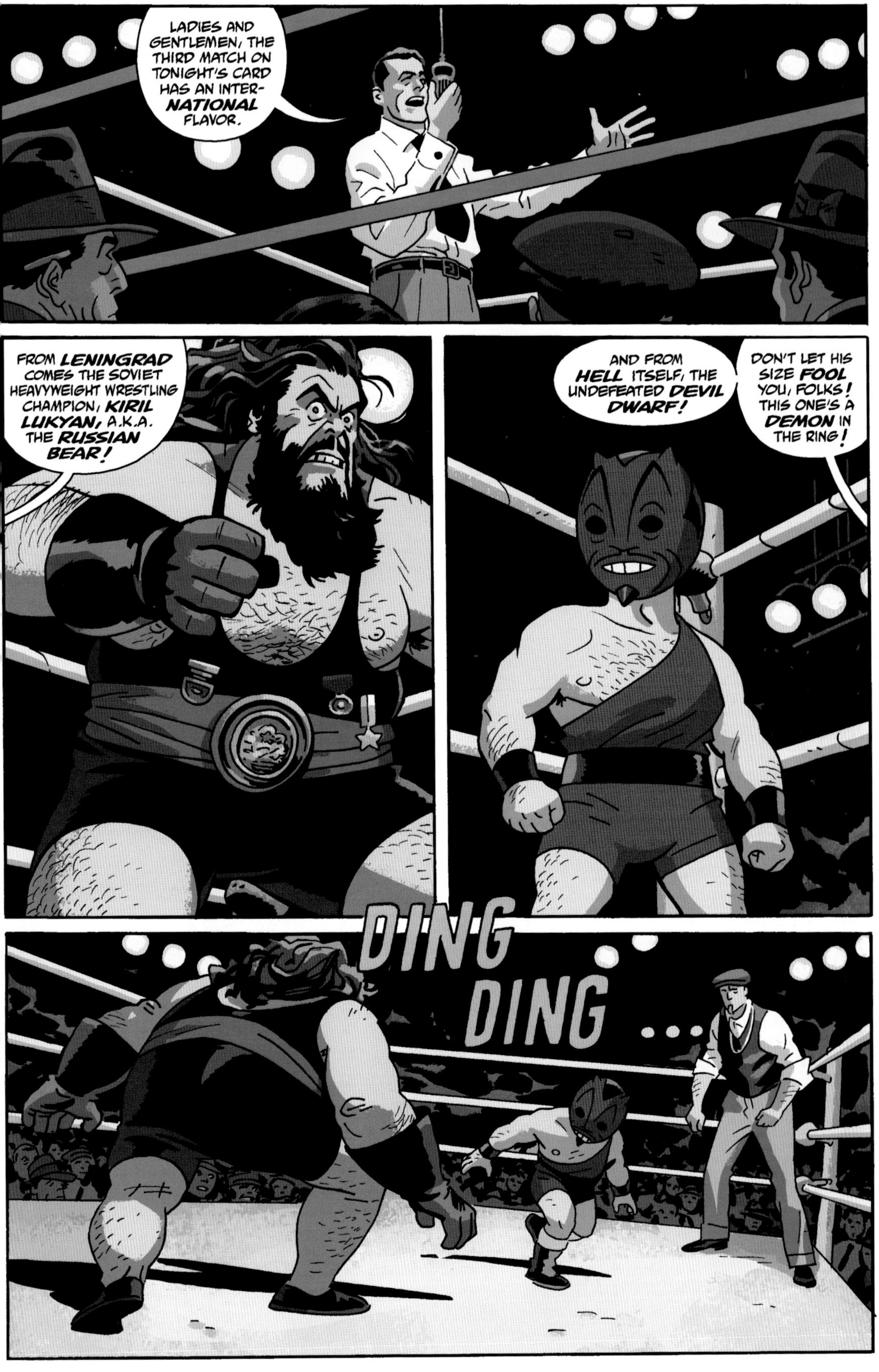

LADIES AND GENTLEMEN, THE THIRD MATCH ON TONIGHT'S CARD HAS AN INTER-NATIONAL FLAVOR.
FROM LENINGRAD COMES THE SOVIET HEAVYWEIGHT WRESTLING CHAMPION, KIRIL LUKYAN, A.K.A. THE RUSSIAN BEAR!
AND FROM HELL ITSELF, THE UNDEFEATED DEVIL DWARF!
DON'T LET HIS SIZE FOOL YOU, FOLKS! THIS ONE'S A DEMON IN THE RING!
DING
DING ...

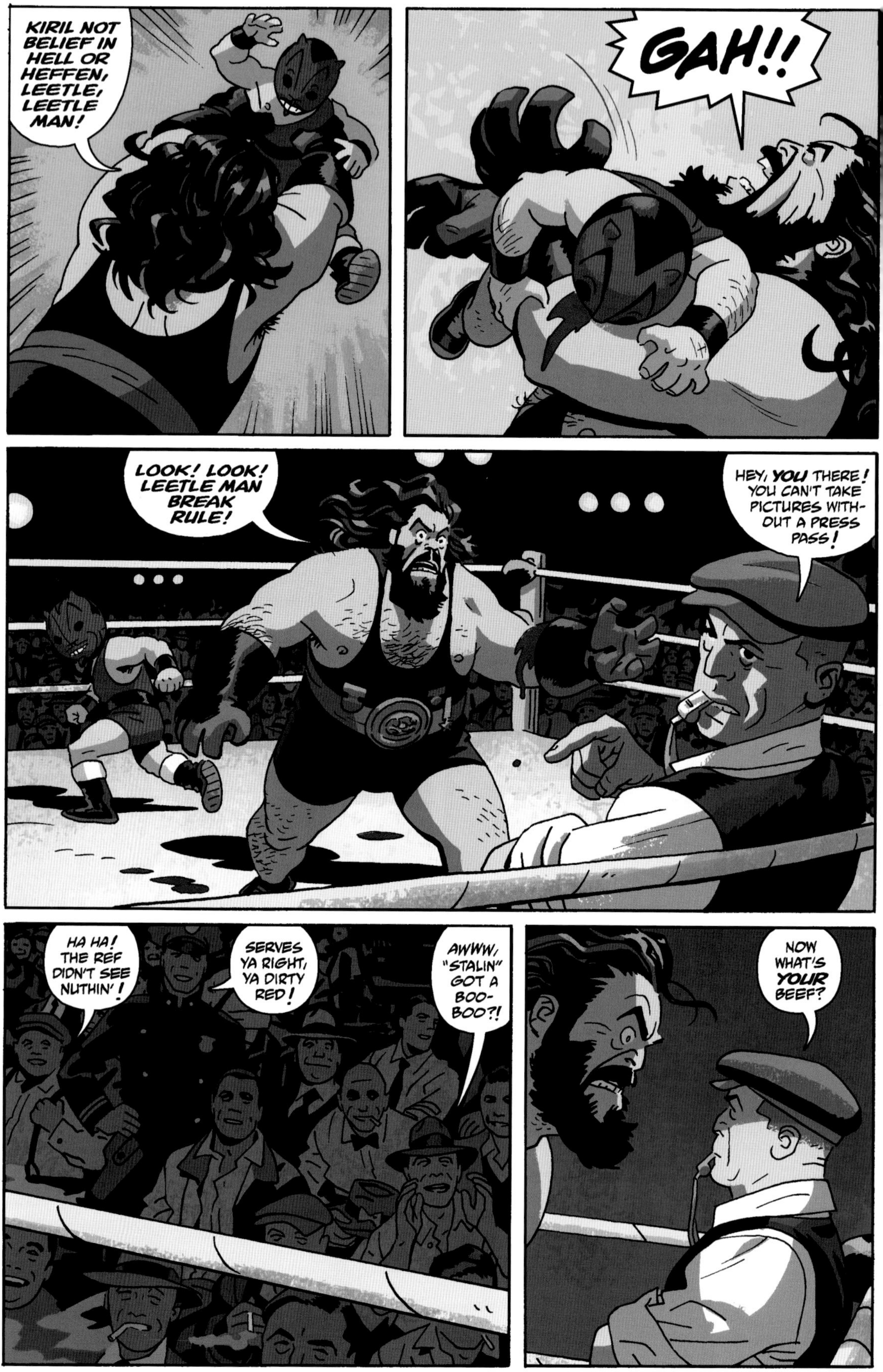
KIRIL NOT BELIEF IN HELL OR HEFFEN, LEETLE, LEETLE MAN!
GAH!!
LOOK! LOOK! LEETLE MAN BREAK RULE!
HEY, YOU THERE! YOU CAN'T TAKE PICTURES WITH-OUT A PRESS PASS!
HA HA! THE REF DIDN'T SEE NUTHIN'!
SERVES YA RIGHT, YA DIRTY RED!
AWWW, "STALIN" GOT A BOO-BOO?!
NOW WHAT'S YOUR BEEF?

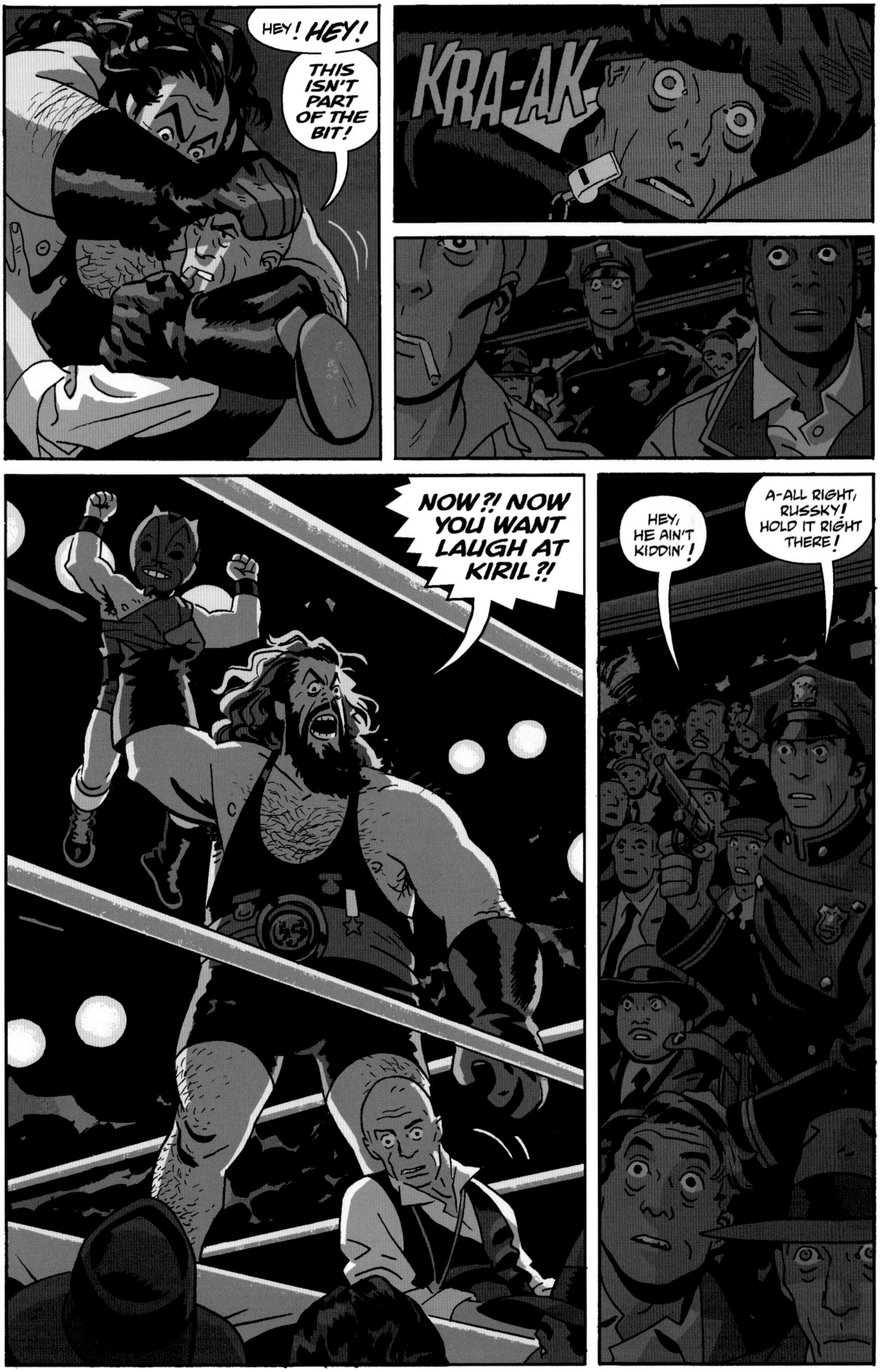
HEY! HEY!
THIS ISN'T PART OF THE BIT!
KRA-AK
NOW?! NOW YOU WANT LAUGH AT KIRIL?!
HEY, HE AIN'T KIDDIN'!
A-ALL RIGHT, RUSSKY! HOLD IT RIGHT THERE!

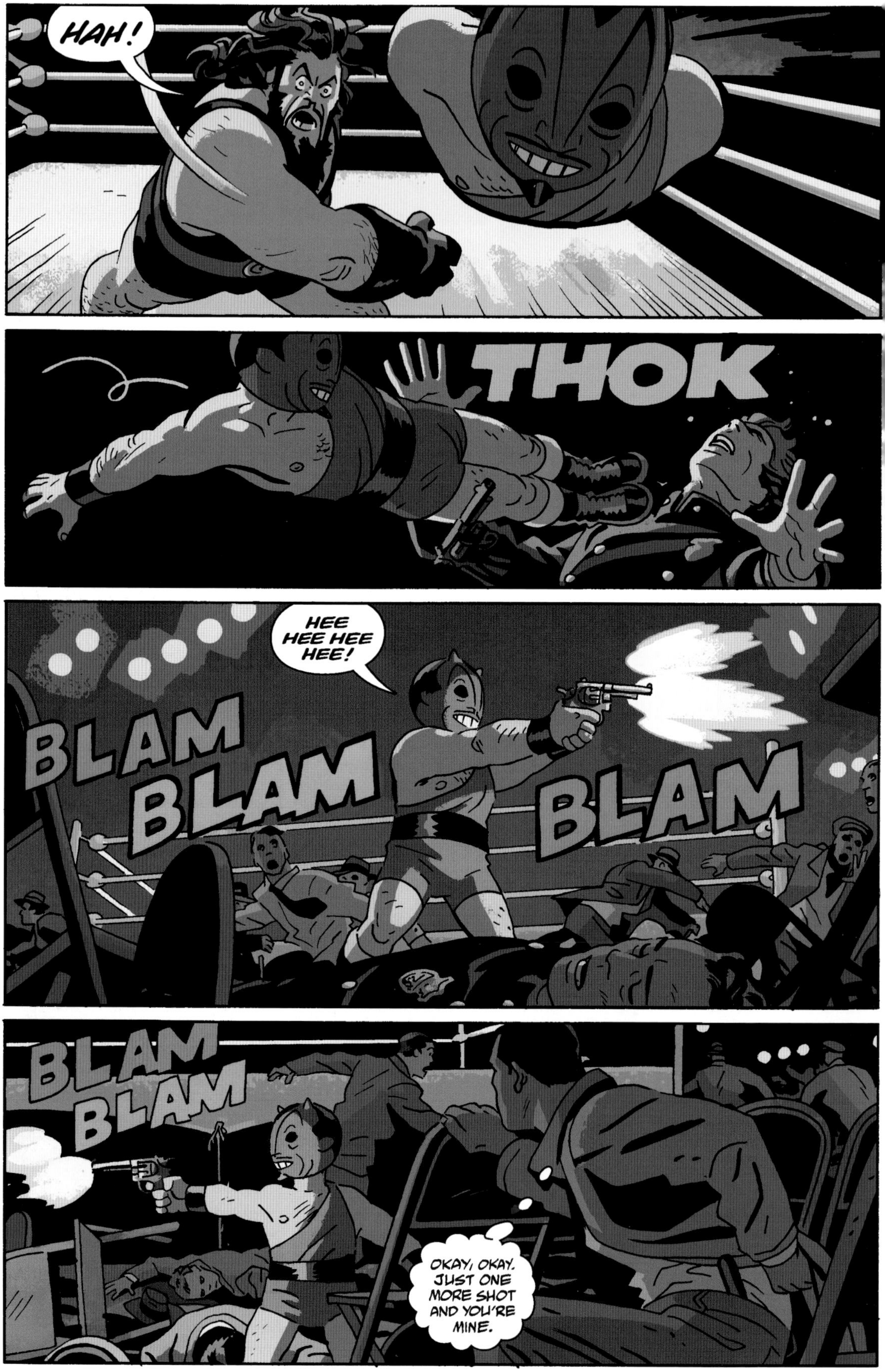

HAH!
THOK
HEE HEE HEE HEE!
BLAM
BLAM
BLAM
BLAM
BLAM
OKAY, OKAY. JUST ONE MORE SHOT AND YOU'RE MINE.

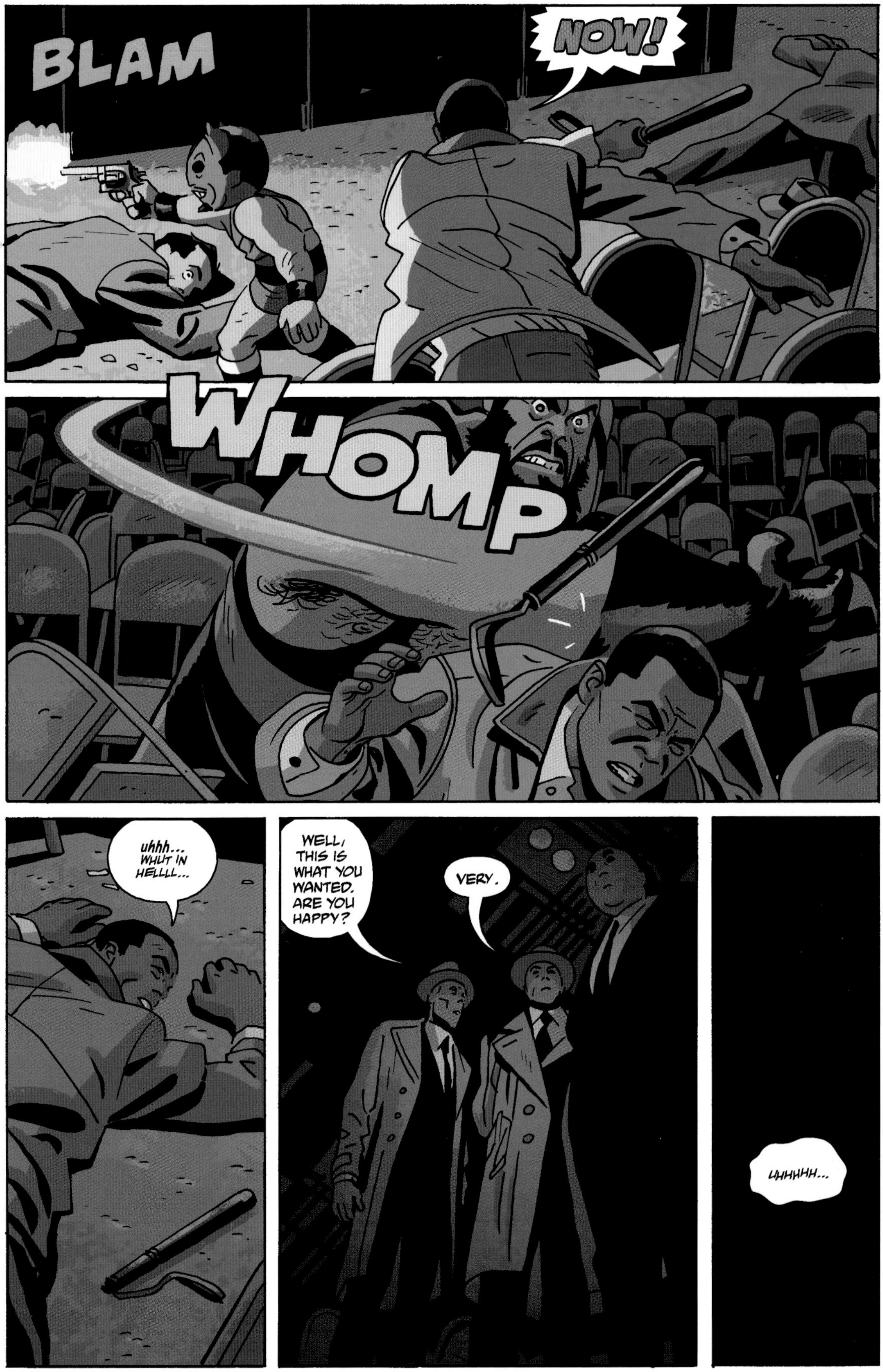
BLAM
NOW!
WHOMP
uhhh... WHUT IN HELLLL...
WELL, THIS IS WHAT YOU WANTED. ARE YOU HAPPY?
VERY.
UHHHHH...

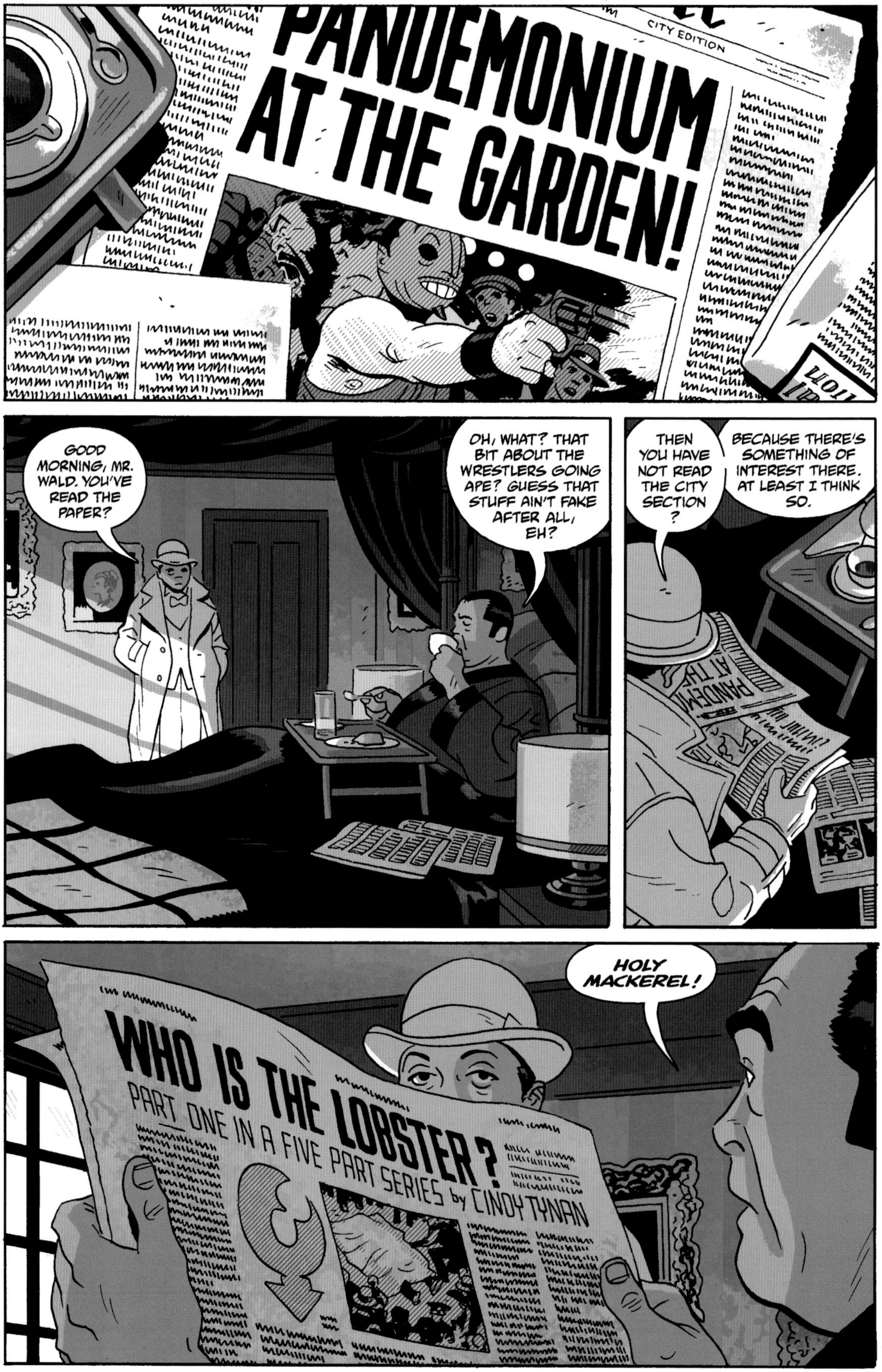

PANDEMONIUM AT THE GARDEN!
CITY EDITION
GOOD MORNING, MR. WALD. YOU'VE READ THE PAPER?
OH, WHAT? THAT BIT ABOUT THE WRESTLERS GOING APE? GUESS THAT STUFF AIN'T FAKE AFTER ALL, EH?
THEN YOU HAVE NOT READ THE CITY SECTION?
BECAUSE THERE'S SOMETHING OF INTEREST THERE. AT LEAST I THINK SO.
HOLY MACKEREL!
WHO IS THE LOBSTER?
PART ONE IN A FIVE PART SERIES by CINDY TYNAN

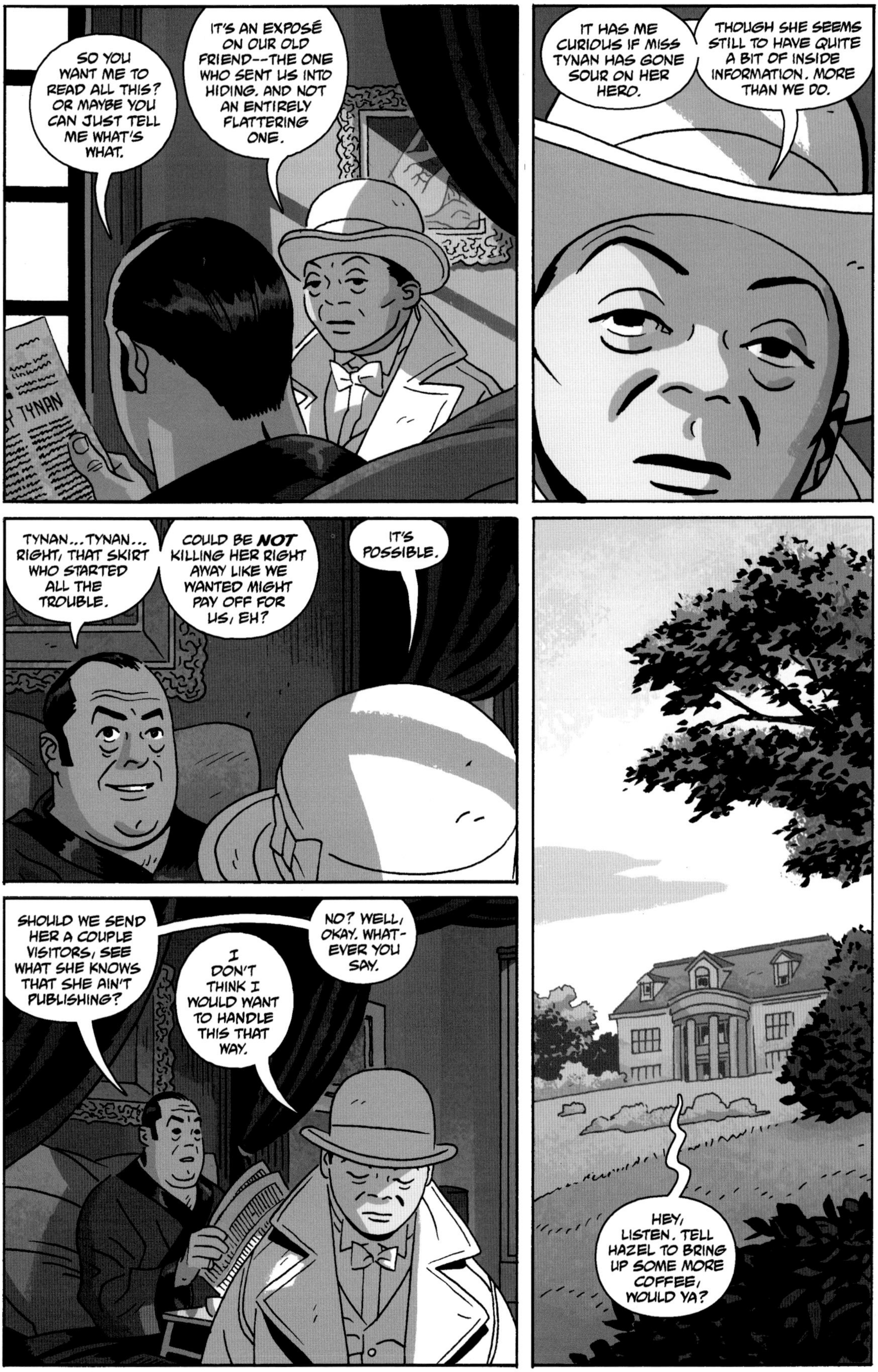
SO YOU WANT ME TO READ ALL THIS? OR MAYBE YOU CAN JUST TELL ME WHAT'S WHAT.
IT'S AN EXPOSÉ ON OUR OLD FRIEND--THE ONE WHO SENT US INTO HIDING. AND NOT AN ENTIRELY FLATTERING ONE.
TYNAN
IT HAS ME CURIOUS IF MISS TYNAN HAS GONE SOUR ON HER HERO.
THOUGH SHE SEEMS STILL TO HAVE QUITE A BIT OF INSIDE INFORMATION. MORE THAN WE DO.
TYNAN... TYNAN... RIGHT, THAT SKIRT WHO STARTED ALL THE TROUBLE.
COULD BE **NOT** KILLING HER RIGHT AWAY LIKE WE WANTED MIGHT PAY OFF FOR US, EH?
IT'S POSSIBLE.
SHOULD WE SEND HER A COUPLE VISITORS, SEE WHAT SHE KNOWS THAT SHE AIN'T PUBLISHING?
I DON'T THINK I WOULD WANT TO HANDLE THIS THAT WAY.
NO? WELL, OKAY. WHATEVER YOU SAY.
HEY, LISTEN. TELL HAZEL TO BRING UP SOME MORE COFFEE, WOULD YA?

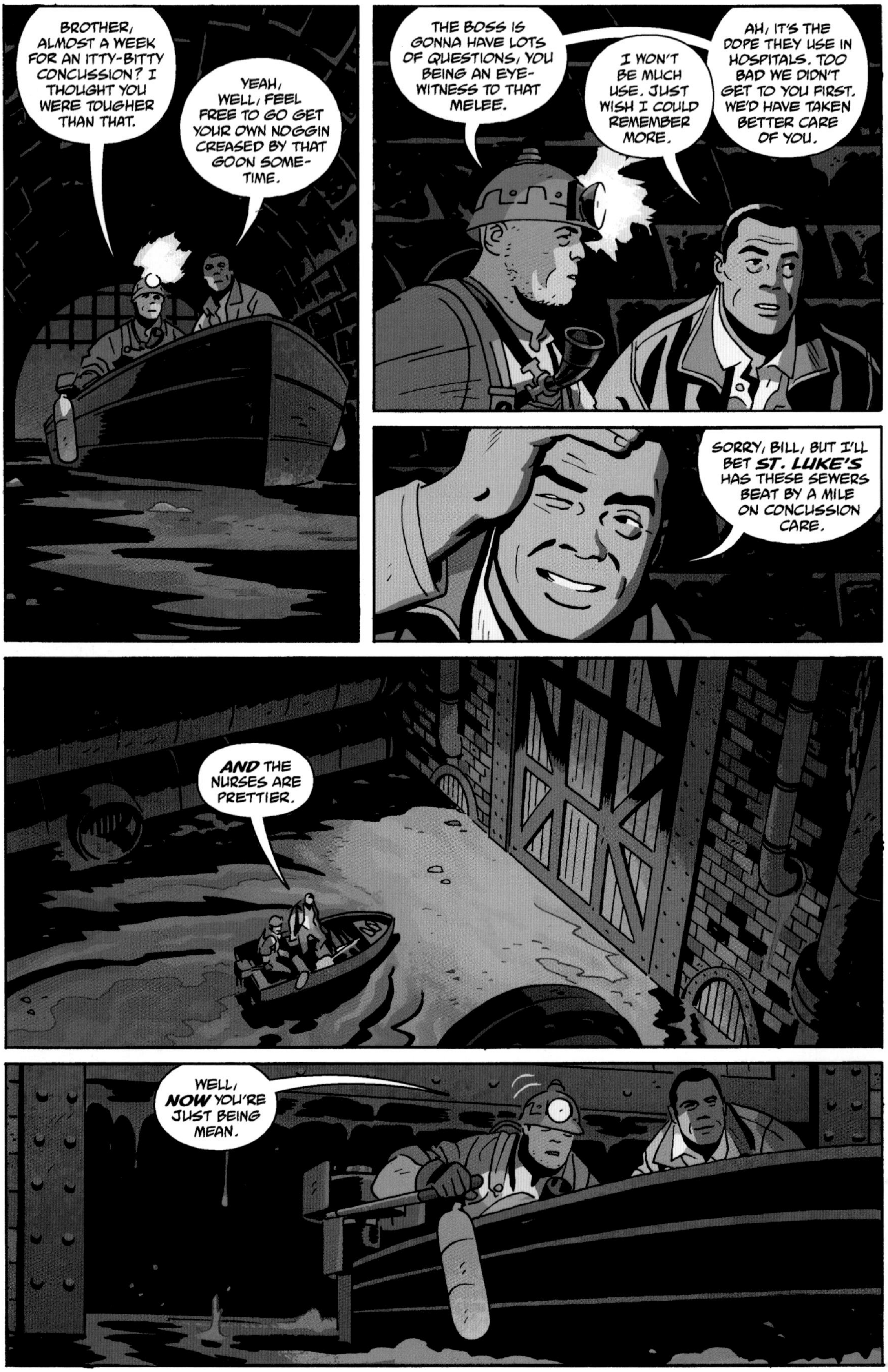
BROTHER, ALMOST A WEEK FOR AN ITTY-BITTY CONCUSSION? I THOUGHT YOU WERE TOUGHER THAN THAT.
YEAH, WELL, FEEL FREE TO GO GET YOUR OWN NOGGIN CREASED BY THAT GOON SOME-TIME.
THE BOSS IS GONNA HAVE LOTS OF QUESTIONS, YOU BEING AN EYE-WITNESS TO THAT MELEE.
I WON'T BE MUCH USE. JUST WISH I COULD REMEMBER MORE.
AH, IT'S THE DOPE THEY USE IN HOSPITALS. TOO BAD WE DIDN'T GET TO YOU FIRST. WE'D HAVE TAKEN BETTER CARE OF YOU.
SORRY, BILL, BUT I'LL BET ST. LUKE'S HAS THESE SEWERS BEAT BY A MILE ON CONCUSSION CARE.
AND THE NURSES ARE PRETTIER.
WELL, NOW YOU'RE JUST BEING MEAN.

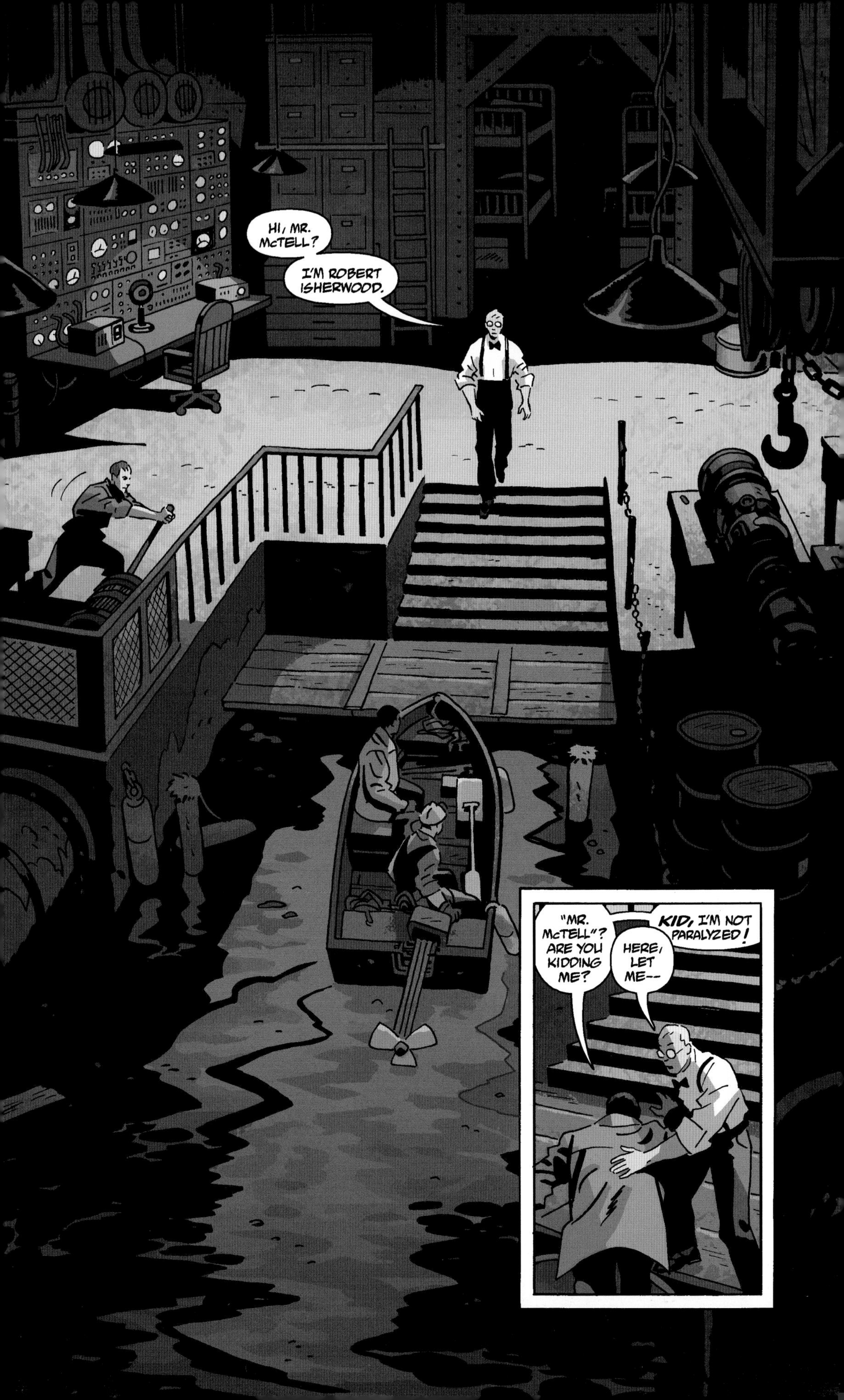
HI, MR. McTELL?
I'M ROBERT ISHERWOOD.
"MR. McTELL"? ARE YOU KIDDING ME?
HERE, LET ME--
KID, I'M NOT PARALYZED!

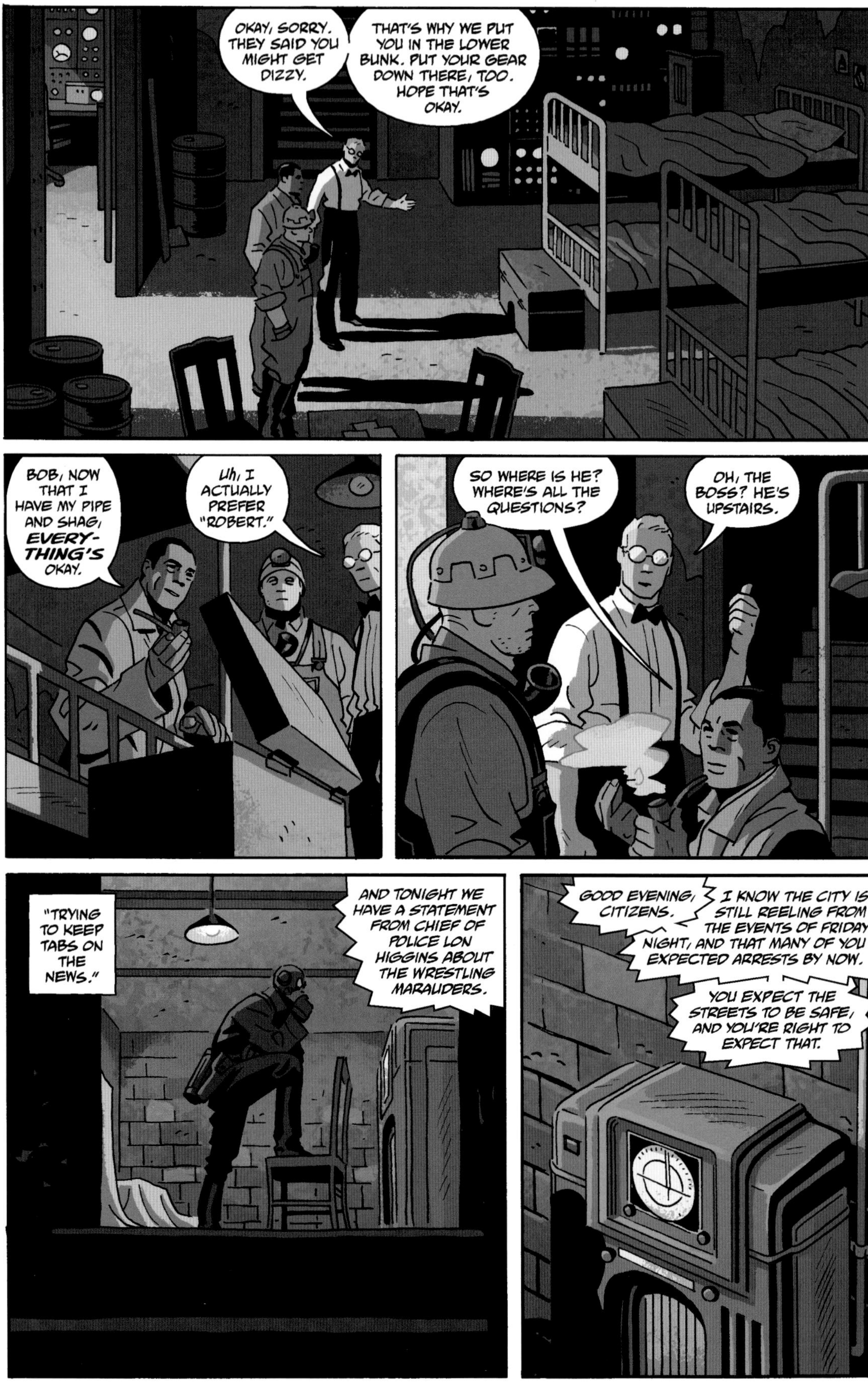
OKAY, SORRY. THEY SAID YOU MIGHT GET DIZZY.
THAT'S WHY WE PUT YOU IN THE LOWER BUNK. PUT YOUR GEAR DOWN THERE, TOO. HOPE THAT'S OKAY.
BOB, NOW THAT I HAVE MY PIPE AND SHAG, EVERY-THING'S OKAY.
UH, I ACTUALLY PREFER "ROBERT."
SO WHERE IS HE? WHERE'S ALL THE QUESTIONS?
OH, THE BOSS? HE'S UPSTAIRS.
"TRYING TO KEEP TABS ON THE NEWS."
AND TONIGHT WE HAVE A STATEMENT FROM CHIEF OF POLICE LON HIGGINS ABOUT THE WRESTLING MARAUDERS.
GOOD EVENING, CITIZENS.
I KNOW THE CITY IS STILL REELING FROM THE EVENTS OF FRIDAY NIGHT, AND THAT MANY OF YOU EXPECTED ARRESTS BY NOW.
YOU EXPECT THE STREETS TO BE SAFE, AND YOU'RE RIGHT TO EXPECT THAT.

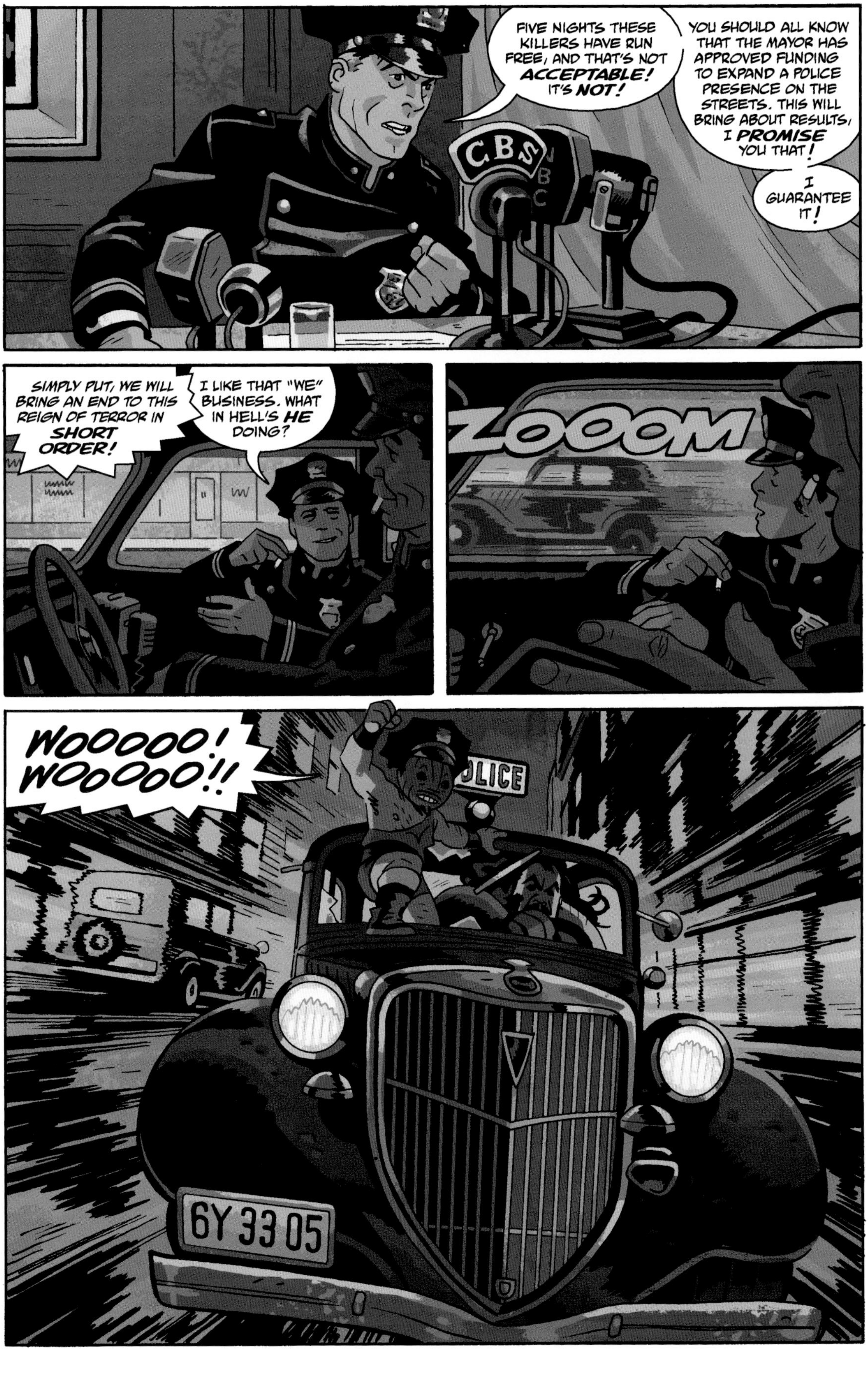
FIVE NIGHTS THESE KILLERS HAVE RUN FREE, AND THAT'S NOT ACCEPTABLE! IT'S NOT!
YOU SHOULD ALL KNOW THAT THE MAYOR HAS APPROVED FUNDING TO EXPAND A POLICE PRESENCE ON THE STREETS. THIS WILL BRING ABOUT RESULTS, I PROMISE YOU THAT!
I GUARANTEE IT!
CBS
NBC
SIMPLY PUT, WE WILL BRING AN END TO THIS REIGN OF TERROR IN SHORT ORDER!
I LIKE THAT "WE" BUSINESS. WHAT IN HELL'S HE DOING?
ZOOOM
WOOOOO! WOOOOO!!
POLICE
6Y 33 05

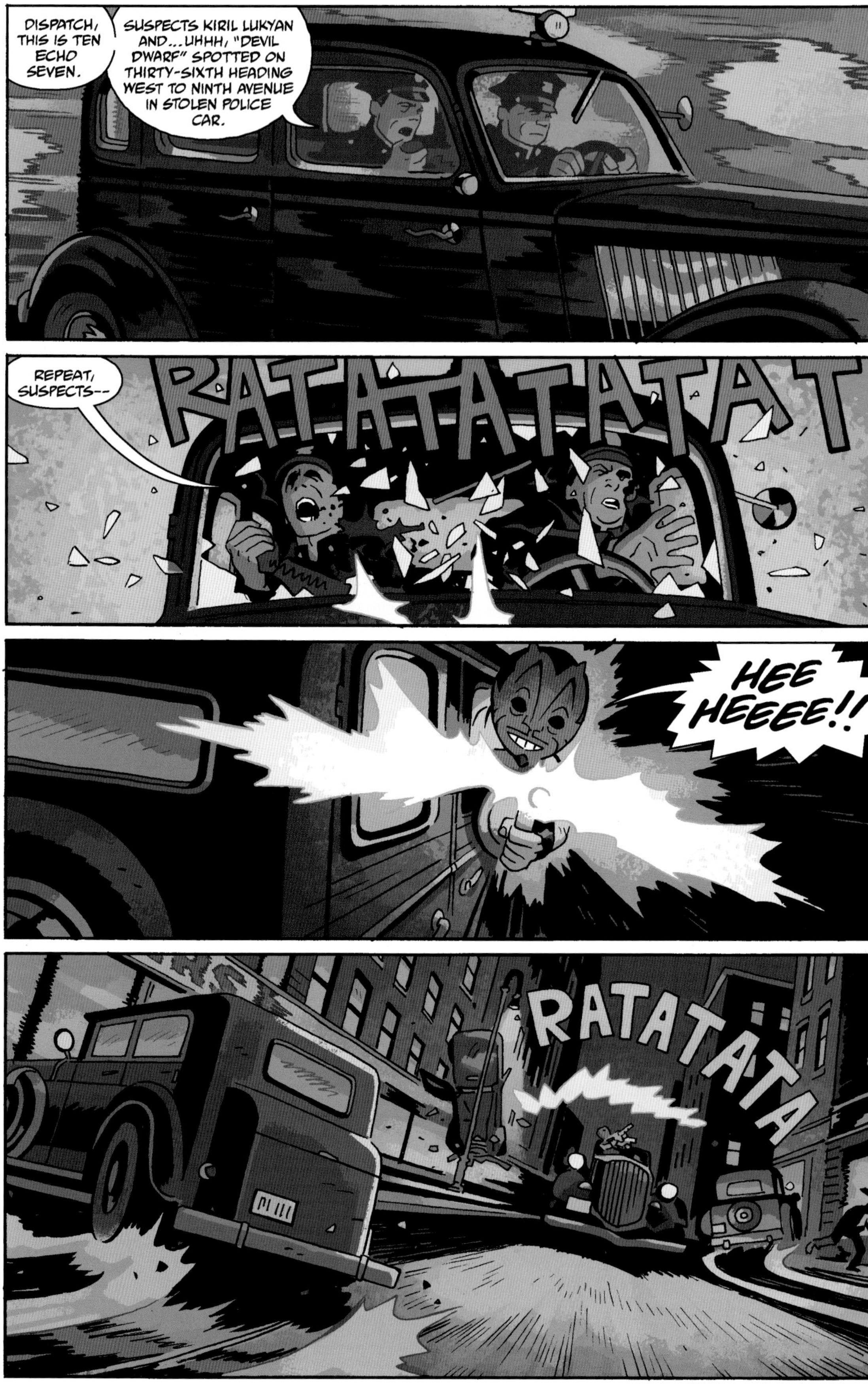
DISPATCH, THIS IS TEN ECHO SEVEN.
SUSPECTS KIRIL LUKYAN AND...UHHH, "DEVIL DWARF" SPOTTED ON THIRTY-SIXTH HEADING WEST TO NINTH AVENUE IN STOLEN POLICE CAR.
REPEAT, SUSPECTS--
RATATATATAT
HEE HEEEEE!!
RATATATA

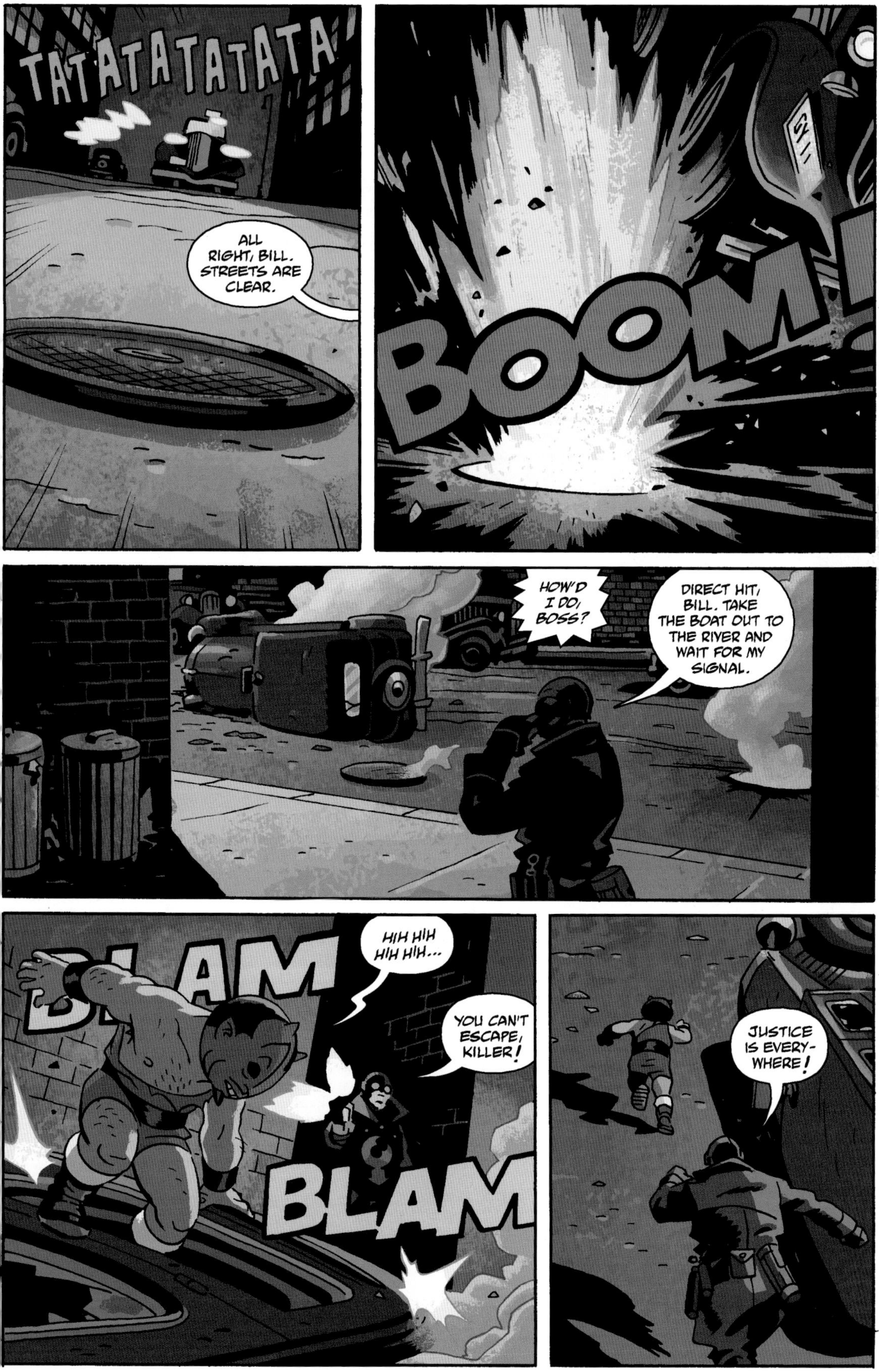
TATATATATATA
ALL RIGHT, BILL. STREETS ARE CLEAR.
BOOM!
HOW'D I DO, BOSS?
DIRECT HIT, BILL. TAKE THE BOAT OUT TO THE RIVER AND WAIT FOR MY SIGNAL.
BLAM
HIH HIH HIH HIH...
YOU CAN'T ESCAPE, KILLER!
BLAM
JUSTICE IS EVERY-WHERE!

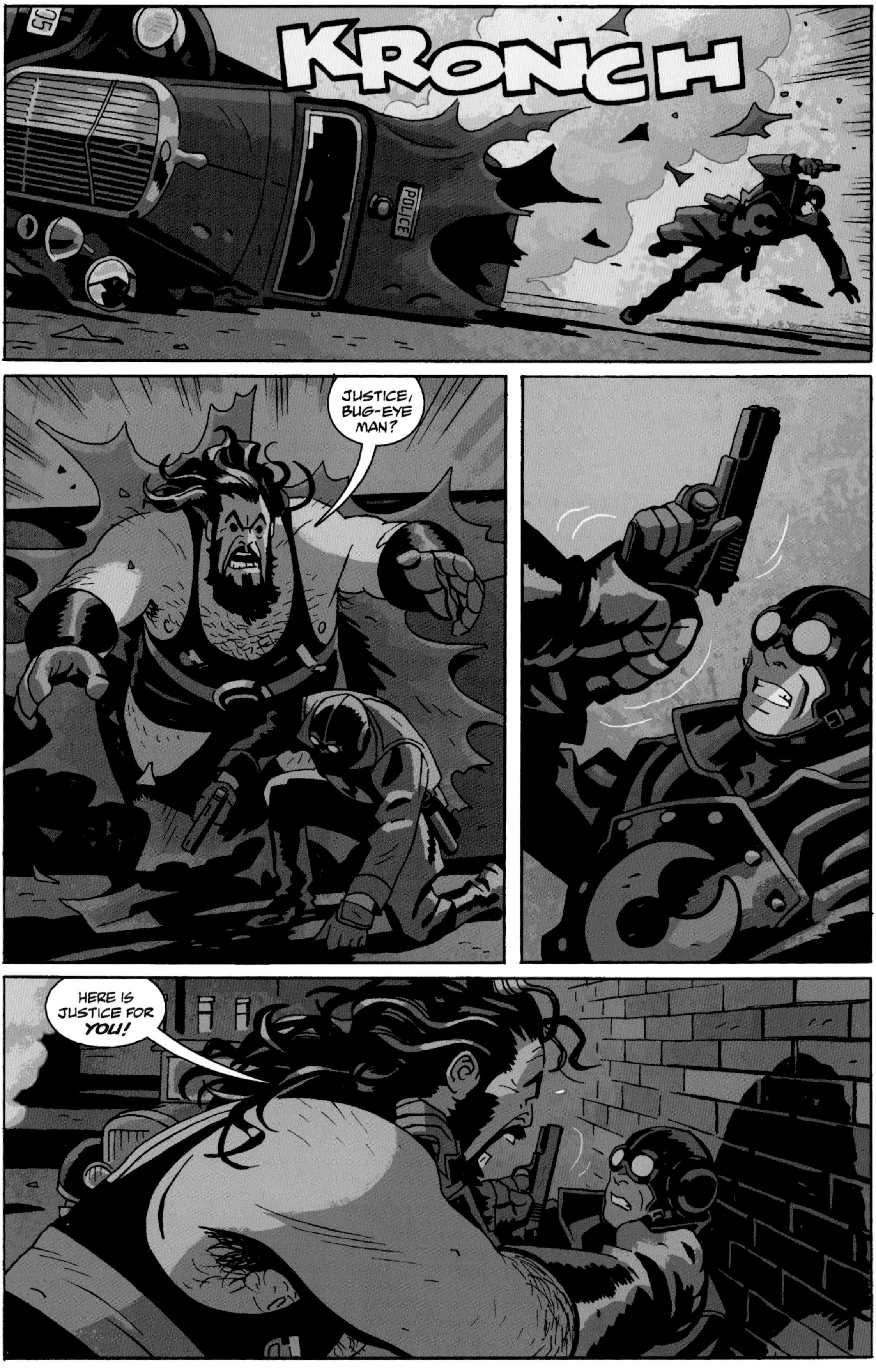
KRONCH
05
POLICE
JUSTICE, BUG-EYE MAN?
HERE IS JUSTICE FOR *YOU!*

UHF!

BLAM
BLAM

BUG-EYE STING LIKE BUG! LEETLE BUG!

BAM

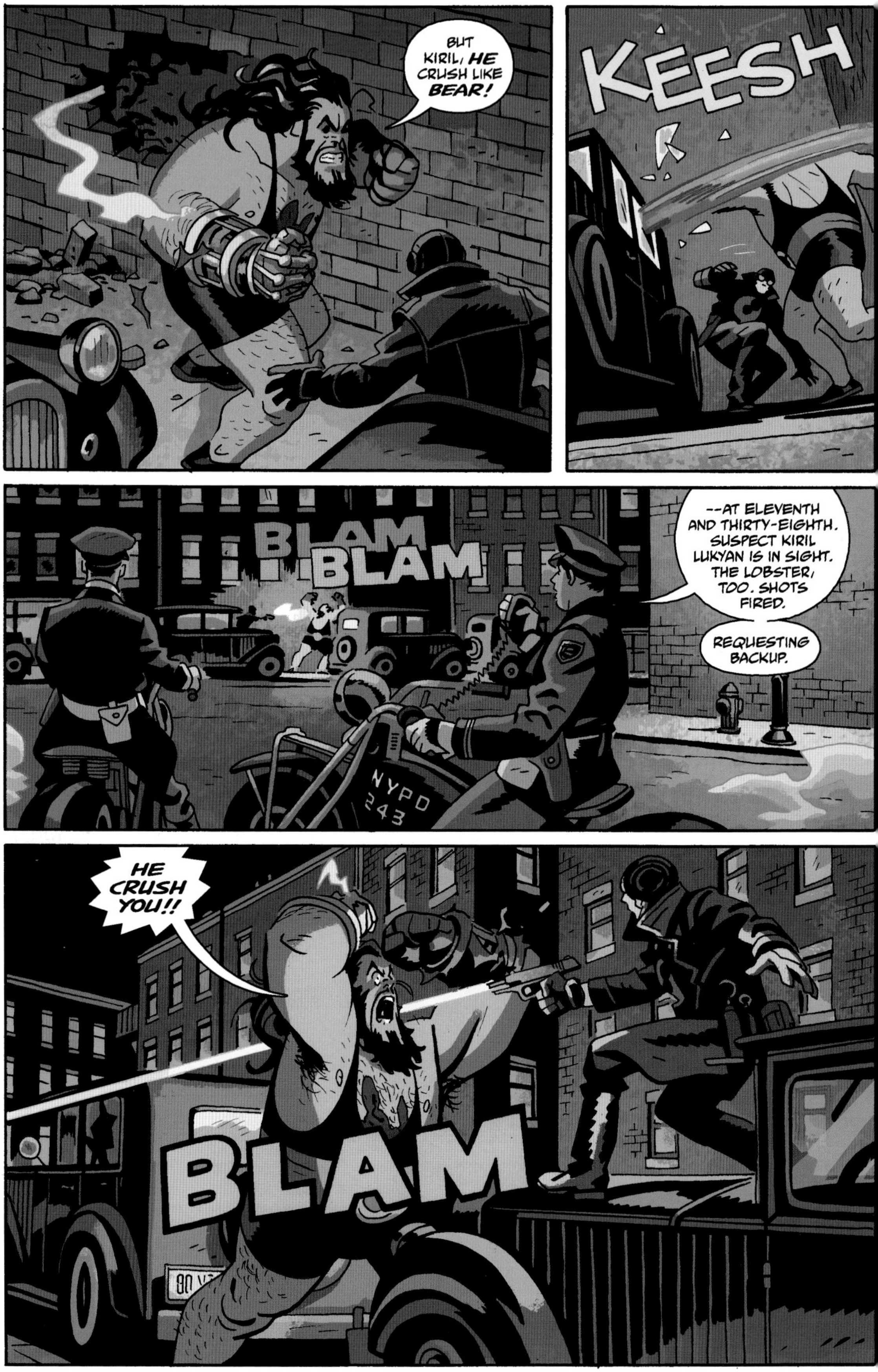
BUT KIRIL, HE CRUSH LIKE BEAR!
KEESH
BLAM
BLAM
--AT ELEVENTH AND THIRTY-EIGHTH. SUSPECT KIRIL LUKYAN IS IN SIGHT. THE LOBSTER, TOO. SHOTS FIRED.
REQUESTING BACKUP.
NYPD 243
HE CRUSH YOU!!
BLAM

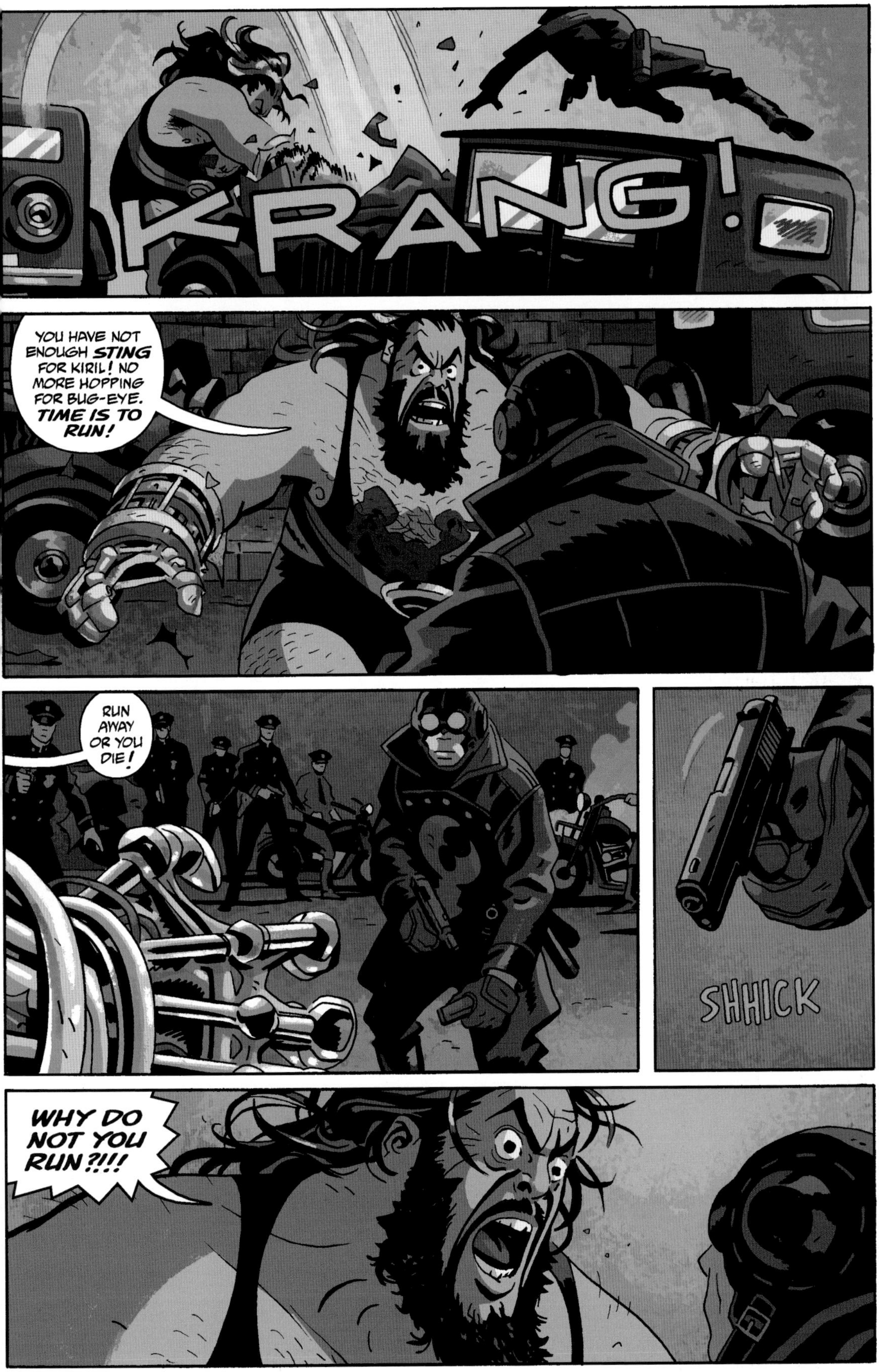
KRANG!
YOU HAVE NOT ENOUGH STING FOR KIRIL! NO MORE HOPPING FOR BUG-EYE. TIME IS TO RUN!
RUN AWAY OR YOU DIE!
SHHICK
WHY DO NOT YOU RUN?!!!

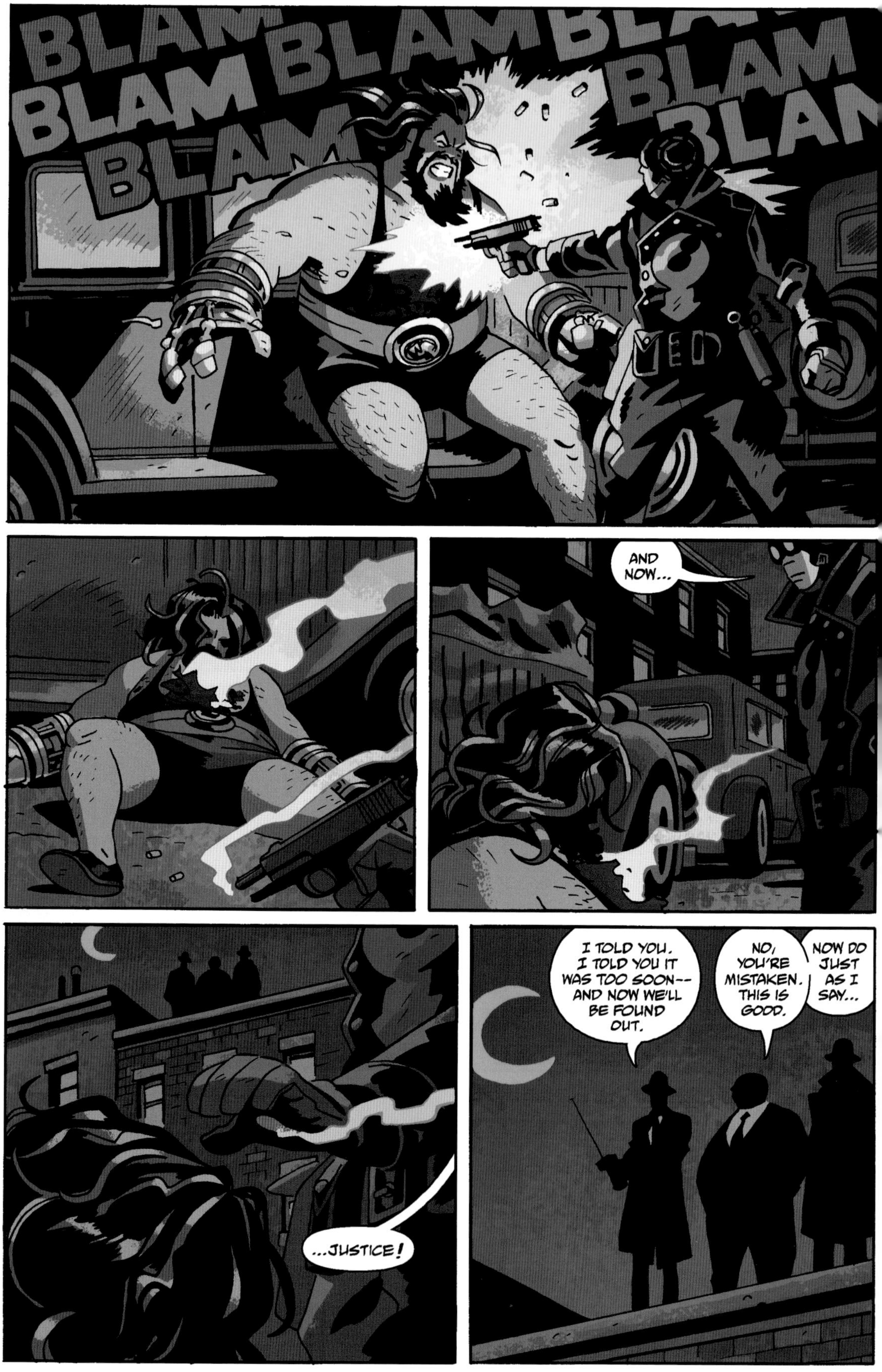
BLAM BLAM BLAM BLAM BLAM BLAM BLAM BLAM
AND NOW...
...JUSTICE!
I TOLD YOU. I TOLD YOU IT WAS TOO SOON-- AND NOW WE'LL BE FOUND OUT.
NO, YOU'RE MISTAKEN. THIS IS GOOD.
NOW DO JUST AS I SAY...

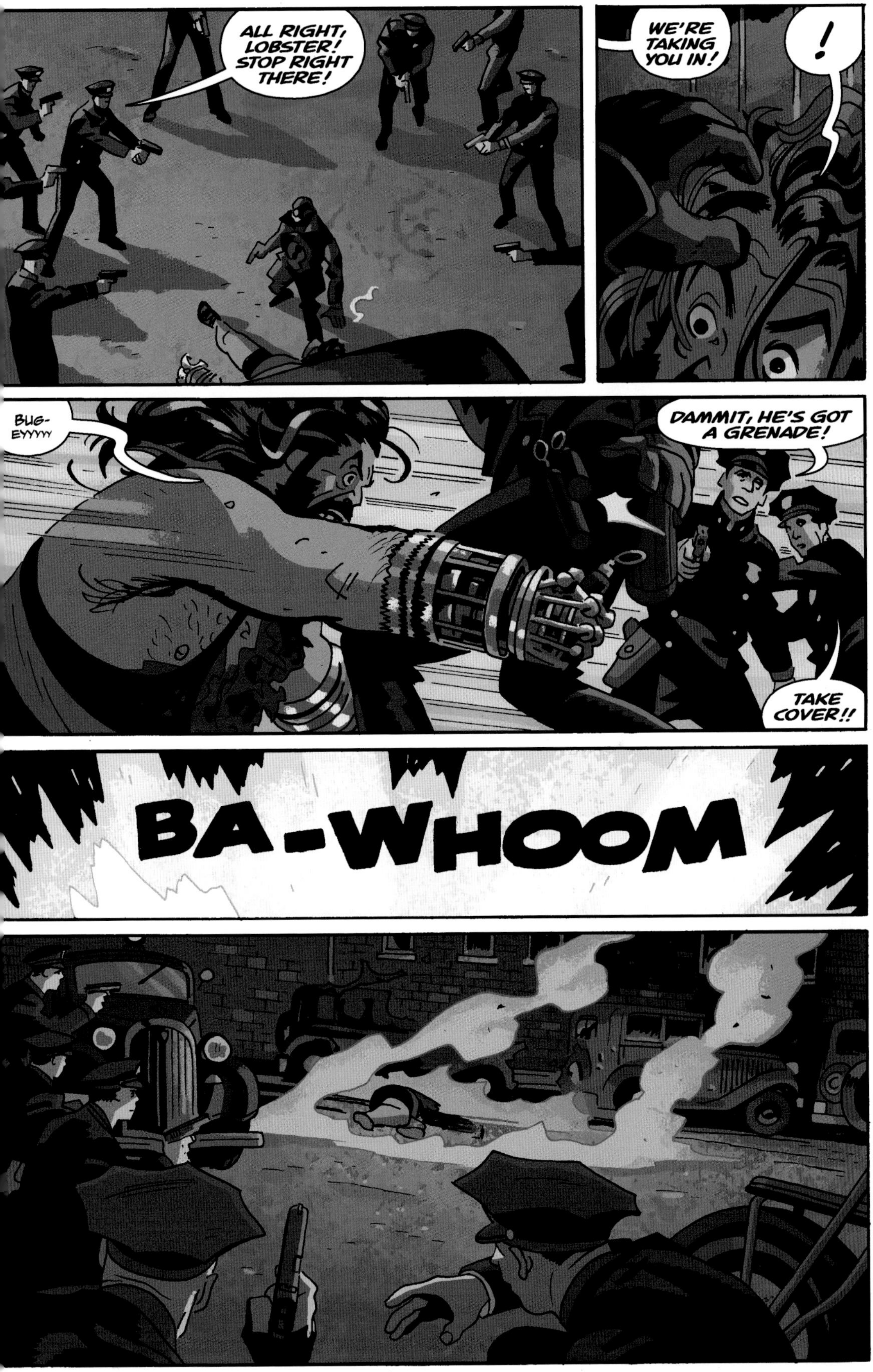
ALL RIGHT, LOBSTER! STOP RIGHT THERE!
WE'RE TAKING YOU IN!
!
BUG-EYYYYY
DAMMIT, HE'S GOT A GRENADE!
TAKE COVER!!
BA-WHOOM

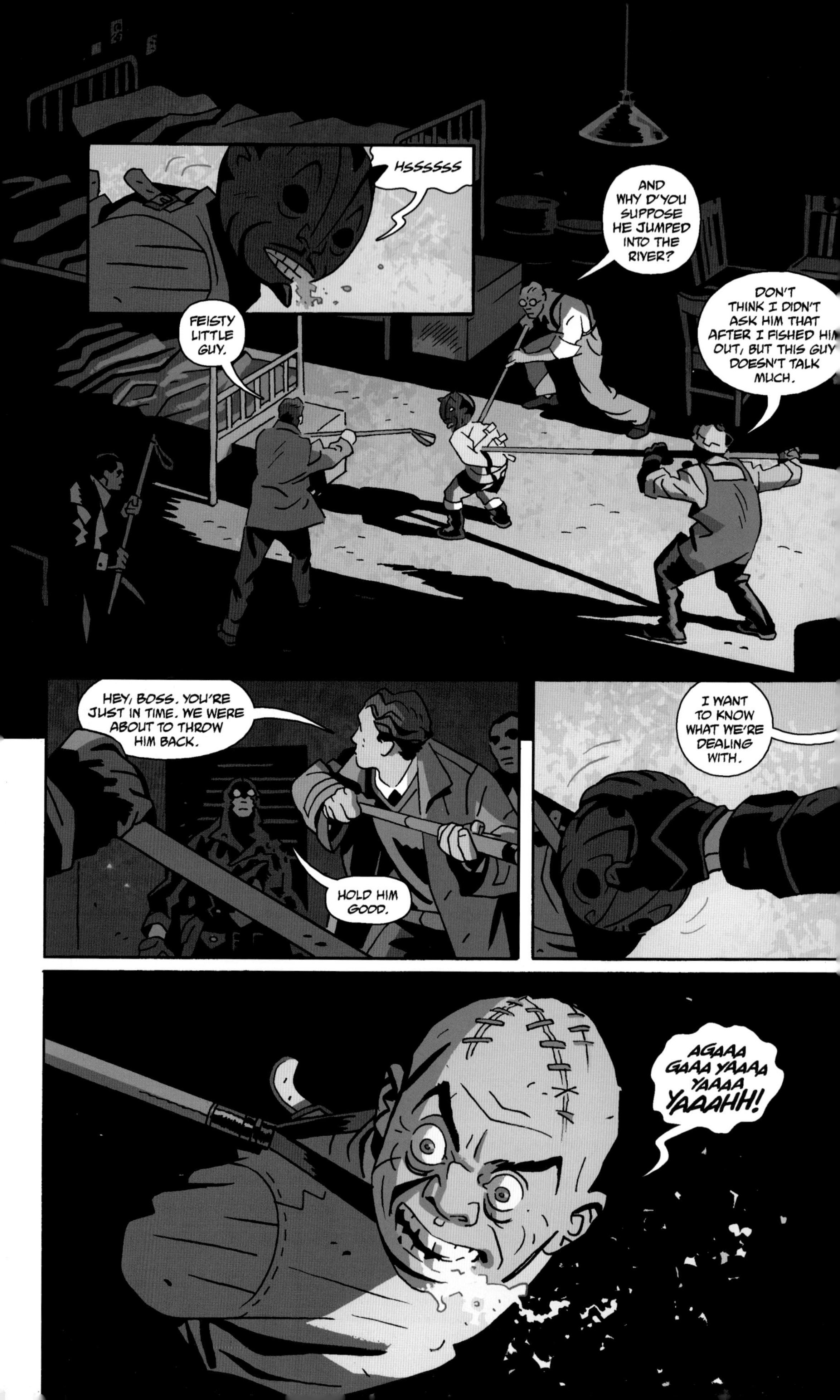
HSSSSSS
FEISTY LITTLE GUY.
AND WHY D'YOU SUPPOSE HE JUMPED INTO THE RIVER?
DON'T THINK I DIDN'T ASK HIM THAT AFTER I FISHED HIM OUT, BUT THIS GUY DOESN'T TALK MUCH.
HEY, BOSS. YOU'RE JUST IN TIME. WE WERE ABOUT TO THROW HIM BACK.
HOLD HIM GOOD.
I WANT TO KNOW WHAT WE'RE DEALING WITH.
AGAAA GAAA YAAAA YAAAA YAAAHH!

CHAPTER TWO

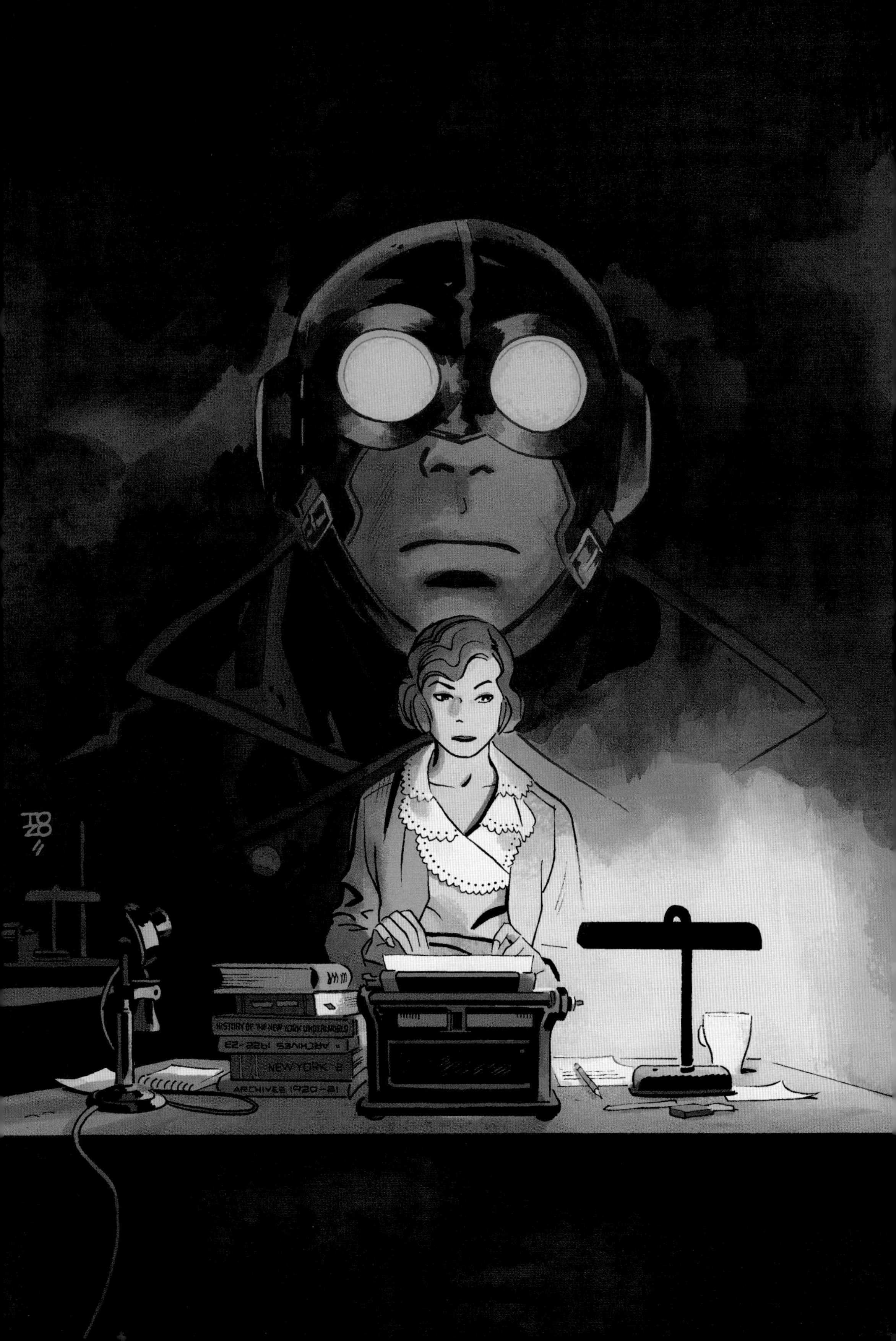
HISTORY OF THE NEW YORK UNDERWORLD
ARCHIVES 1925-29
NEW YORK 8
ARCHIVES 1920-21

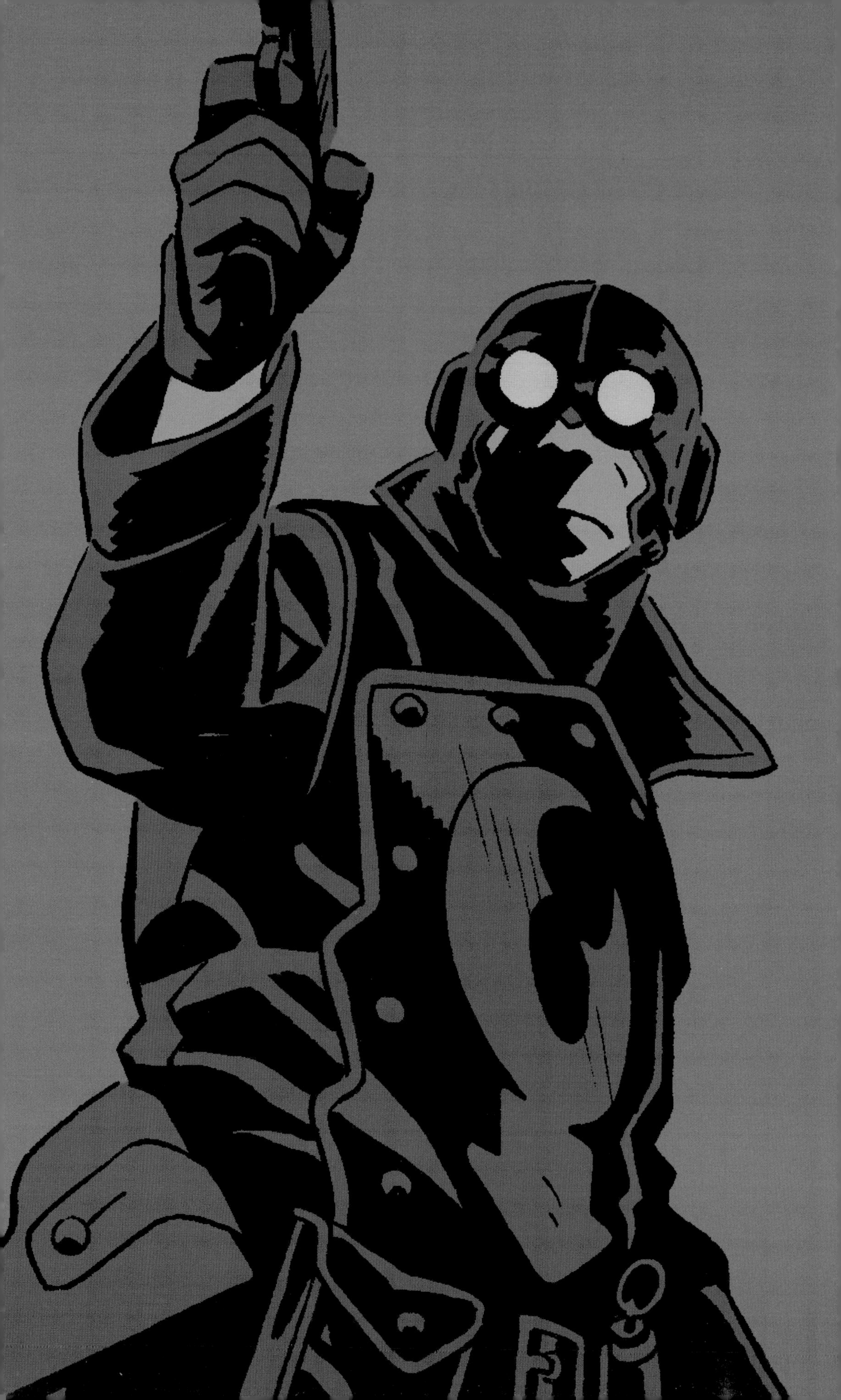

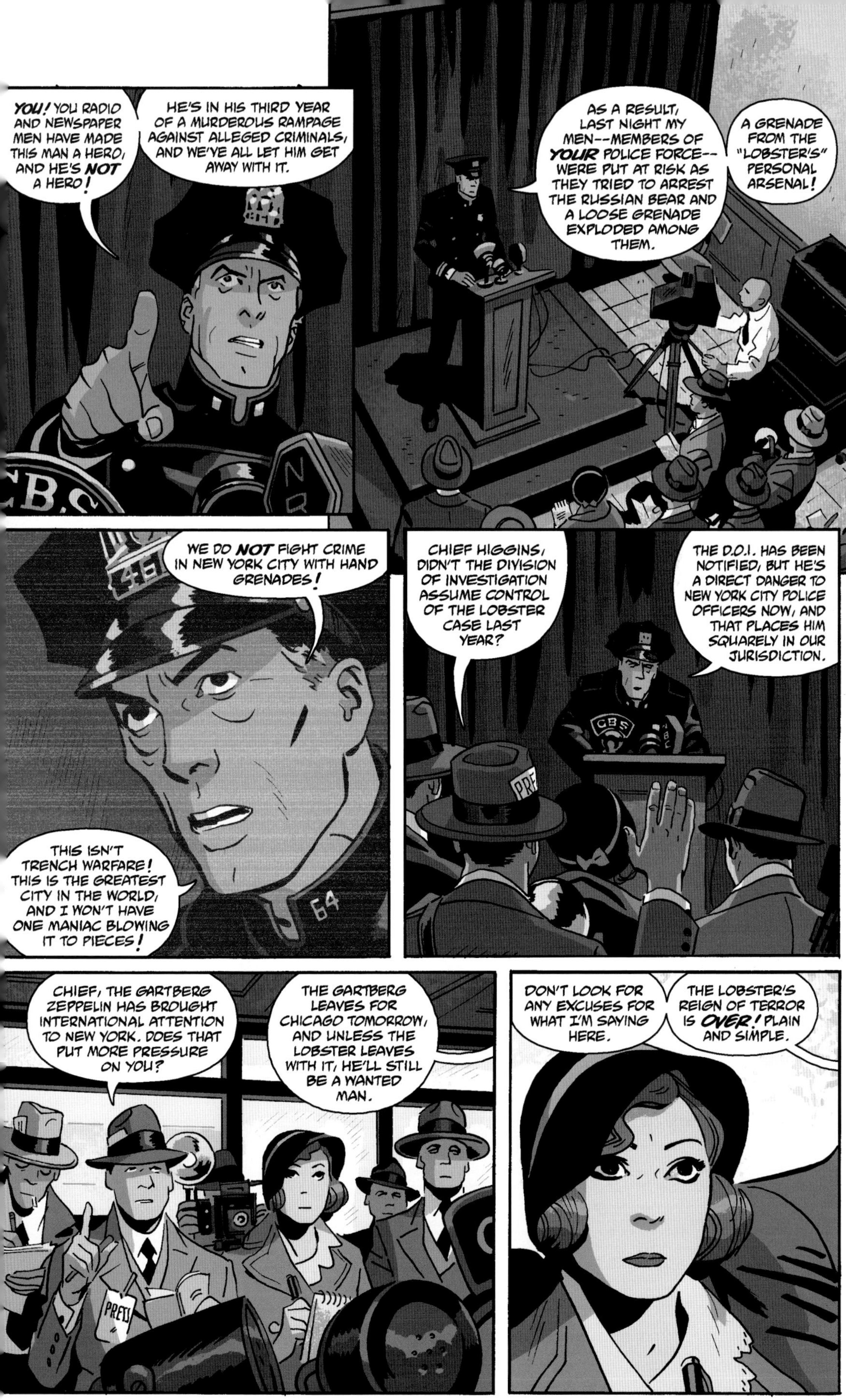
YOU! YOU RADIO AND NEWSPAPER MEN HAVE MADE THIS MAN A HERO, AND HE'S NOT A HERO!
HE'S IN HIS THIRD YEAR OF A MURDEROUS RAMPAGE AGAINST ALLEGED CRIMINALS, AND WE'VE ALL LET HIM GET AWAY WITH IT.
AS A RESULT, LAST NIGHT MY MEN--MEMBERS OF YOUR POLICE FORCE--WERE PUT AT RISK AS THEY TRIED TO ARREST THE RUSSIAN BEAR AND A LOOSE GRENADE EXPLODED AMONG THEM.
A GRENADE FROM THE "LOBSTER'S" PERSONAL ARSENAL!
WE DO NOT FIGHT CRIME IN NEW YORK CITY WITH HAND GRENADES!
THIS ISN'T TRENCH WARFARE! THIS IS THE GREATEST CITY IN THE WORLD, AND I WON'T HAVE ONE MANIAC BLOWING IT TO PIECES!
CHIEF HIGGINS, DIDN'T THE DIVISION OF INVESTIGATION ASSUME CONTROL OF THE LOBSTER CASE LAST YEAR?
THE D.O.I. HAS BEEN NOTIFIED, BUT HE'S A DIRECT DANGER TO NEW YORK CITY POLICE OFFICERS NOW, AND THAT PLACES HIM SQUARELY IN OUR JURISDICTION.
CHIEF, THE GARTBERG ZEPPELIN HAS BROUGHT INTERNATIONAL ATTENTION TO NEW YORK. DOES THAT PUT MORE PRESSURE ON YOU?
THE GARTBERG LEAVES FOR CHICAGO TOMORROW, AND UNLESS THE LOBSTER LEAVES WITH IT, HE'LL STILL BE A WANTED MAN.
DON'T LOOK FOR ANY EXCUSES FOR WHAT I'M SAYING HERE.
THE LOBSTER'S REIGN OF TERROR IS OVER! PLAIN AND SIMPLE.

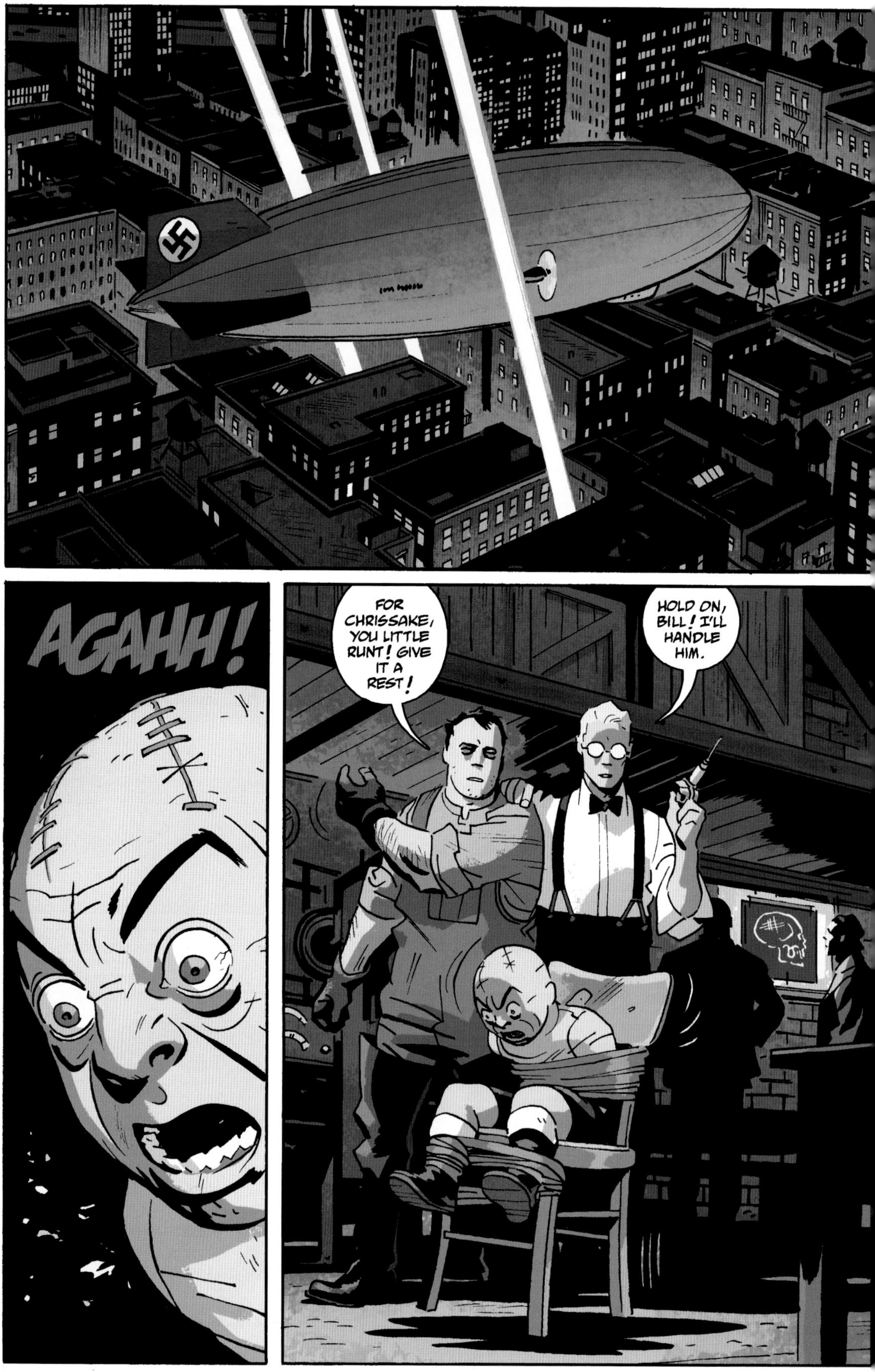
AGAHH!
FOR CHRISSAKE, YOU LITTLE RUNT! GIVE IT A REST!
HOLD ON, BILL! I'LL HANDLE HIM.

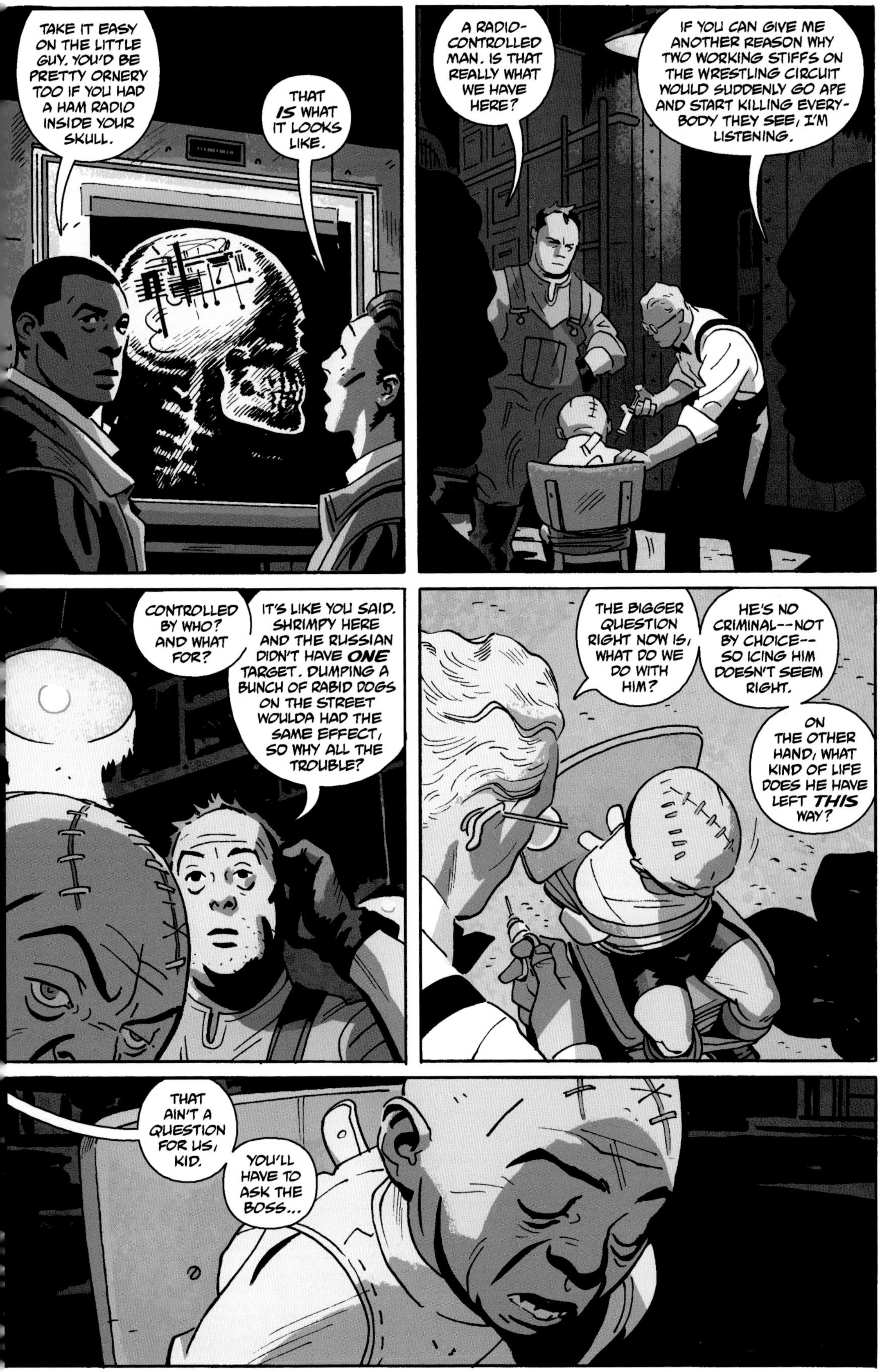
TAKE IT EASY ON THE LITTLE GUY. YOU'D BE PRETTY ORNERY TOO IF YOU HAD A HAM RADIO INSIDE YOUR SKULL.
THAT *IS* WHAT IT LOOKS LIKE.
A RADIO-CONTROLLED MAN. IS THAT REALLY WHAT WE HAVE HERE?
IF YOU CAN GIVE ME ANOTHER REASON WHY TWO WORKING STIFFS ON THE WRESTLING CIRCUIT WOULD SUDDENLY GO APE AND START KILLING EVERY-BODY THEY SEE, I'M LISTENING.
CONTROLLED BY WHO? AND WHAT FOR?
IT'S LIKE YOU SAID. SHRIMPY HERE AND THE RUSSIAN DIDN'T HAVE *ONE* TARGET. DUMPING A BUNCH OF RABID DOGS ON THE STREET WOULDA HAD THE SAME EFFECT, SO WHY ALL THE TROUBLE?
THE BIGGER QUESTION RIGHT NOW IS, WHAT DO WE DO WITH HIM?
HE'S NO CRIMINAL--NOT BY CHOICE--SO ICING HIM DOESN'T SEEM RIGHT.
ON THE OTHER HAND, WHAT KIND OF LIFE DOES HE HAVE LEFT *THIS* WAY?
THAT AIN'T A QUESTION FOR US, KID.
YOU'LL HAVE TO ASK THE BOSS...

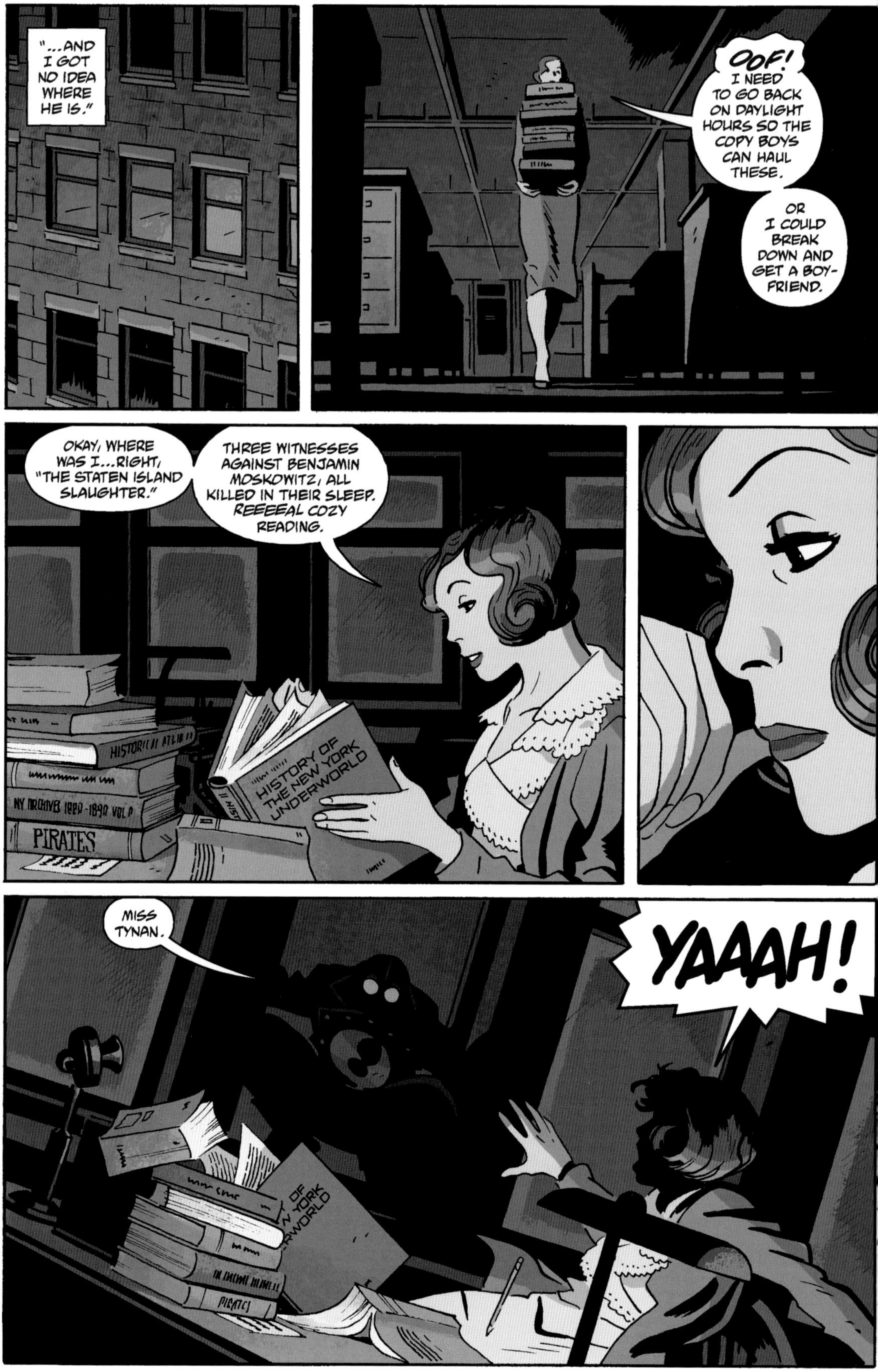
"...AND I GOT NO IDEA WHERE HE IS."
OOF! I NEED TO GO BACK ON DAYLIGHT HOURS SO THE COPY BOYS CAN HAUL THESE.
OR I COULD BREAK DOWN AND GET A BOY-FRIEND.
OKAY, WHERE WAS I...RIGHT, "THE STATEN ISLAND SLAUGHTER."
THREE WITNESSES AGAINST BENJAMIN MOSKOWITZ, ALL KILLED IN THEIR SLEEP. REEEEAL COZY READING.
HISTORICAL ATLAS
NY ARCHIVES 1880-1890 VOL 0
PIRATES
HISTORY OF THE NEW YORK UNDERWORLD
MISS TYNAN.
YAAAH!
PIRATES

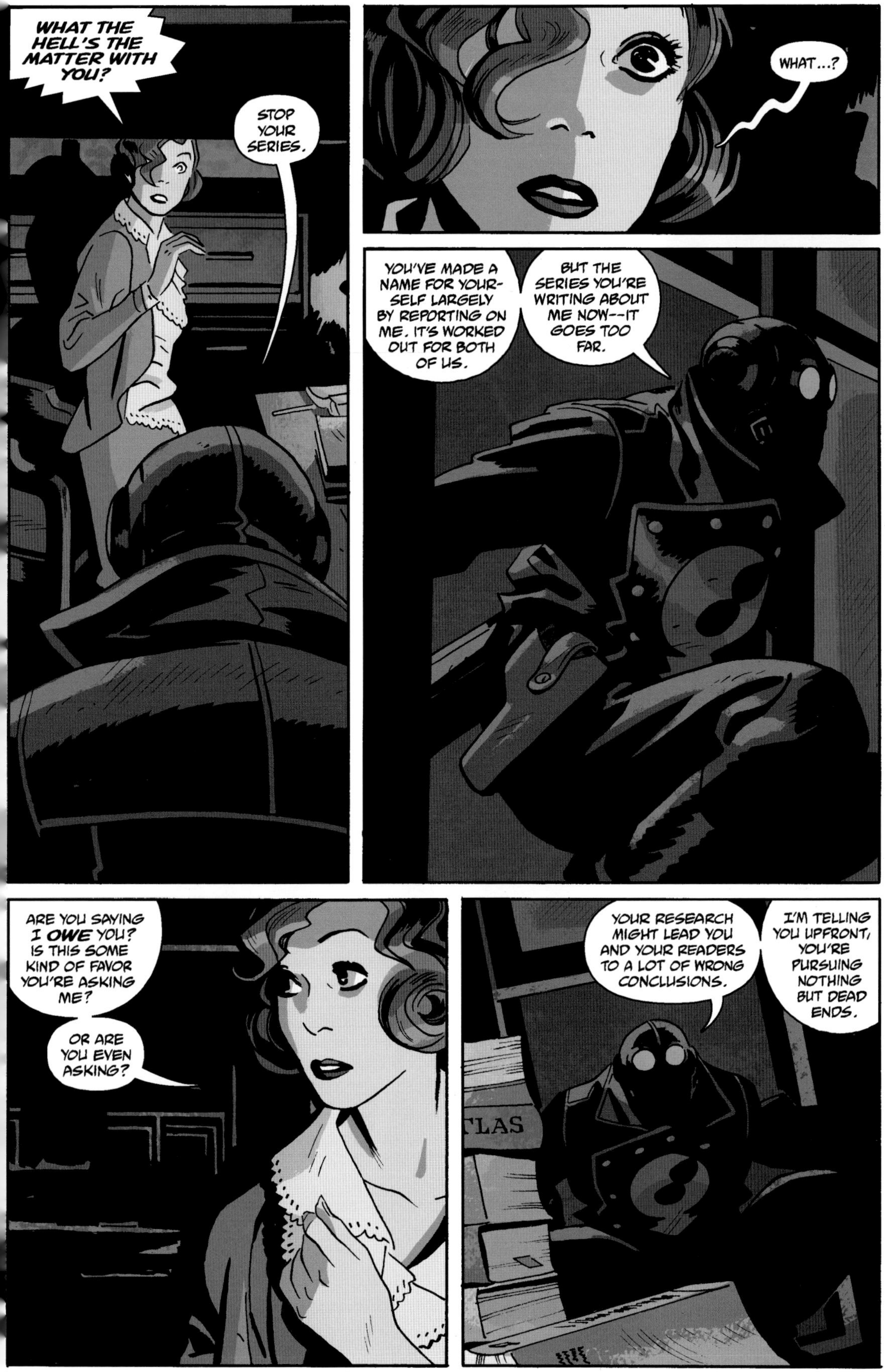
WHAT THE HELL'S THE MATTER WITH YOU?
STOP YOUR SERIES.
WHAT...?
YOU'VE MADE A NAME FOR YOURSELF LARGELY BY REPORTING ON ME. IT'S WORKED OUT FOR BOTH OF US.
BUT THE SERIES YOU'RE WRITING ABOUT ME NOW--IT GOES TOO FAR.
ARE YOU SAYING I *OWE* YOU? IS THIS SOME KIND OF FAVOR YOU'RE ASKING ME?
OR ARE YOU EVEN ASKING?
YOUR RESEARCH MIGHT LEAD YOU AND YOUR READERS TO A LOT OF WRONG CONCLUSIONS.
I'M TELLING YOU UPFRONT, YOU'RE PURSUING NOTHING BUT DEAD ENDS.
TLAS

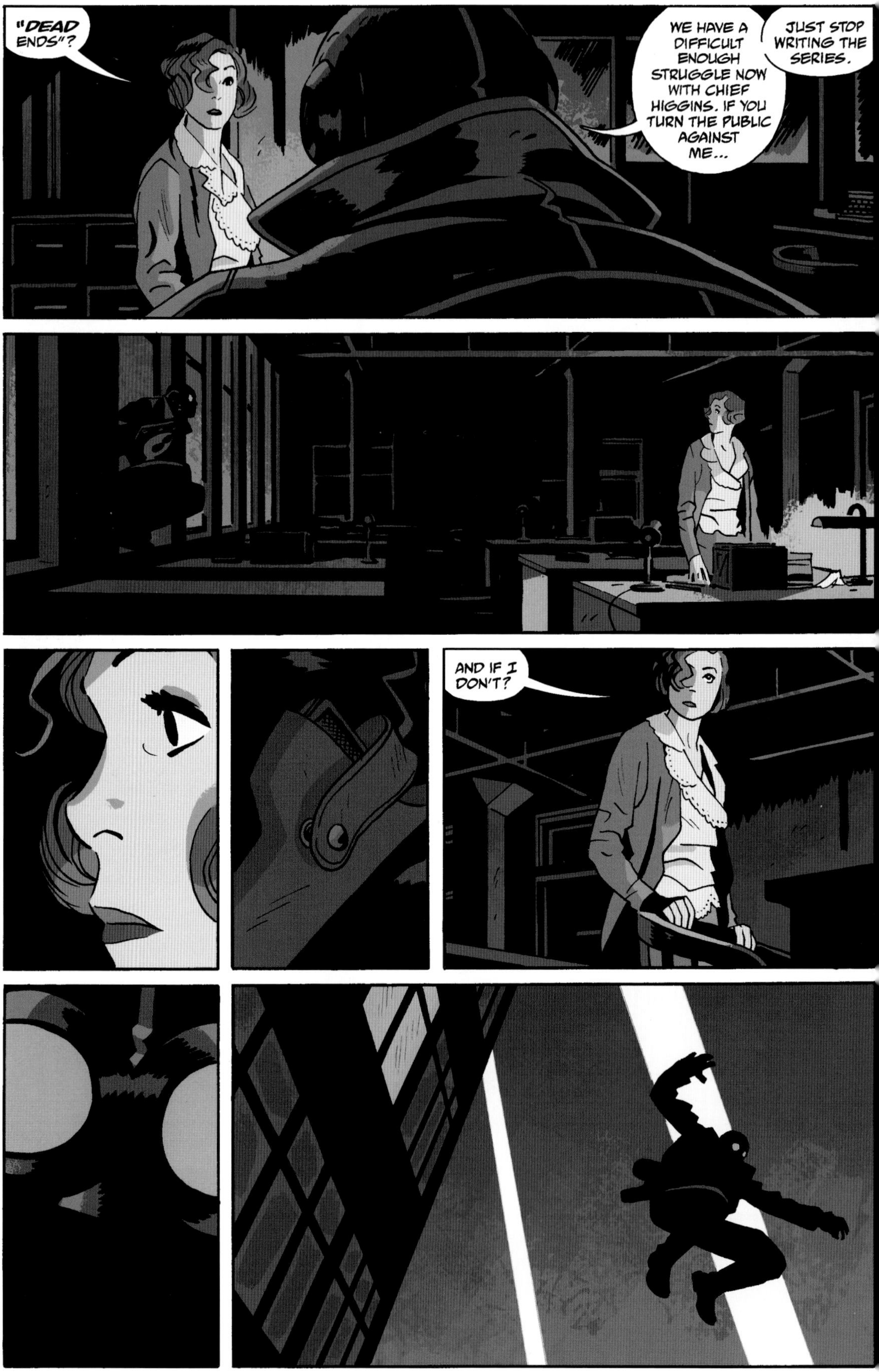
"DEAD ENDS"?
WE HAVE A DIFFICULT ENOUGH STRUGGLE NOW WITH CHIEF HIGGINS. IF YOU TURN THE PUBLIC AGAINST ME...
JUST STOP WRITING THE SERIES.
AND IF I DON'T?

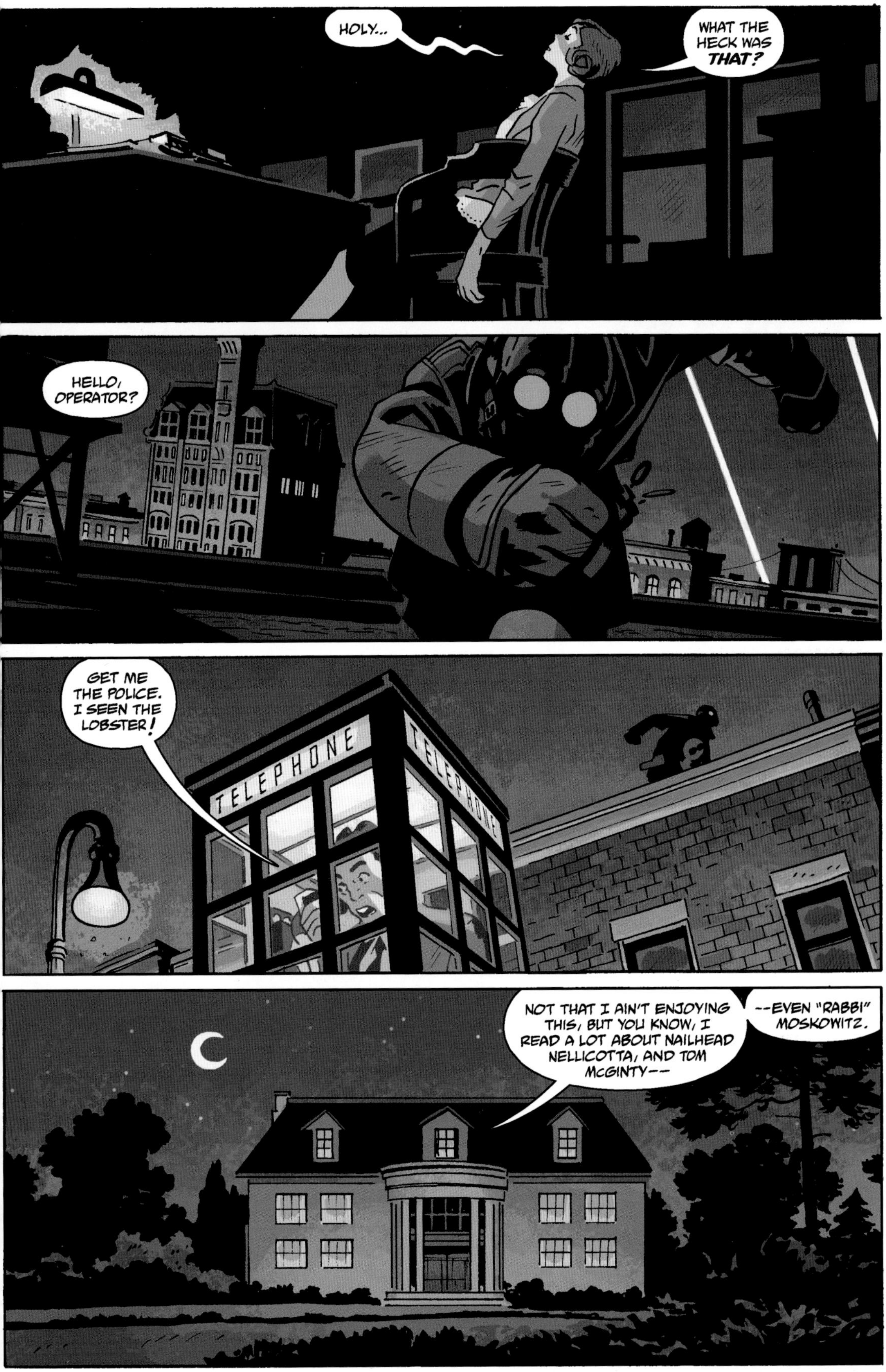
HOLY...
WHAT THE HECK WAS *THAT?*
HELLO, OPERATOR?
GET ME THE POLICE. I SEEN THE LOBSTER!
TELEPHONE
TELEPHONE
TELEPHONE
NOT THAT I AIN'T ENJOYING THIS, BUT YOU KNOW, I READ A LOT ABOUT NAILHEAD NELLICOTTA, AND TOM McGINTY--
--EVEN "RABBI" MOSKOWITZ.

BUT SHE DON'T MENTION ME EVEN ONCE-- IN EITHER CHAPTER.

NOT BY NAME, ANYHOW.

WHATEVER HAPPENED IN THE WINTER OF 1932, MR. WALD, YOU WERE NEVER SO MUCH AS QUESTIONED.

AND LIBEL, IT IS EXPENSIVE FOR NEWSPAPERS.

WHO AM I ABOUT TO SUE? MANHATTAN D.A. FINDS OUT WHERE I AM, IT'S WARRANTS ALL AROUND.

WHO IS THE LOBSTER?

PART TWO: MINTS PARKER AND THE EAST RIVER DRIVE

by CYNTHIA TYNAN

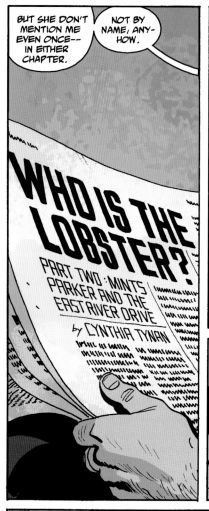

YOU SURE WERE RIGHT, THOUGH! *THIS* DAME'S GOT THE INSIDE TRACK.

REMEMBER ALL THAT MESS A WHILE BACK WITH THE GERMANS? APPARENTLY "CRAB BOY" WAS BACK OF ALL THAT.

YES, SIR. I READ IT THIS MORNING.

OKAY, SO YOU'RE AHEAD OF ME. WHAT'S NEW?

WAY I SEE IT, THAT *STILL* PUTS YOU A FEW STEPS BEHIND THE TYNAN DOLL, DON'T IT?

WHO
LORS

FOR THE MOMENT.

EDWARD GIBBON

"--LEFT HIM RIGHT OUT IN FRONT OF THE ADMITTING OFFICE. YOU KNOW, LIKE THEY DO BABIES IN THE MOVIES."

AND HAVE YOU SEEN HIM? HE'S NOT MUCH *BIGGER* THAN A BABY, EITHER!

RING RING

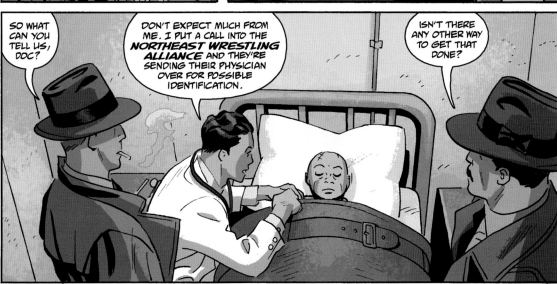

SO WHAT CAN YOU TELL US, DOC?

DON'T EXPECT MUCH FROM ME. I PUT A CALL INTO THE *NORTHEAST WRESTLING ALLIANCE* AND THEY'RE SENDING THEIR PHYSICIAN OVER FOR POSSIBLE IDENTIFICATION.

ISN'T THERE ANY OTHER WAY TO GET THAT DONE?

WE TOOK SOME FILMS, BUT I DON'T SEE HOW THEY CAN TELL US DEFINITIVELY IF THIS IS THE SAME MAN WHO'S BEEN SHOOTING UP THE CITY.

WELL, I'D SAY HE AT LEAST MAKES THE "SHORT" LIST, RIGHT?

CAN'T BELIEVE IT TOOK YOU *THIS* LONG TO GET THERE, HANSON.

EXCUSE ME, DETECTIVE ECKERD?

THERE'S A PHONE CALL FOR YOU OUT AT THE DESK. IT SOUNDS IMPORTANT.

OKAY, THANKS.

THAT'S THE LAST WE'LL SEE OF HIM TONIGHT, I'M BETTING.

SO WHAT DO YOU SAY, DOC? IF YOU CAN WAKE UP TOM THUMB, I GOT A DECK OF CARDS.

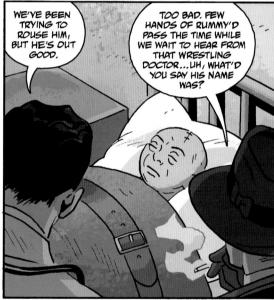

WE'VE BEEN TRYING TO ROUSE HIM, BUT HE'S OUT GOOD.

TOO BAD. FEW HANDS OF RUMMY'D PASS THE TIME WHILE WE WAIT TO HEAR FROM THAT WRESTLING DOCTOR...UH, WHAT'D YOU SAY HIS NAME WAS?

EMERSON.

DR. BOYER EMERSON. NOW LET'S SEE IF I CAN BE OF SOME HELP.

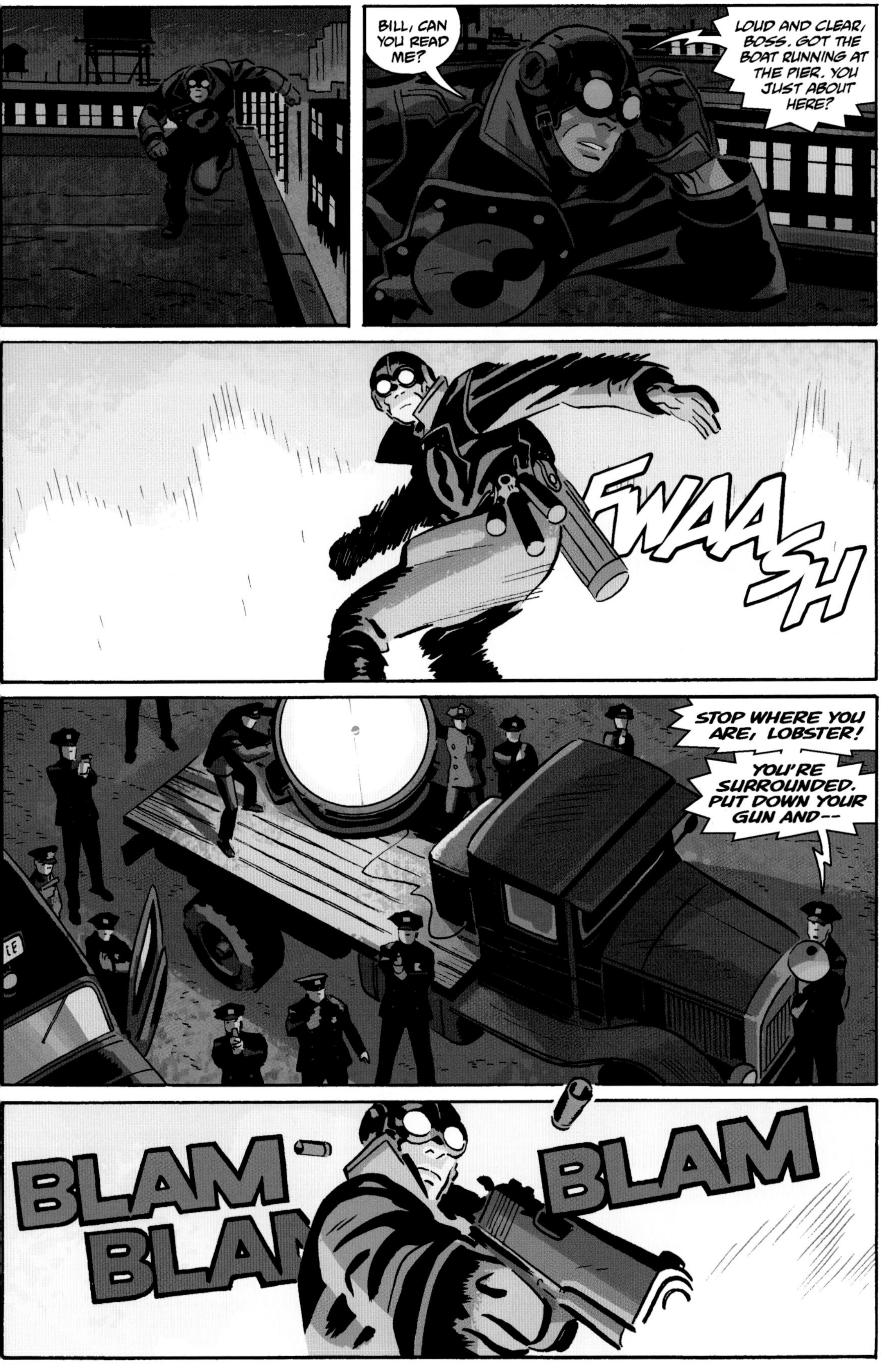

BILL, CAN YOU READ ME?
LOUD AND CLEAR, BOSS. GOT THE BOAT RUNNING AT THE PIER. YOU JUST ABOUT HERE?
FWAASH
STOP WHERE YOU ARE, LOBSTER!
YOU'RE SURROUNDED. PUT DOWN YOUR GUN AND--
BLAM-BLAM
BLAM

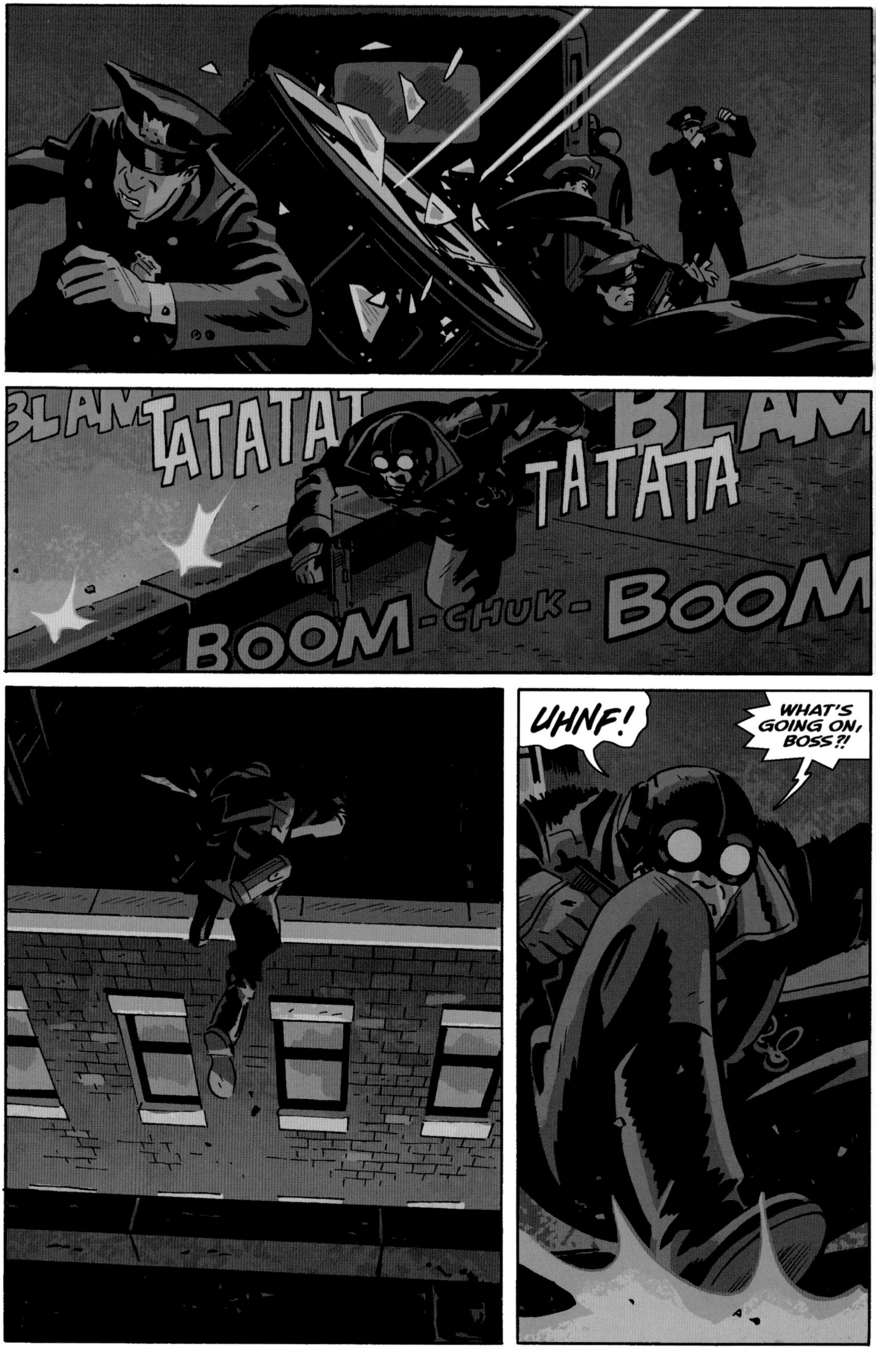
BLAM
TATATAT
BLAM
TATATA
BOOM-CHUK-BOOM
UHNF!
WHAT'S GOING ON, BOSS?!

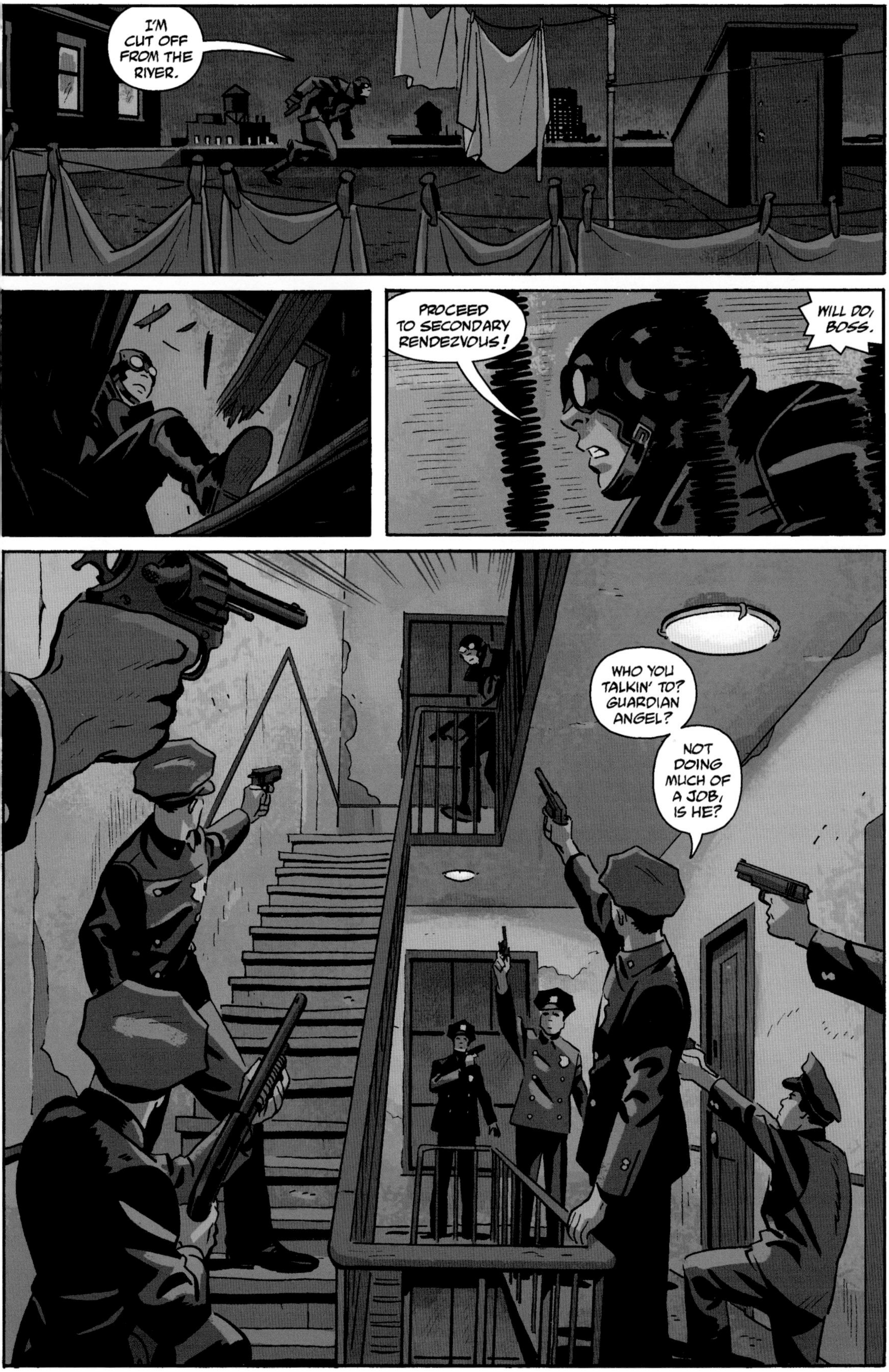
I'M CUT OFF FROM THE RIVER.
PROCEED TO SECONDARY RENDEZVOUS!
WILL DO, BOSS.
WHO YOU TALKIN' TO? GUARDIAN ANGEL?
NOT DOING MUCH OF A JOB, IS HE?

ALL RIGHT, LOBSTER. WE GOT CIVILIANS LIVING HERE.

NO MATTER WHAT HIGGINS SAYS, I *KNOW* YOU DON'T WANT US OPENING FIRE WITH INNOCENT FOLK AROUND.

FOR THE LUVVA MIKE, WHAT'S ALL THE NOI--

GET INSIDE *NOW!*

KEESH

BLAM
BLAM
BLAM
BLAM
BLAM

OH, DEAR! OH MY WORD!

OKAY, CALM DOWN, MA'AM. JUST RELAX.

DONEGAN, IS HE--?

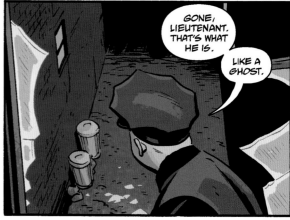

GONE, LIEUTENANT. THAT'S WHAT HE IS.

LIKE A GHOST.

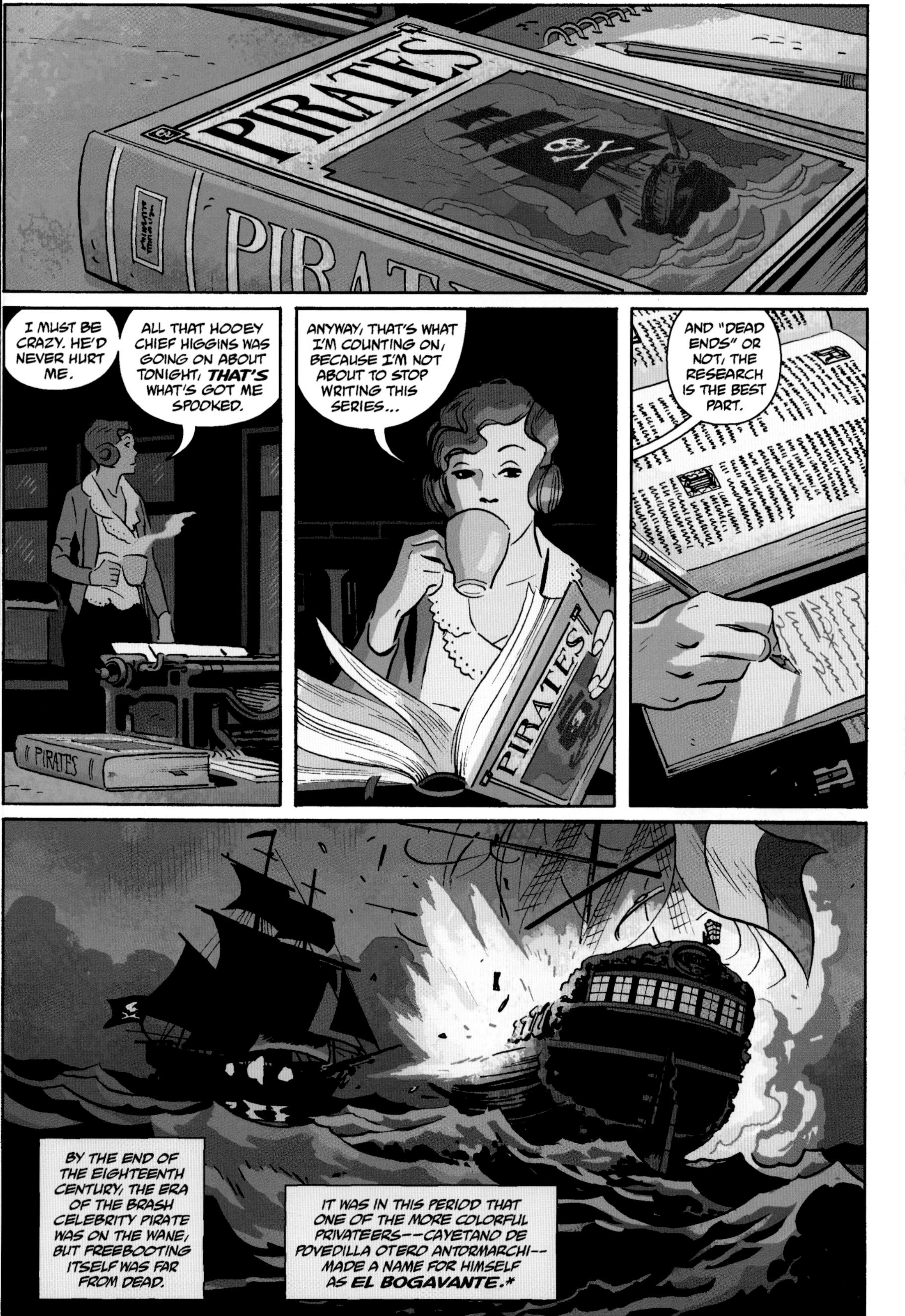
PIRATES
I MUST BE CRAZY. HE'D NEVER HURT ME.
ALL THAT HOOEY CHIEF HIGGINS WAS GOING ON ABOUT TONIGHT, THAT'S WHAT'S GOT ME SPOOKED.
PIRATES
ANYWAY, THAT'S WHAT I'M COUNTING ON, BECAUSE I'M NOT ABOUT TO STOP WRITING THIS SERIES...
PIRATES
AND "DEAD ENDS" OR NOT, THE RESEARCH IS THE BEST PART.
BY THE END OF THE EIGHTEENTH CENTURY, THE ERA OF THE BRASH CELEBRITY PIRATE WAS ON THE WANE, BUT FREEBOOTING ITSELF WAS FAR FROM DEAD.
IT WAS IN THIS PERIOD THAT ONE OF THE MORE COLORFUL PRIVATEERS--CAYETANO DE POVEDILLA OTERO ANTORMARCHI--MADE A NAME FOR HIMSELF AS EL BOGAVANTE.*

*THE LOBSTER.

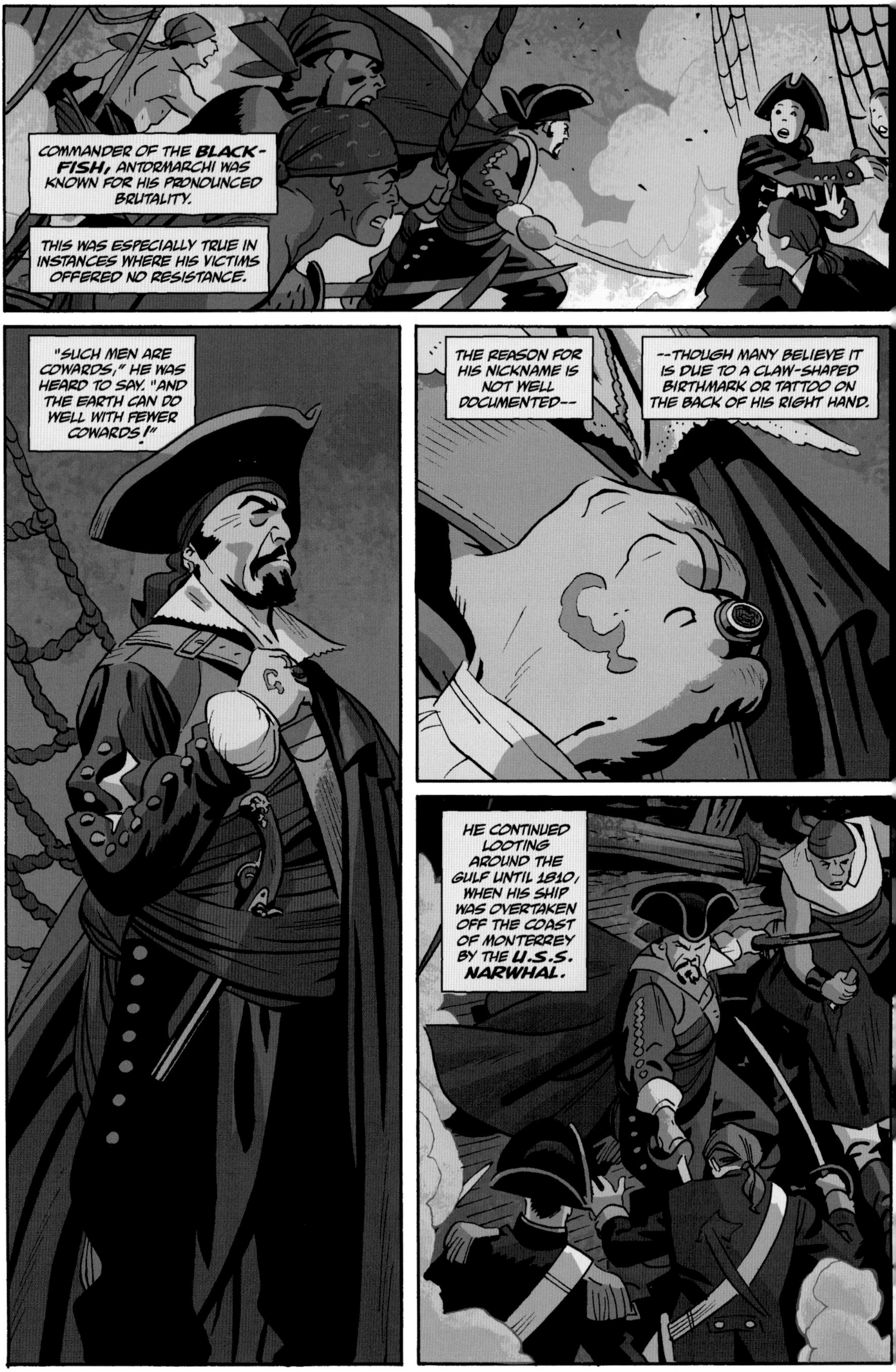
COMMANDER OF THE BLACKFISH, ANTORMARCHI WAS KNOWN FOR HIS PRONOUNCED BRUTALITY.
THIS WAS ESPECIALLY TRUE IN INSTANCES WHERE HIS VICTIMS OFFERED NO RESISTANCE.
"SUCH MEN ARE COWARDS," HE WAS HEARD TO SAY. "AND THE EARTH CAN DO WELL WITH FEWER COWARDS!"
THE REASON FOR HIS NICKNAME IS NOT WELL DOCUMENTED--
--THOUGH MANY BELIEVE IT IS DUE TO A CLAW-SHAPED BIRTHMARK OR TATTOO ON THE BACK OF HIS RIGHT HAND.
HE CONTINUED LOOTING AROUND THE GULF UNTIL 1810, WHEN HIS SHIP WAS OVERTAKEN OFF THE COAST OF MONTERREY BY THE U.S.S. NARWHAL.

BY ALL ACCOUNTS "THE LOBSTER" FOUGHT FEROCIOUSLY AND DEFTLY FOR HOURS.

HE WAS NOT CAPTURED, AND HIS DEATH WAS NEVER CONFIRMED.

MUDDYING THIS ISSUE FURTHER, THERE ARE REPORTS THAT THE SAME NIGHT OF THE BATTLE, THE LOBSTER WAS SEEN IN ST. CROIX.

WHILE THERE HE VISITED THE BROTHEL OF ONE OF HIS MANY PARAMOURS, OLIVIA DASCHER.

THE TWO WERE SAID TO HAVE SPENT A NOT UNEVENTFUL NIGHT TOGETHER--

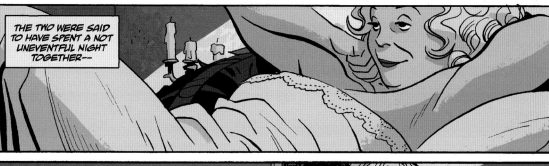

--MAKING THE EVENTS OF THE MORNING TROUBLING INDEED.

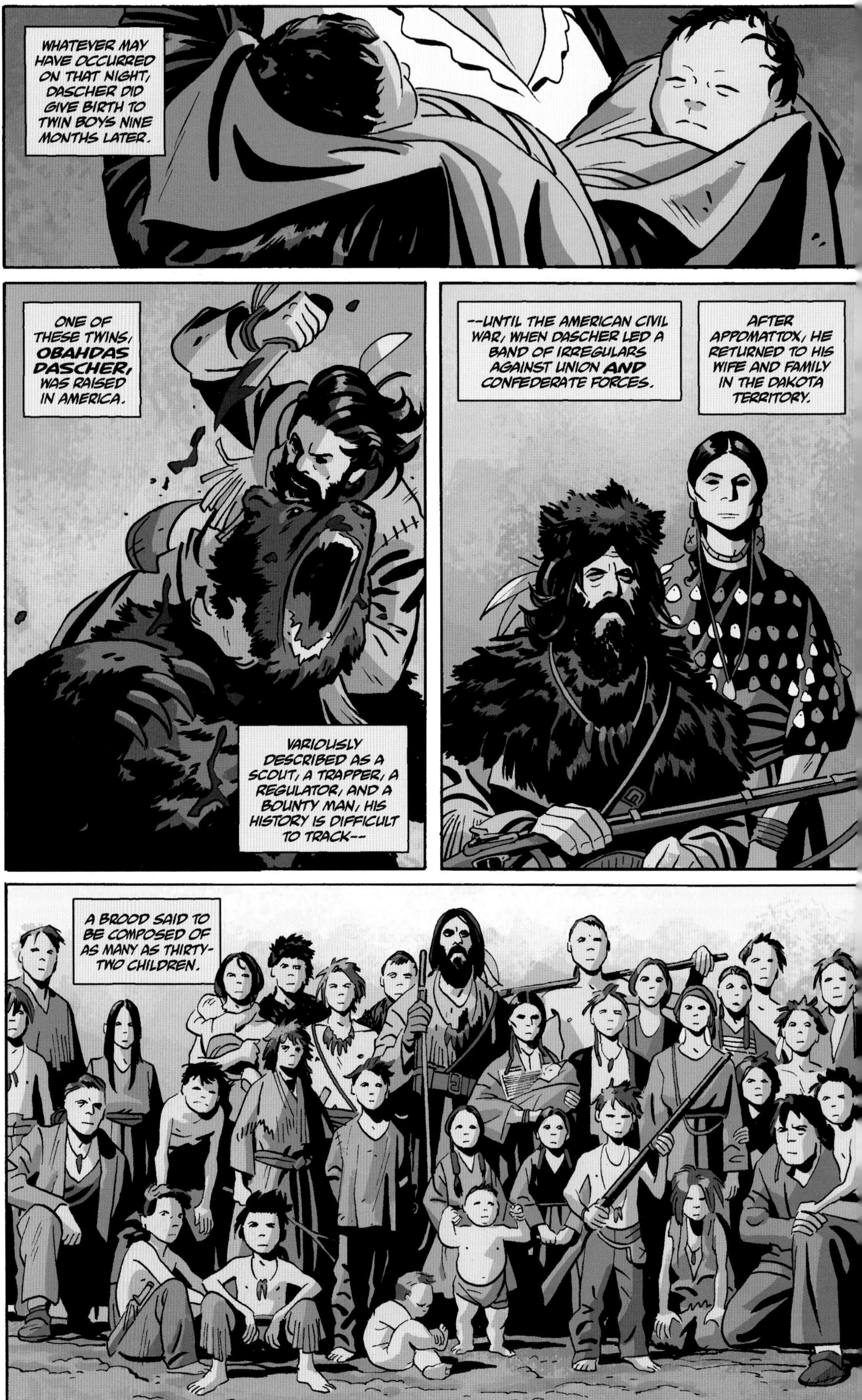
WHATEVER MAY HAVE OCCURRED ON THAT NIGHT, DASCHER DID GIVE BIRTH TO TWIN BOYS NINE MONTHS LATER.
ONE OF THESE TWINS, OBAHDAS DASCHER, WAS RAISED IN AMERICA.
VARIOUSLY DESCRIBED AS A SCOUT, A TRAPPER, A REGULATOR, AND A BOUNTY MAN, HIS HISTORY IS DIFFICULT TO TRACK--
--UNTIL THE AMERICAN CIVIL WAR, WHEN DASCHER LED A BAND OF IRREGULARS AGAINST UNION AND CONFEDERATE FORCES.
AFTER APPOMATTOX, HE RETURNED TO HIS WIFE AND FAMILY IN THE DAKOTA TERRITORY.
A BROOD SAID TO BE COMPOSED OF AS MANY AS THIRTY-TWO CHILDREN.

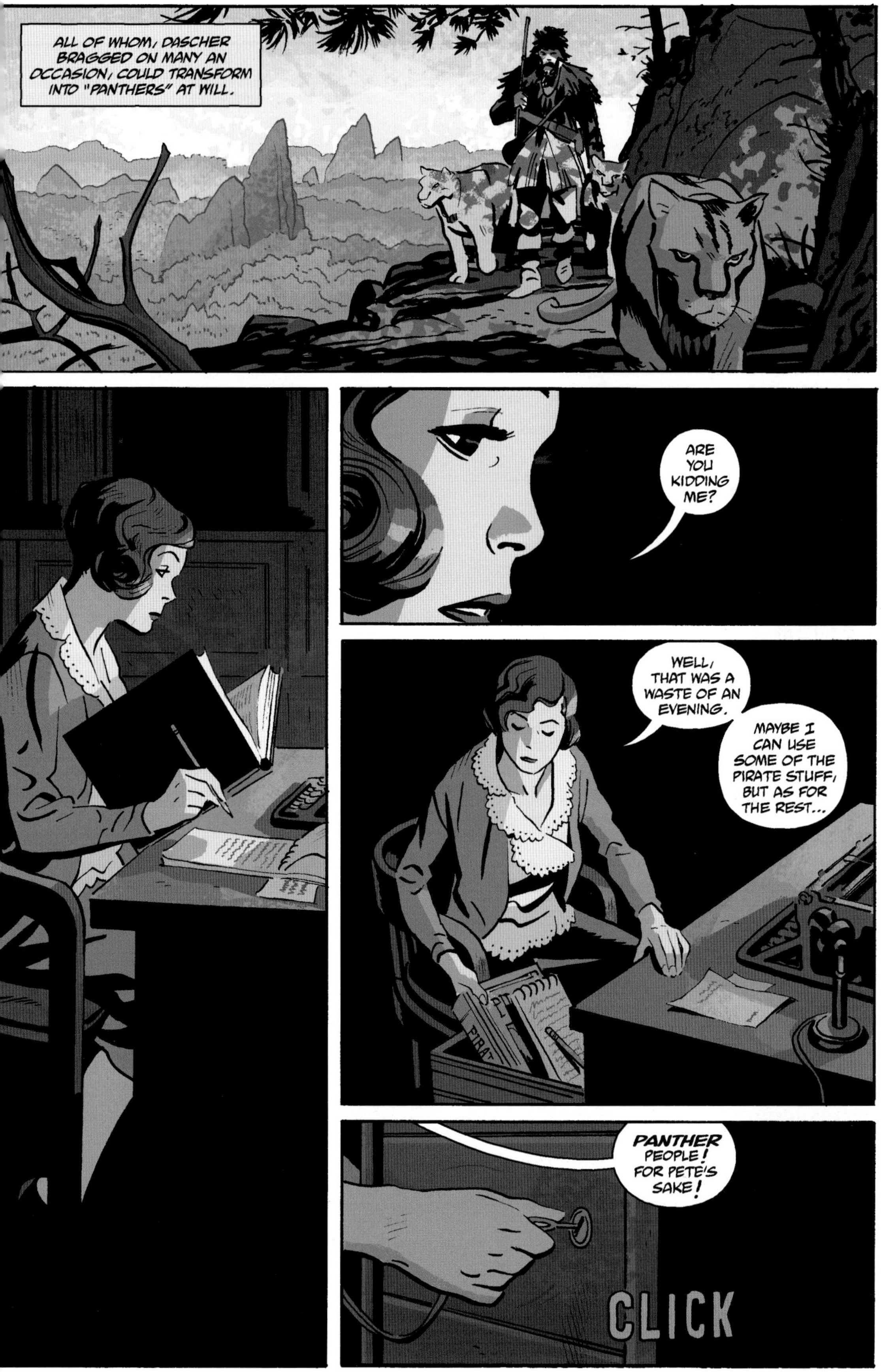
ALL OF WHOM, DASCHER BRAGGED ON MANY AN OCCASION, COULD TRANSFORM INTO "PANTHERS" AT WILL.
ARE YOU KIDDING ME?
WELL, THAT WAS A WASTE OF AN EVENING.
MAYBE I CAN USE SOME OF THE PIRATE STUFF, BUT AS FOR THE REST...
PANTHER PEOPLE! FOR PETE'S SAKE!
CLICK

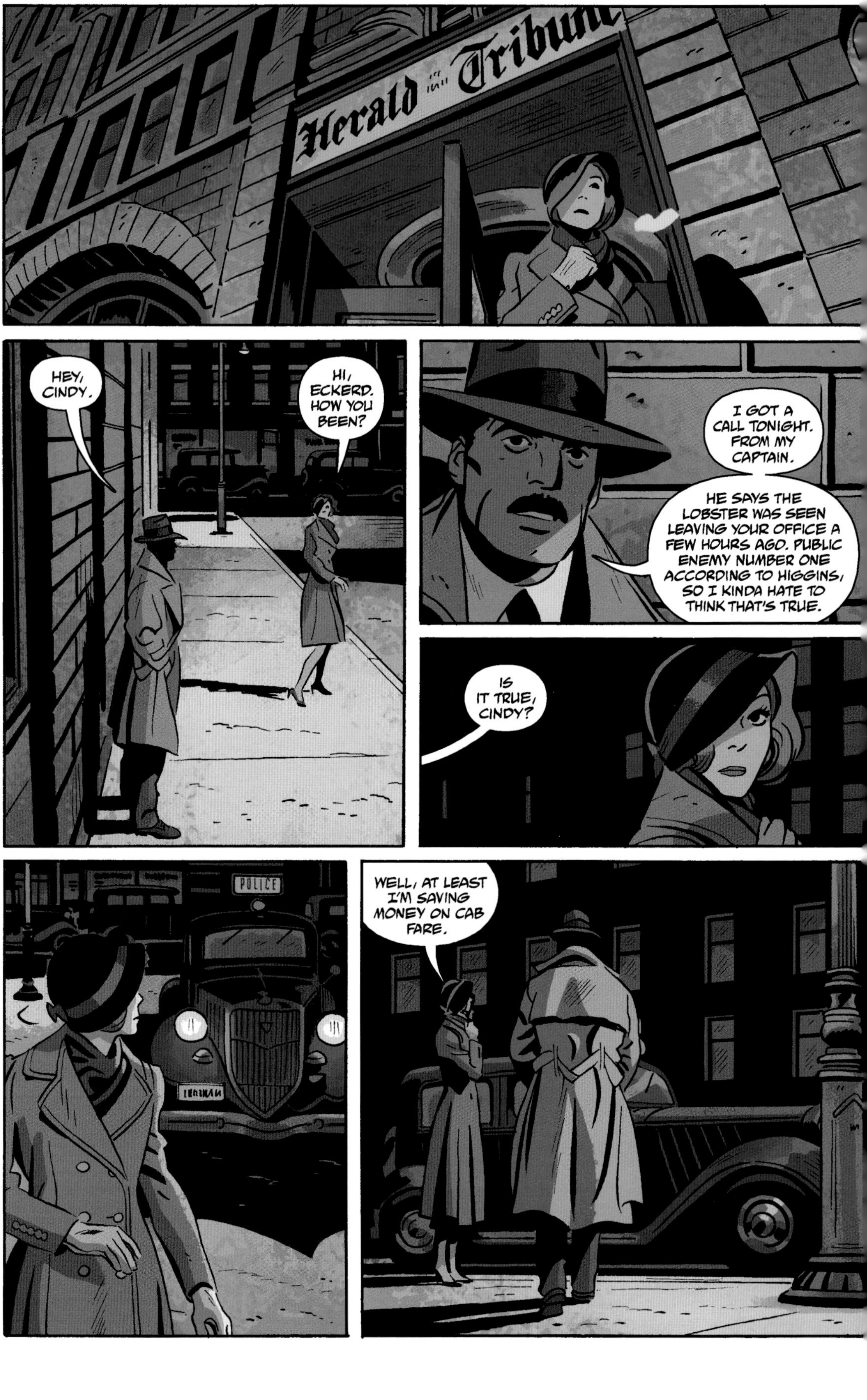
Herald Tribune
HEY, CINDY.
HI, ECKERD. HOW YOU BEEN?
I GOT A CALL TONIGHT. FROM MY CAPTAIN.
HE SAYS THE LOBSTER WAS SEEN LEAVING YOUR OFFICE A FEW HOURS AGO. PUBLIC ENEMY NUMBER ONE ACCORDING TO HIGGINS, SO I KINDA HATE TO THINK THAT'S TRUE.
IS IT TRUE, CINDY?
POLICE
WELL, AT LEAST I'M SAVING MONEY ON CAB FARE.

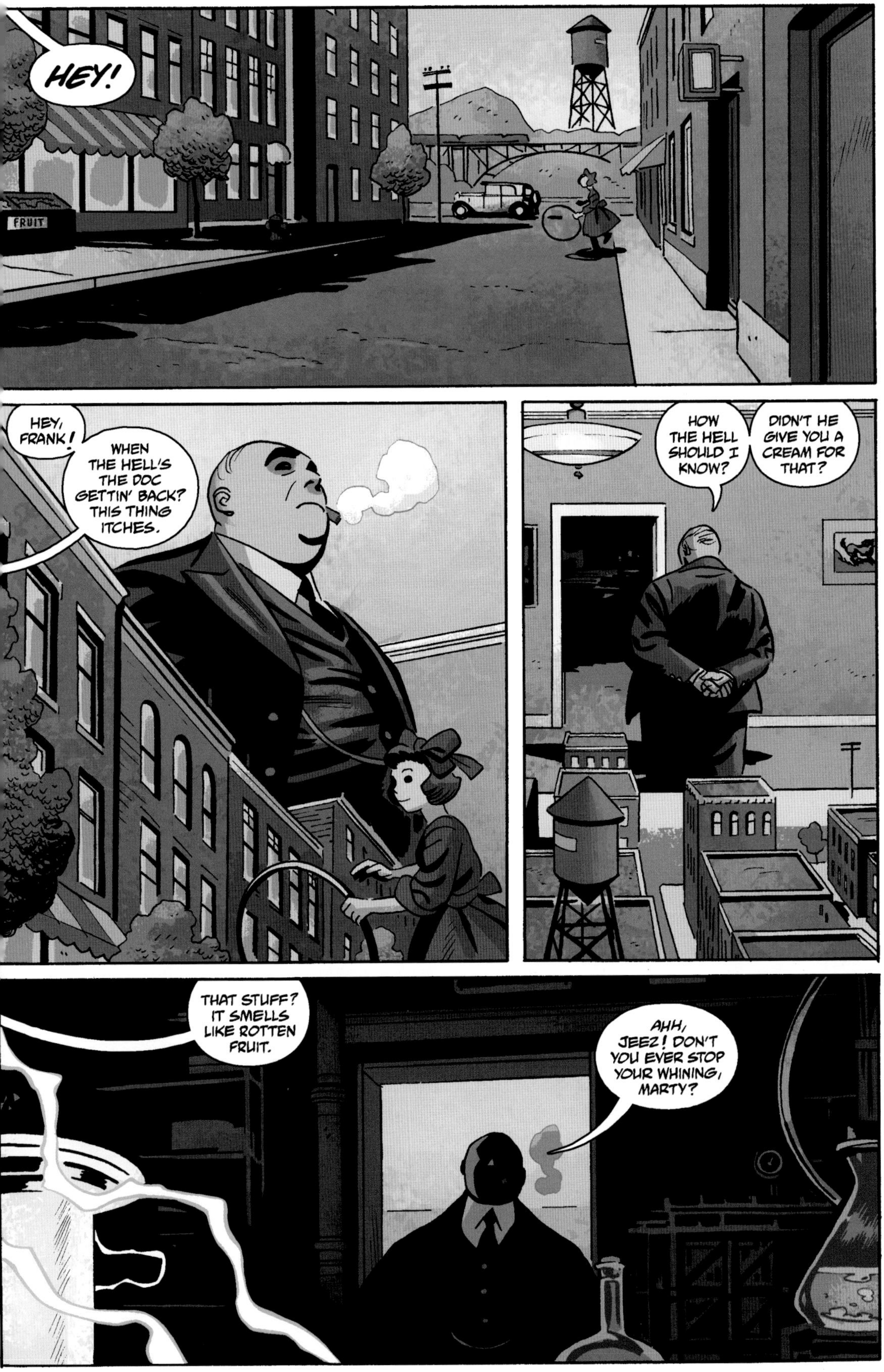
HEY!
FRUIT
HEY, FRANK!
WHEN THE HELL'S THE DOC GETTIN' BACK? THIS THING ITCHES.
HOW THE HELL SHOULD I KNOW?
DIDN'T HE GIVE YOU A CREAM FOR THAT?
THAT STUFF? IT SMELLS LIKE ROTTEN FRUIT.
AHH, JEEZ! DON'T YOU EVER STOP YOUR WHINING, MARTY?

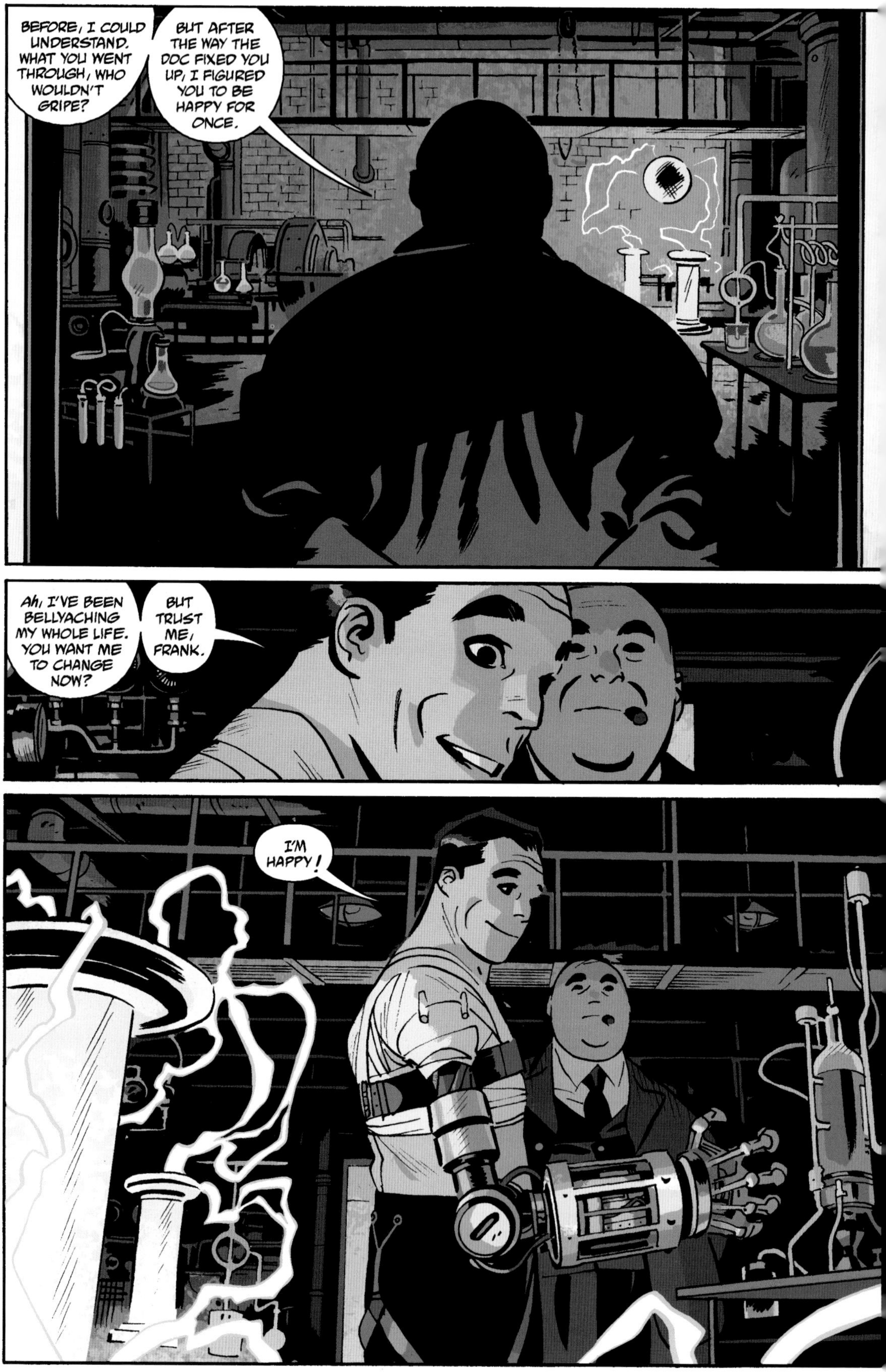
BEFORE, I COULD UNDERSTAND. WHAT YOU WENT THROUGH, WHO WOULDN'T GRIPE?
BUT AFTER THE WAY THE DOC FIXED YOU UP, I FIGURED YOU TO BE HAPPY FOR ONCE.
Ah, I'VE BEEN BELLYACHING MY WHOLE LIFE. YOU WANT ME TO CHANGE NOW?
BUT TRUST ME, FRANK.
I'M HAPPY!

CHAPTER THREE

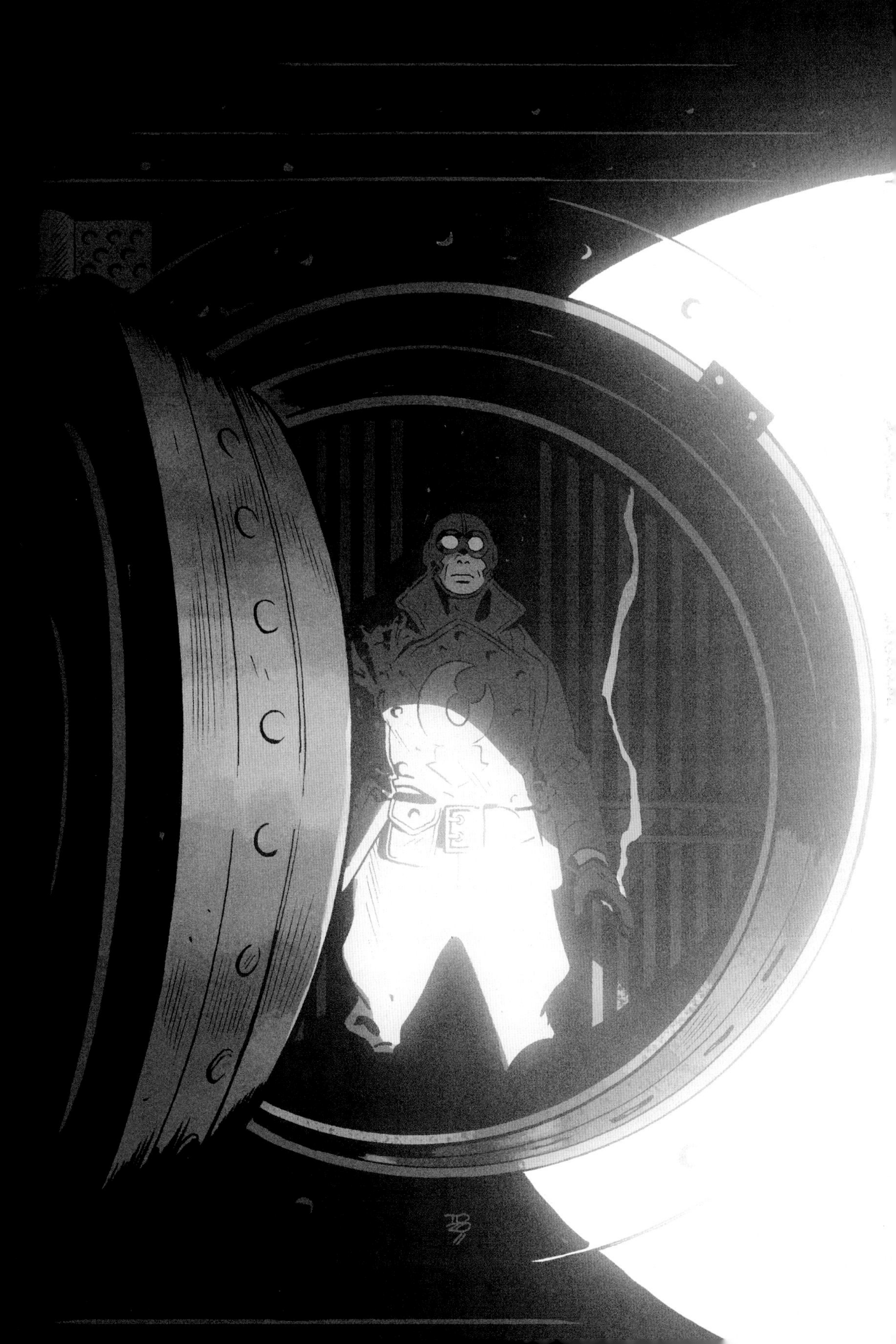

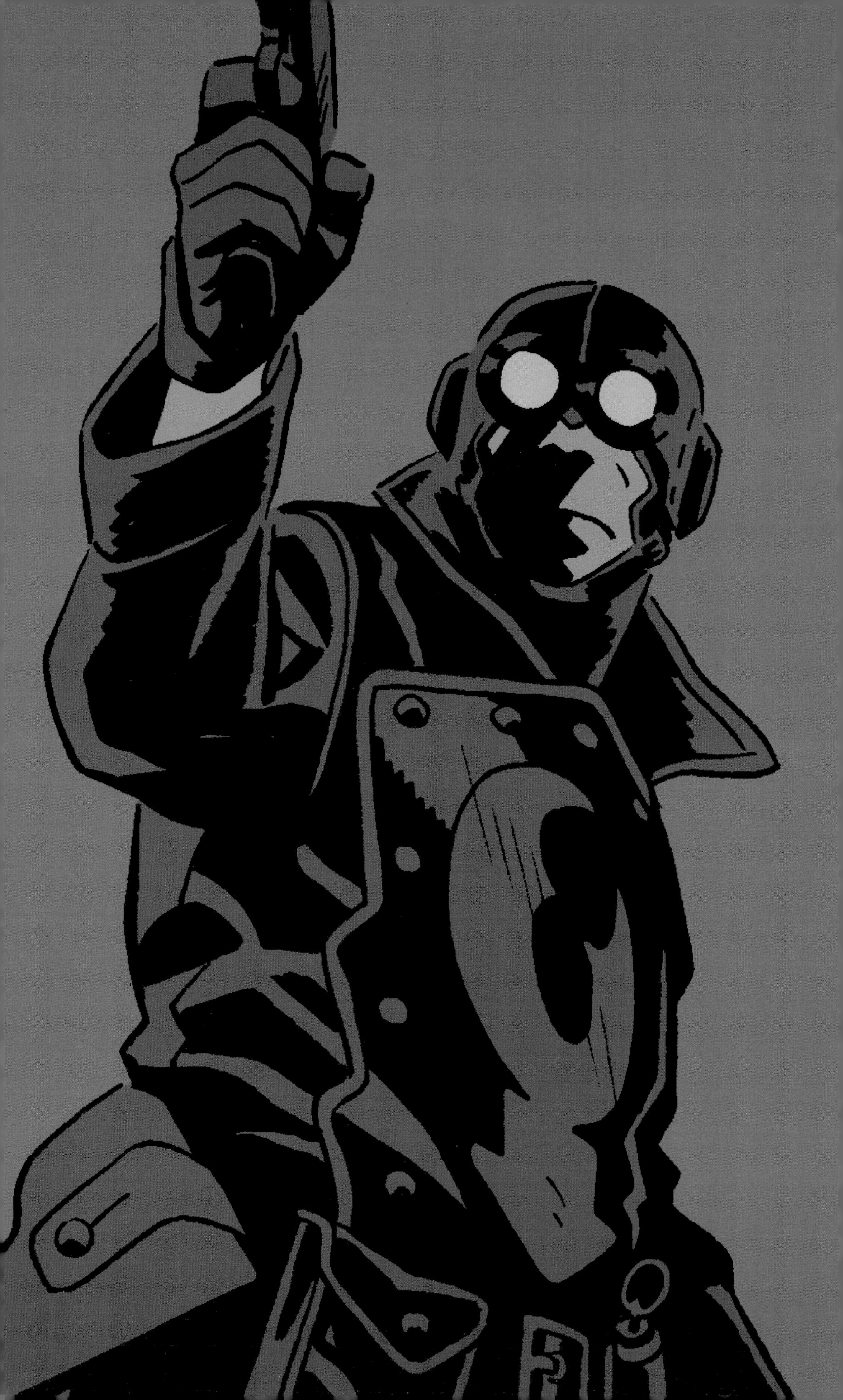

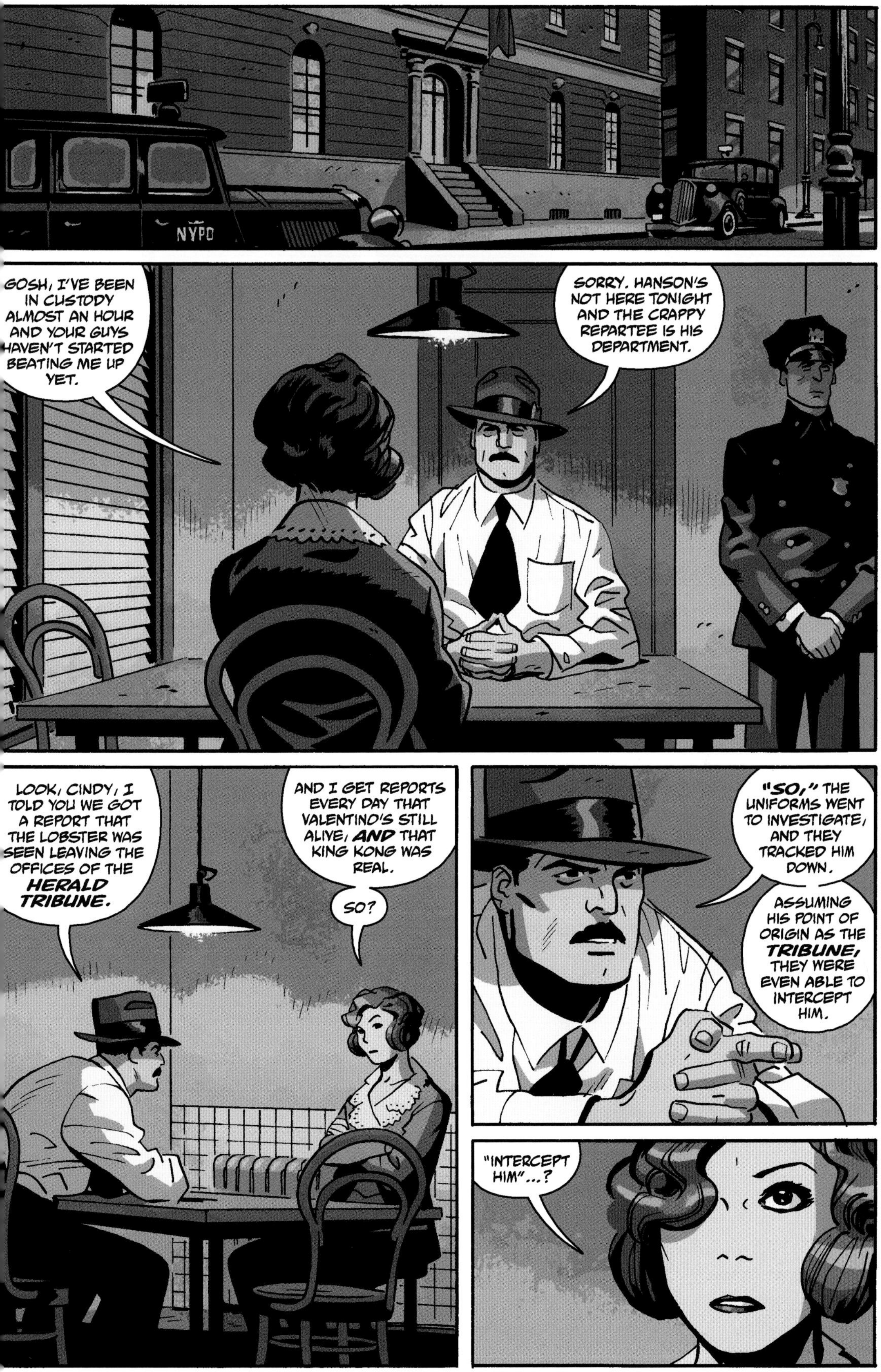
NYPD
GOSH, I'VE BEEN IN CUSTODY ALMOST AN HOUR AND YOUR GUYS HAVEN'T STARTED BEATING ME UP YET.
SORRY. HANSON'S NOT HERE TONIGHT AND THE CRAPPY REPARTEE IS HIS DEPARTMENT.
LOOK, CINDY, I TOLD YOU WE GOT A REPORT THAT THE LOBSTER WAS SEEN LEAVING THE OFFICES OF THE HERALD TRIBUNE.
AND I GET REPORTS EVERY DAY THAT VALENTINO'S STILL ALIVE, AND THAT KING KONG WAS REAL.
SO?
"SO," THE UNIFORMS WENT TO INVESTIGATE, AND THEY TRACKED HIM DOWN.
ASSUMING HIS POINT OF ORIGIN AS THE TRIBUNE, THEY WERE EVEN ABLE TO INTERCEPT HIM.
"INTERCEPT HIM"...?

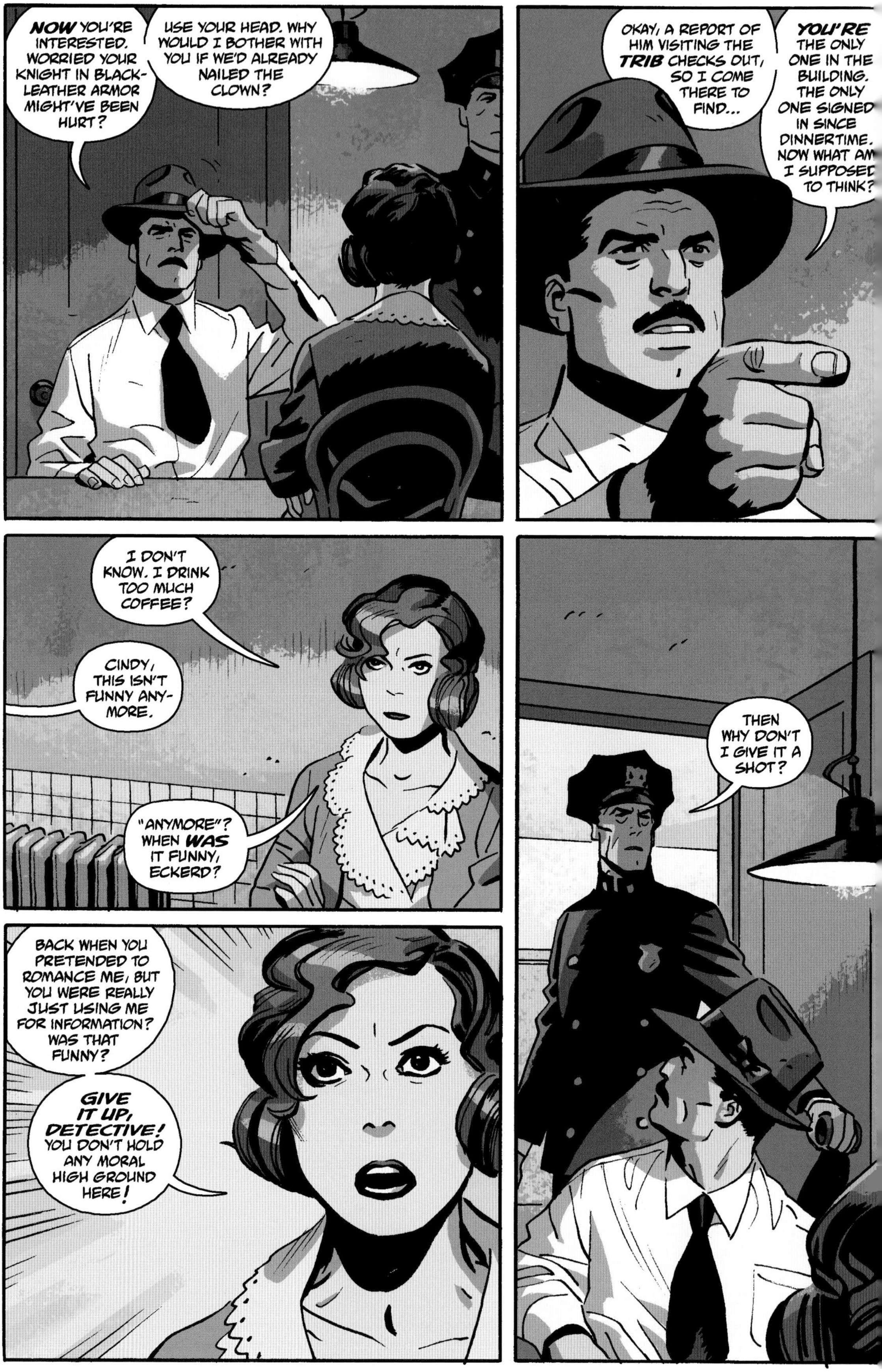
NOW YOU'RE INTERESTED. WORRIED YOUR KNIGHT IN BLACK-LEATHER ARMOR MIGHT'VE BEEN HURT?
USE YOUR HEAD. WHY WOULD I BOTHER WITH YOU IF WE'D ALREADY NAILED THE CLOWN?
OKAY, A REPORT OF HIM VISITING THE TRIB CHECKS OUT, SO I COME THERE TO FIND...
YOU'RE THE ONLY ONE IN THE BUILDING. THE ONLY ONE SIGNED IN SINCE DINNERTIME. NOW WHAT AM I SUPPOSED TO THINK?
I DON'T KNOW. I DRINK TOO MUCH COFFEE?
CINDY, THIS ISN'T FUNNY ANYMORE.
"ANYMORE"? WHEN WAS IT FUNNY, ECKERD?
THEN WHY DON'T I GIVE IT A SHOT?
BACK WHEN YOU PRETENDED TO ROMANCE ME, BUT YOU WERE REALLY JUST USING ME FOR INFORMATION? WAS THAT FUNNY?
GIVE IT UP, DETECTIVE! YOU DON'T HOLD ANY MORAL HIGH GROUND HERE!

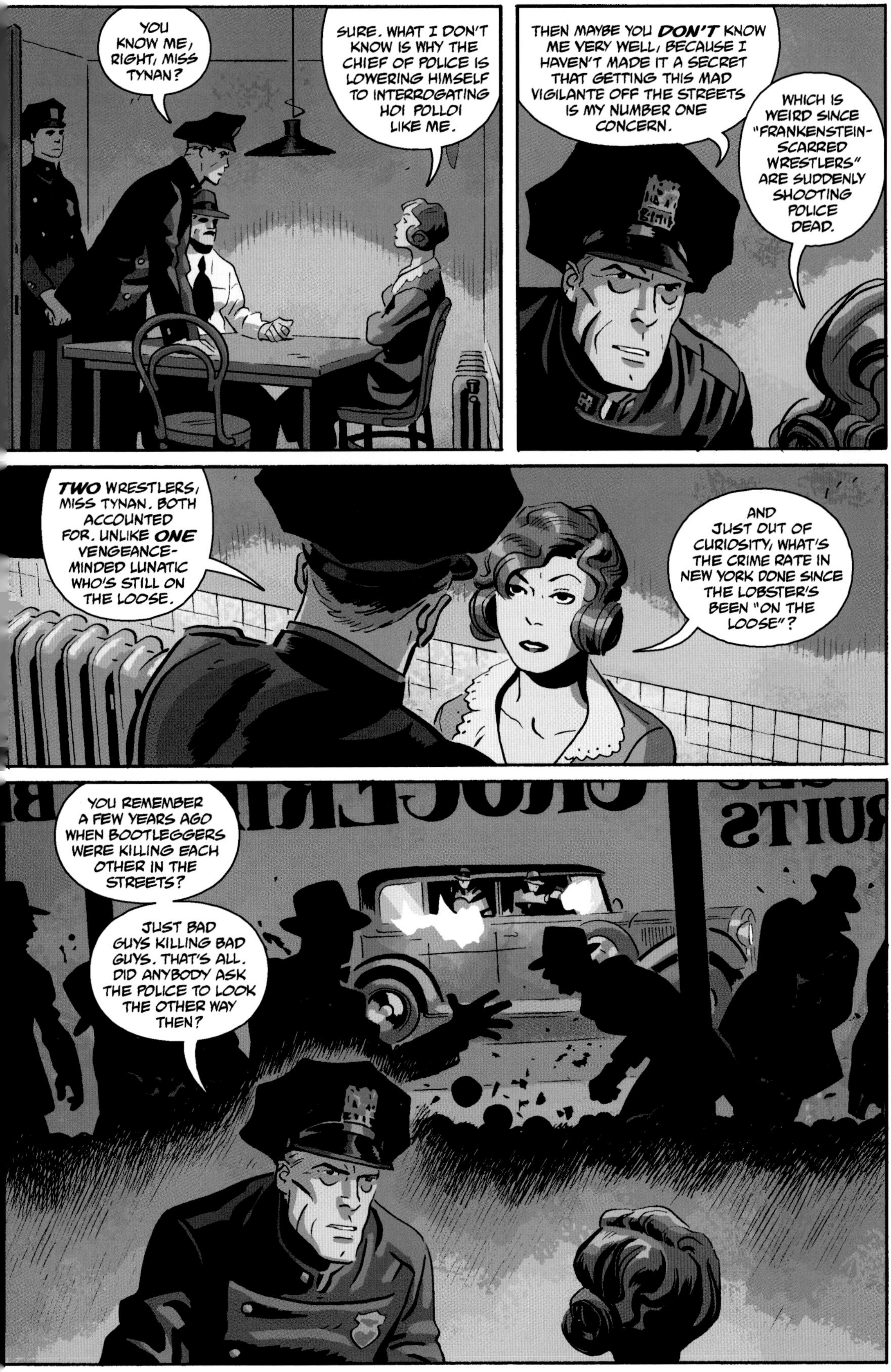
YOU KNOW ME, RIGHT, MISS TYNAN?
SURE. WHAT I DON'T KNOW IS WHY THE CHIEF OF POLICE IS LOWERING HIMSELF TO INTERROGATING HOI POLLOI LIKE ME.
THEN MAYBE YOU **DON'T** KNOW ME VERY WELL, BECAUSE I HAVEN'T MADE IT A SECRET THAT GETTING THIS MAD VIGILANTE OFF THE STREETS IS MY NUMBER ONE CONCERN.
WHICH IS WEIRD SINCE "FRANKENSTEIN-SCARRED WRESTLERS" ARE SUDDENLY SHOOTING POLICE DEAD.
TWO WRESTLERS, MISS TYNAN. BOTH ACCOUNTED FOR. UNLIKE **ONE** VENGEANCE-MINDED LUNATIC WHO'S STILL ON THE LOOSE.
AND JUST OUT OF CURIOSITY, WHAT'S THE CRIME RATE IN NEW YORK DONE SINCE THE LOBSTER'S BEEN "ON THE LOOSE"?
YOU REMEMBER A FEW YEARS AGO WHEN BOOTLEGGERS WERE KILLING EACH OTHER IN THE STREETS?
JUST BAD GUYS KILLING BAD GUYS. THAT'S ALL. DID ANYBODY ASK THE POLICE TO LOOK THE OTHER WAY THEN?

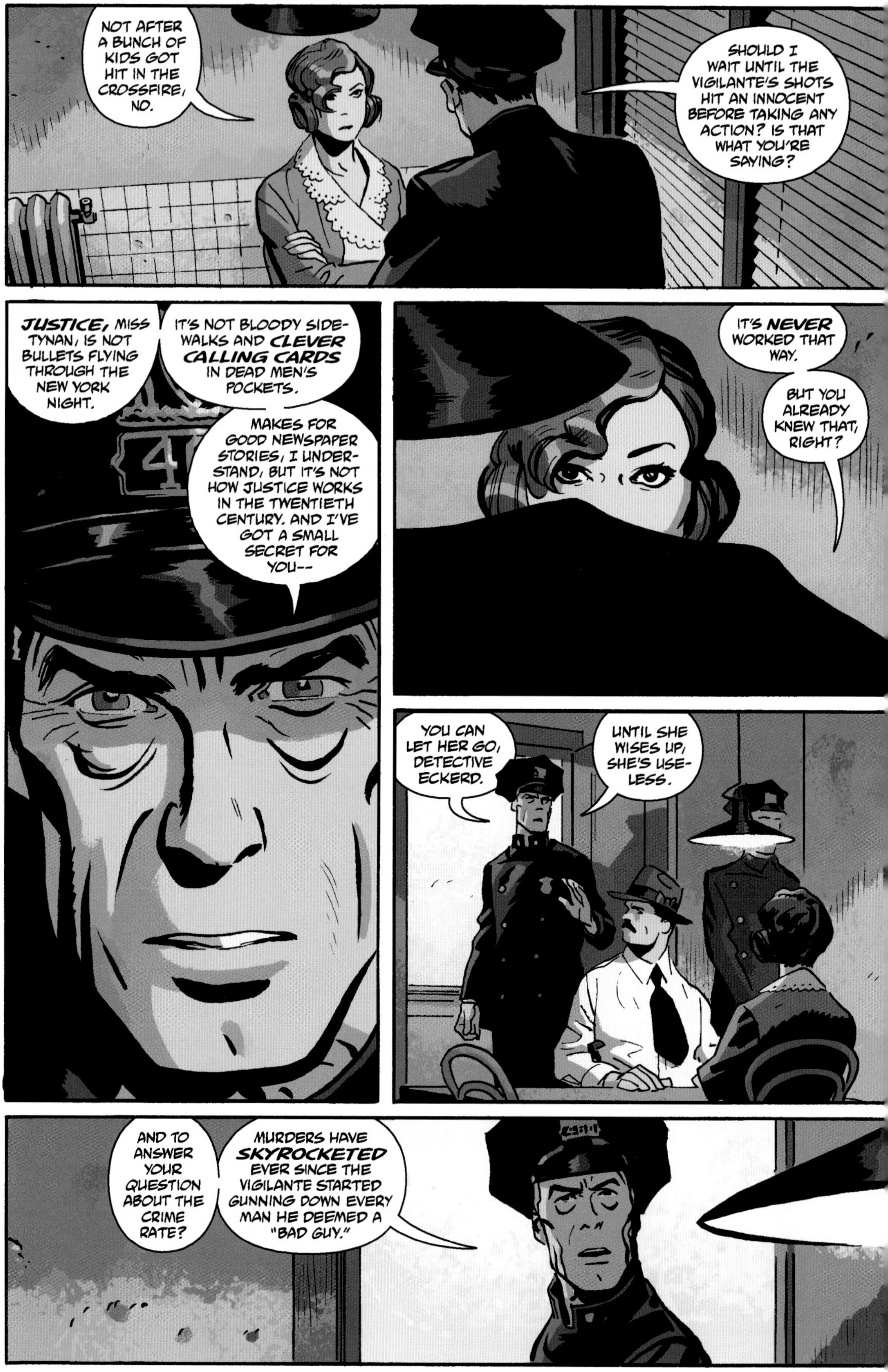

NOT AFTER A BUNCH OF KIDS GOT HIT IN THE CROSSFIRE, NO.
SHOULD I WAIT UNTIL THE VIGILANTE'S SHOTS HIT AN INNOCENT BEFORE TAKING ANY ACTION? IS THAT WHAT YOU'RE SAYING?
JUSTICE, MISS TYNAN, IS NOT BULLETS FLYING THROUGH THE NEW YORK NIGHT.
IT'S NOT BLOODY SIDE-WALKS AND CLEVER CALLING CARDS IN DEAD MEN'S POCKETS.
MAKES FOR GOOD NEWSPAPER STORIES, I UNDER-STAND, BUT IT'S NOT HOW JUSTICE WORKS IN THE TWENTIETH CENTURY. AND I'VE GOT A SMALL SECRET FOR YOU--
IT'S NEVER WORKED THAT WAY.
BUT YOU ALREADY KNEW THAT, RIGHT?
YOU CAN LET HER GO, DETECTIVE ECKERD.
UNTIL SHE WISES UP, SHE'S USE-LESS.
AND TO ANSWER YOUR QUESTION ABOUT THE CRIME RATE?
MURDERS HAVE SKYROCKETED EVER SINCE THE VIGILANTE STARTED GUNNING DOWN EVERY MAN HE DEEMED A "BAD GUY."

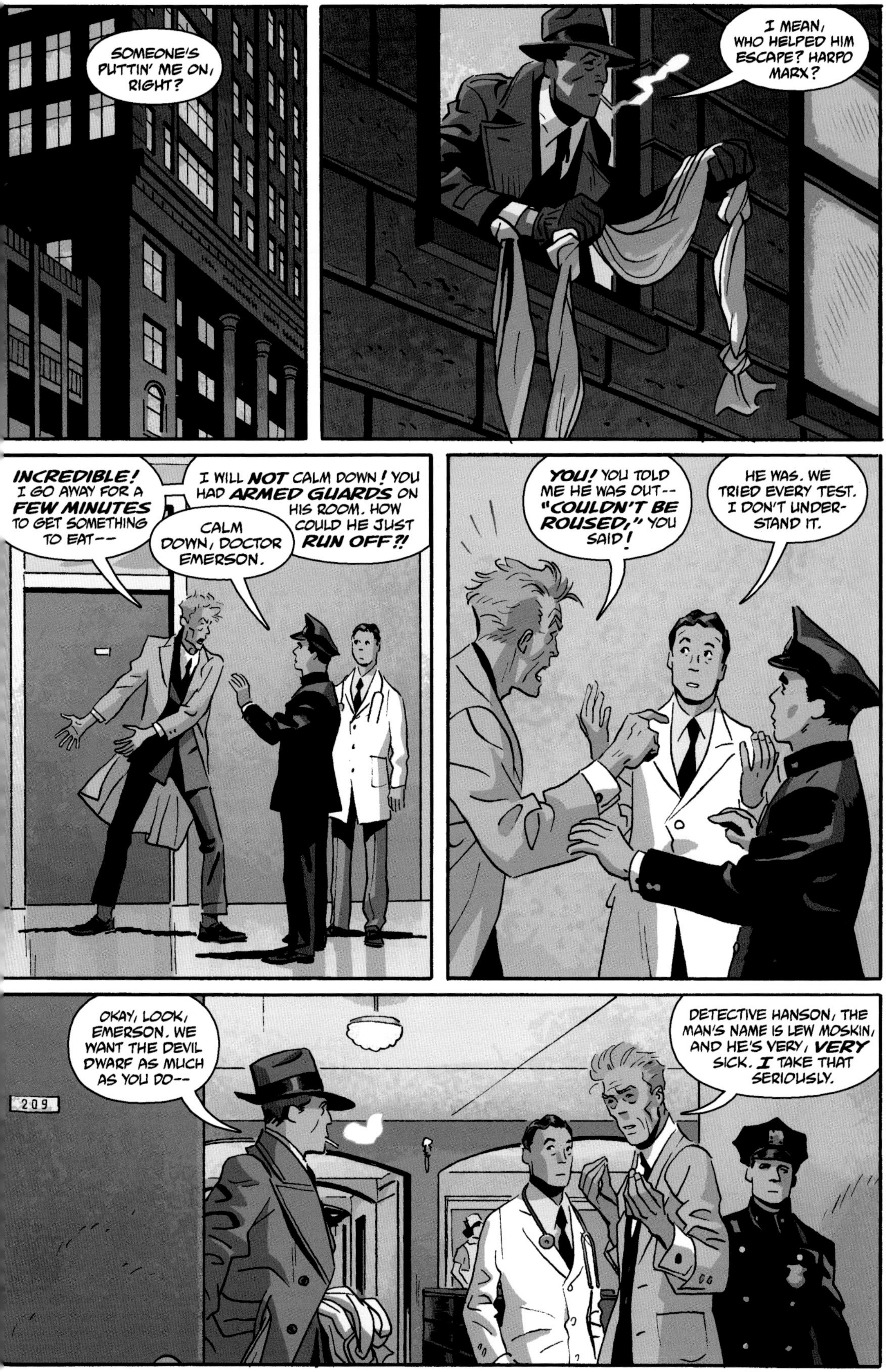

SOMEONE'S PUTTIN' ME ON, RIGHT?
I MEAN, WHO HELPED HIM ESCAPE? HARPO MARX?
INCREDIBLE! I GO AWAY FOR A FEW MINUTES TO GET SOMETHING TO EAT--
CALM DOWN, DOCTOR EMERSON.
I WILL NOT CALM DOWN! YOU HAD ARMED GUARDS ON HIS ROOM. HOW COULD HE JUST RUN OFF?!
YOU! YOU TOLD ME HE WAS OUT-- "COULDN'T BE ROUSED," YOU SAID!
HE WAS. WE TRIED EVERY TEST. I DON'T UNDERSTAND IT.
OKAY, LOOK, EMERSON. WE WANT THE DEVIL DWARF AS MUCH AS YOU DO--
209
DETECTIVE HANSON, THE MAN'S NAME IS LEW MOSKIN, AND HE'S VERY, VERY SICK. I TAKE THAT SERIOUSLY.

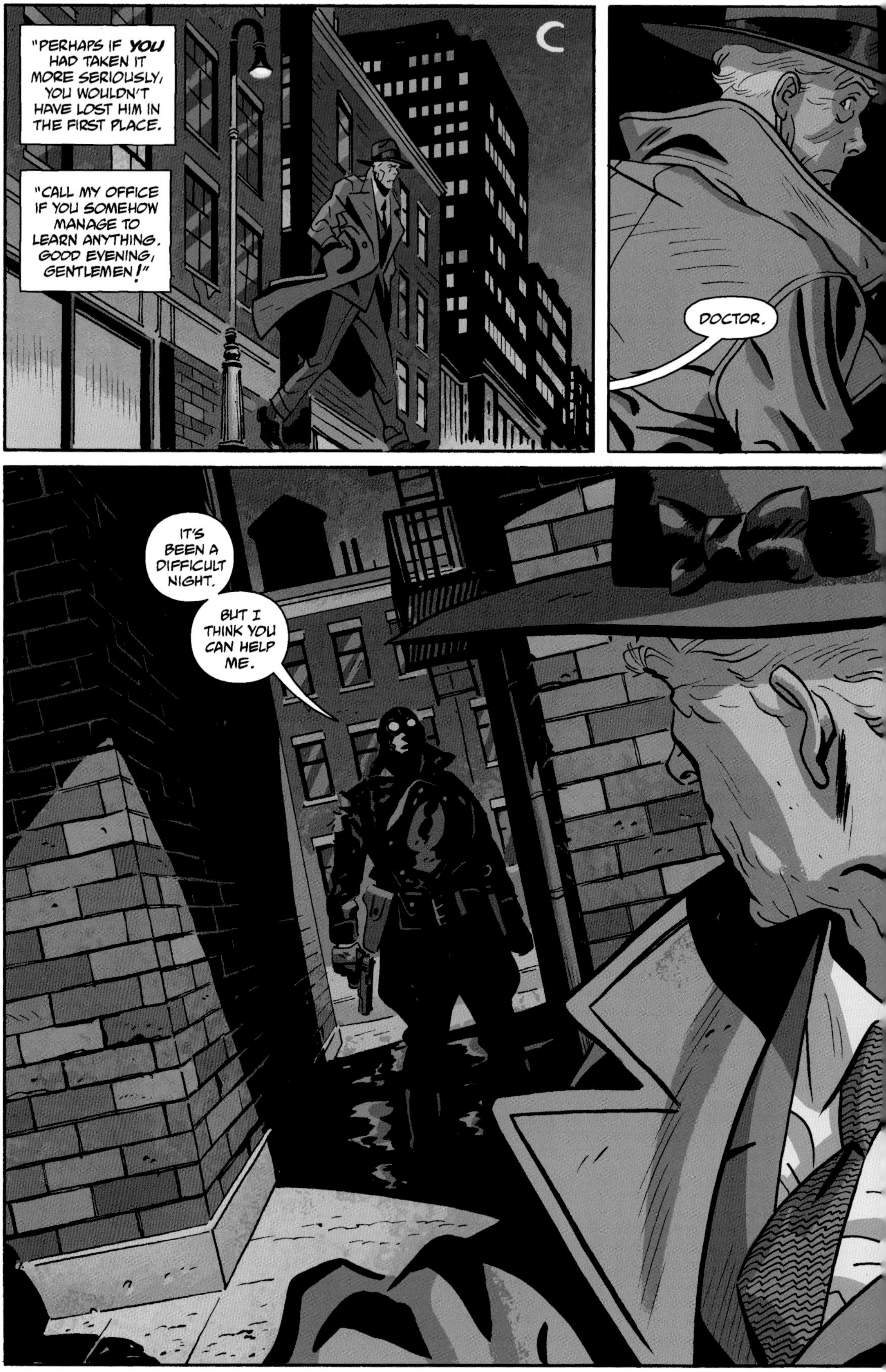
"PERHAPS IF YOU HAD TAKEN IT MORE SERIOUSLY, YOU WOULDN'T HAVE LOST HIM IN THE FIRST PLACE.
"CALL MY OFFICE IF YOU SOMEHOW MANAGE TO LEARN ANYTHING. GOOD EVENING, GENTLEMEN!"
DOCTOR.
IT'S BEEN A DIFFICULT NIGHT.
BUT I THINK YOU CAN HELP ME.

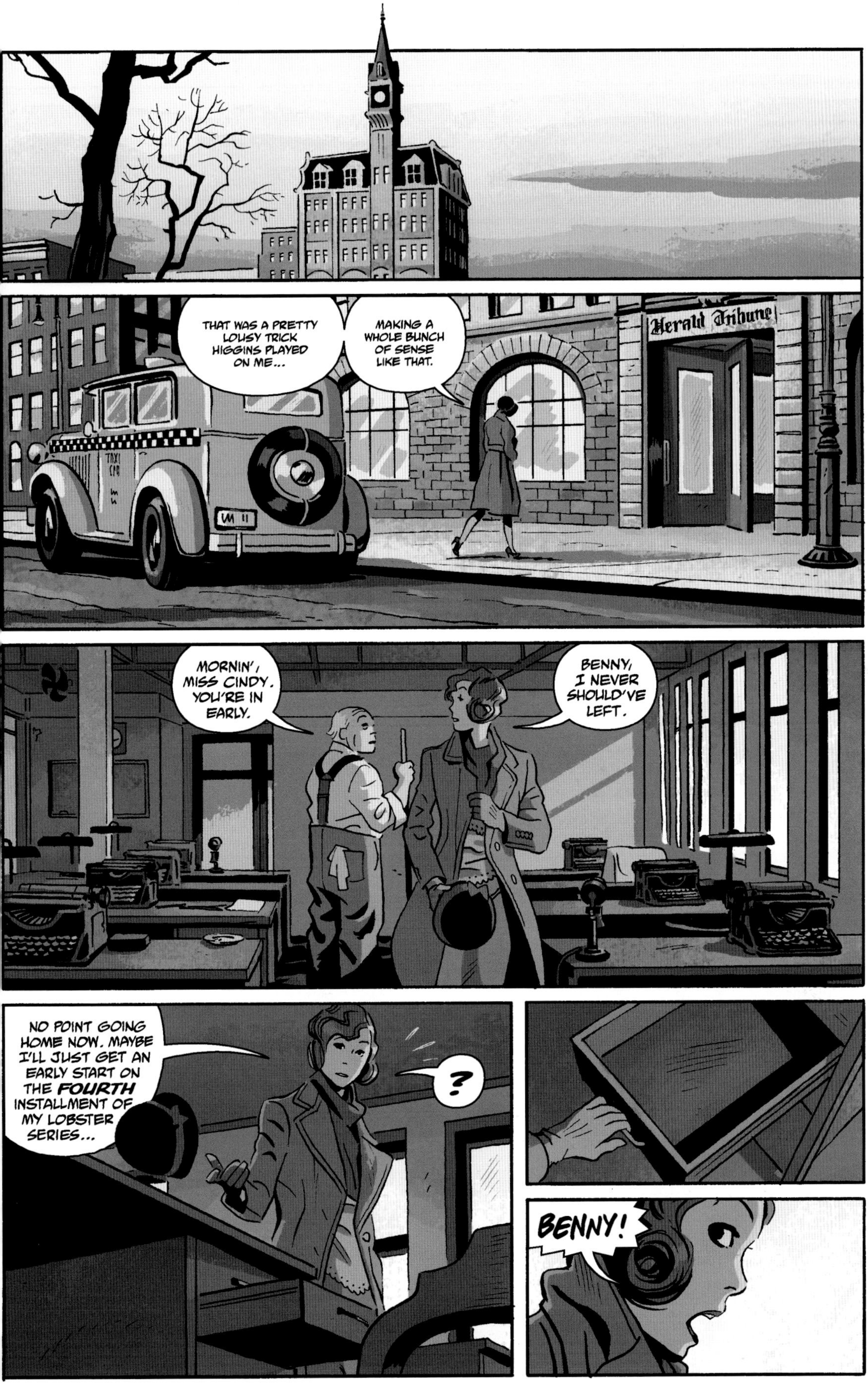

THAT WAS A PRETTY LOUSY TRICK HIGGINS PLAYED ON ME...
MAKING A WHOLE BUNCH OF SENSE LIKE THAT.
Herald Tribune
MORNIN', MISS CINDY. YOU'RE IN EARLY.
BENNY, I NEVER SHOULD'VE LEFT.
NO POINT GOING HOME NOW. MAYBE I'LL JUST GET AN EARLY START ON THE FOURTH INSTALLMENT OF MY LOBSTER SERIES...
?
BENNY!

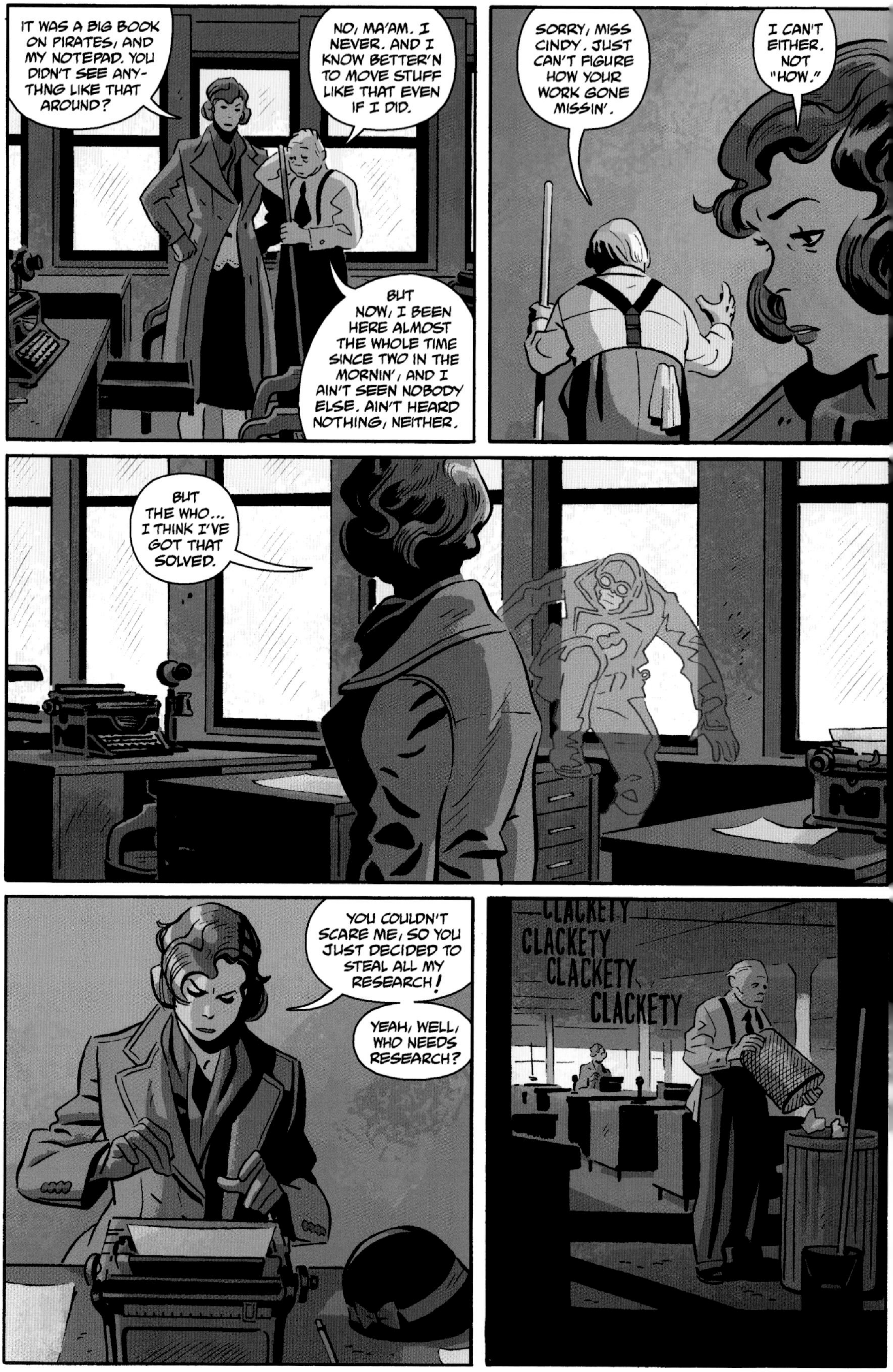
IT WAS A BIG BOOK ON PIRATES, AND MY NOTEPAD. YOU DIDN'T SEE ANY-THNG LIKE THAT AROUND?
NO, MA'AM. I NEVER. AND I KNOW BETTER'N TO MOVE STUFF LIKE THAT EVEN IF I DID.
BUT NOW, I BEEN HERE ALMOST THE WHOLE TIME SINCE TWO IN THE MORNIN', AND I AIN'T SEEN NOBODY ELSE. AIN'T HEARD NOTHING, NEITHER.
SORRY, MISS CINDY. JUST CAN'T FIGURE HOW YOUR WORK GONE MISSIN'.
I CAN'T EITHER. NOT "HOW."
BUT THE WHO... I THINK I'VE GOT THAT SOLVED.
YOU COULDN'T SCARE ME, SO YOU JUST DECIDED TO STEAL ALL MY RESEARCH!
YEAH, WELL, WHO NEEDS RESEARCH?
CLACKETY
CLACKETY
CLACKETY
CLACKETY

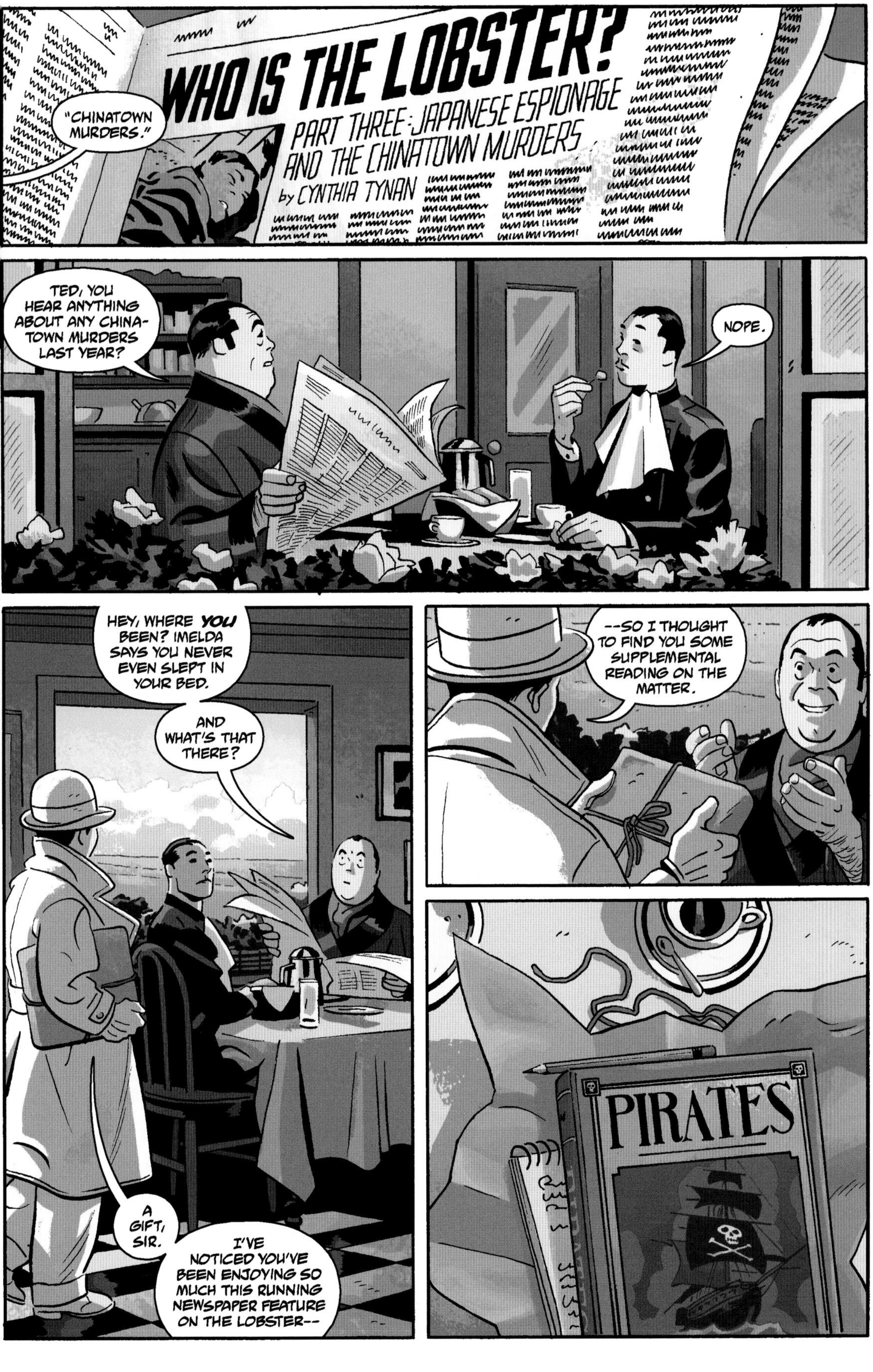
WHO IS THE LOBSTER?
PART THREE: JAPANESE ESPIONAGE AND THE CHINATOWN MURDERS
by CYNTHIA TYNAN
"CHINATOWN MURDERS."
TED, YOU HEAR ANYTHING ABOUT ANY CHINA-TOWN MURDERS LAST YEAR?
NOPE.
HEY, WHERE YOU BEEN? IMELDA SAYS YOU NEVER EVEN SLEPT IN YOUR BED.
AND WHAT'S THAT THERE?
A GIFT, SIR.
I'VE NOTICED YOU'VE BEEN ENJOYING SO MUCH THIS RUNNING NEWSPAPER FEATURE ON THE LOBSTER--
--SO I THOUGHT TO FIND YOU SOME SUPPLEMENTAL READING ON THE MATTER.
PIRATES

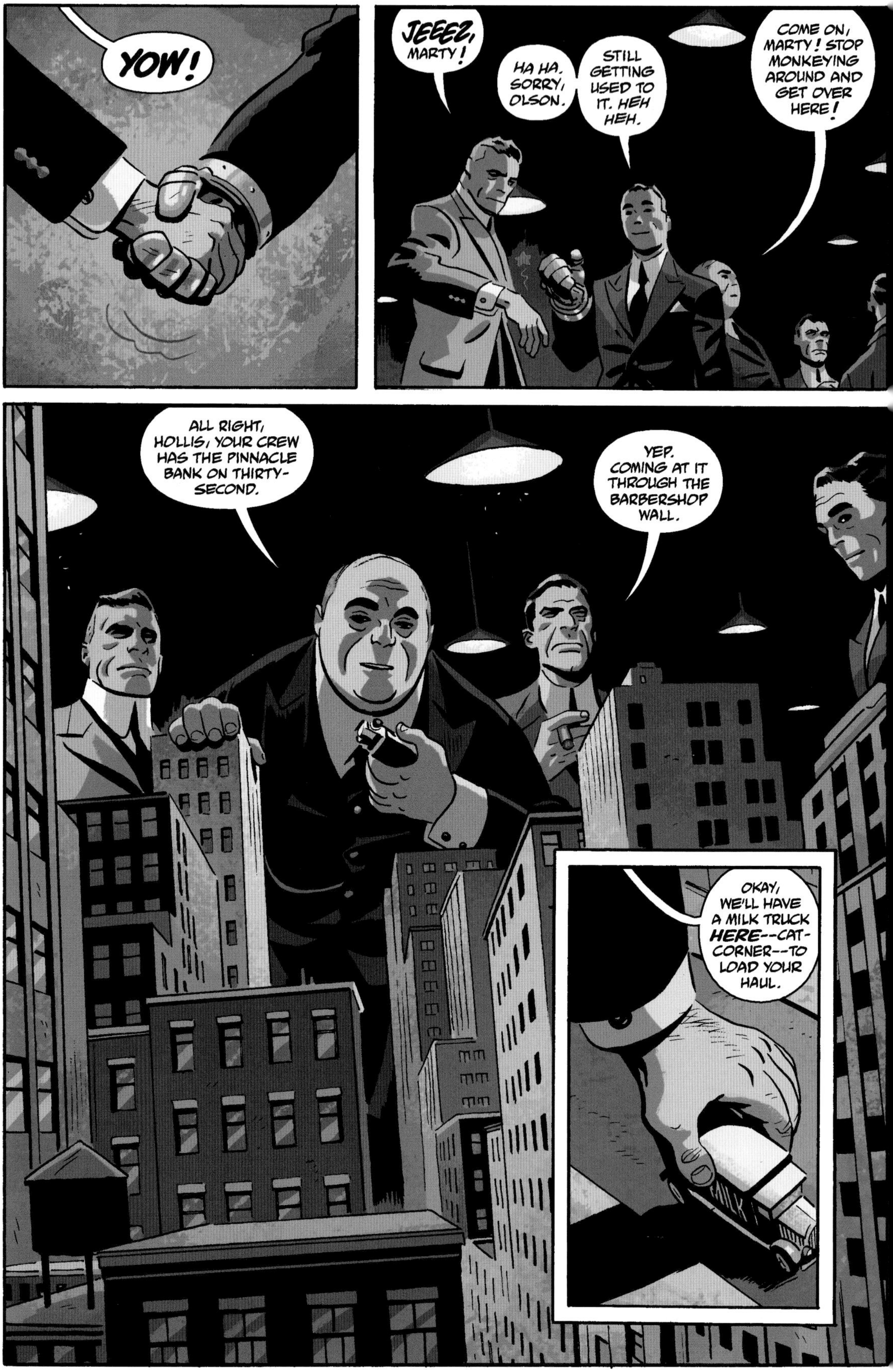
YOW!
JEEEZ, MARTY!
HA HA. SORRY, OLSON.
STILL GETTING USED TO IT. HEH HEH.
COME ON, MARTY! STOP MONKEYING AROUND AND GET OVER HERE!
ALL RIGHT, HOLLIS, YOUR CREW HAS THE PINNACLE BANK ON THIRTY-SECOND.
YEP. COMING AT IT THROUGH THE BARBERSHOP WALL.
OKAY, WE'LL HAVE A MILK TRUCK HERE--CAT-CORNER--TO LOAD YOUR HAUL.
MILK

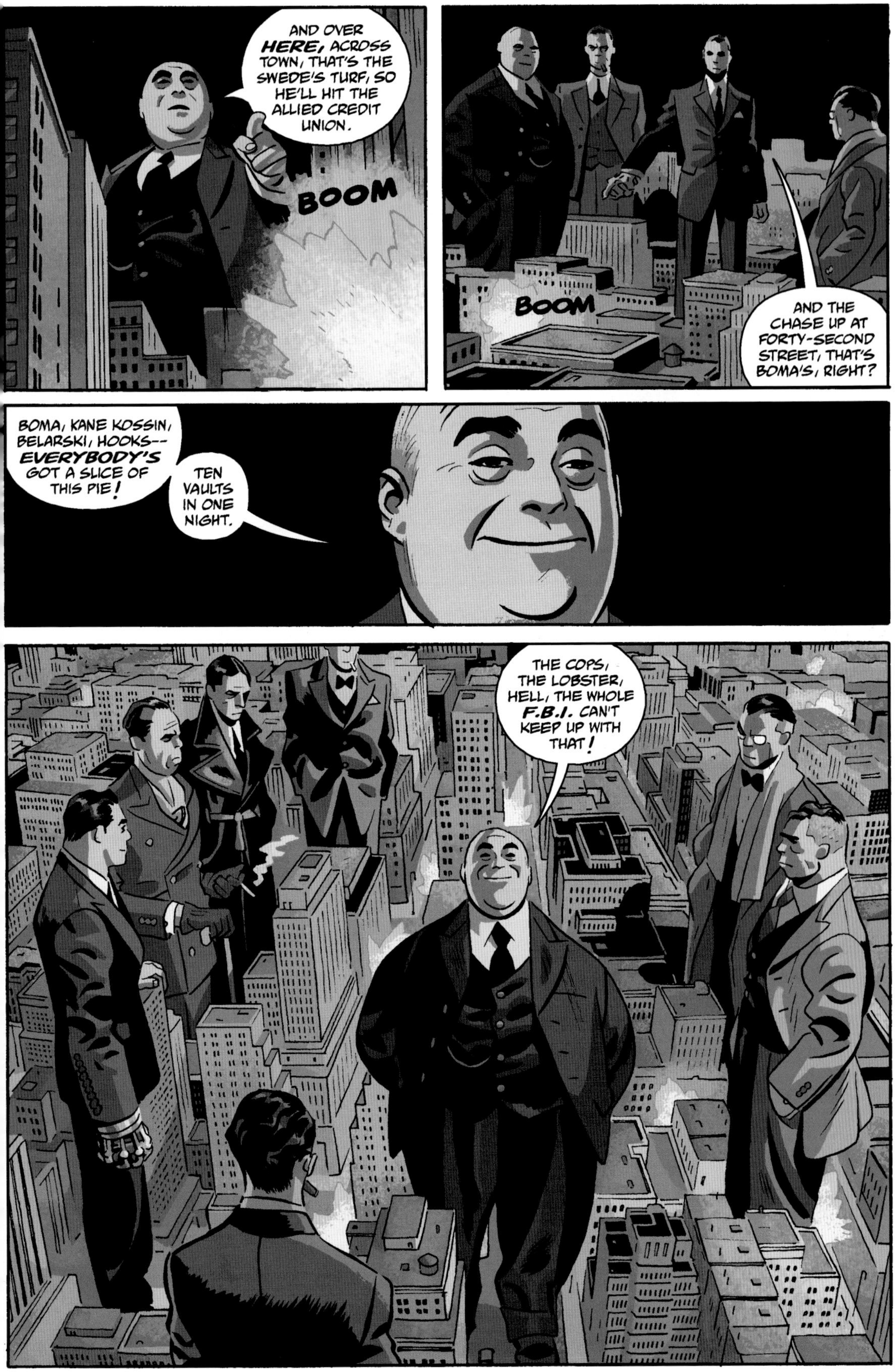
AND OVER HERE, ACROSS TOWN, THAT'S THE SWEDE'S TURF, SO HE'LL HIT THE ALLIED CREDIT UNION.
BOOM
BOOM
AND THE CHASE UP AT FORTY-SECOND STREET, THAT'S BOMA'S, RIGHT?
BOMA, KANE KOSSIN, BELARSKI, HOOKS-- EVERYBODY'S GOT A SLICE OF THIS PIE!
TEN VAULTS IN ONE NIGHT.
THE COPS, THE LOBSTER, HELL, THE WHOLE F.B.I. CAN'T KEEP UP WITH THAT!

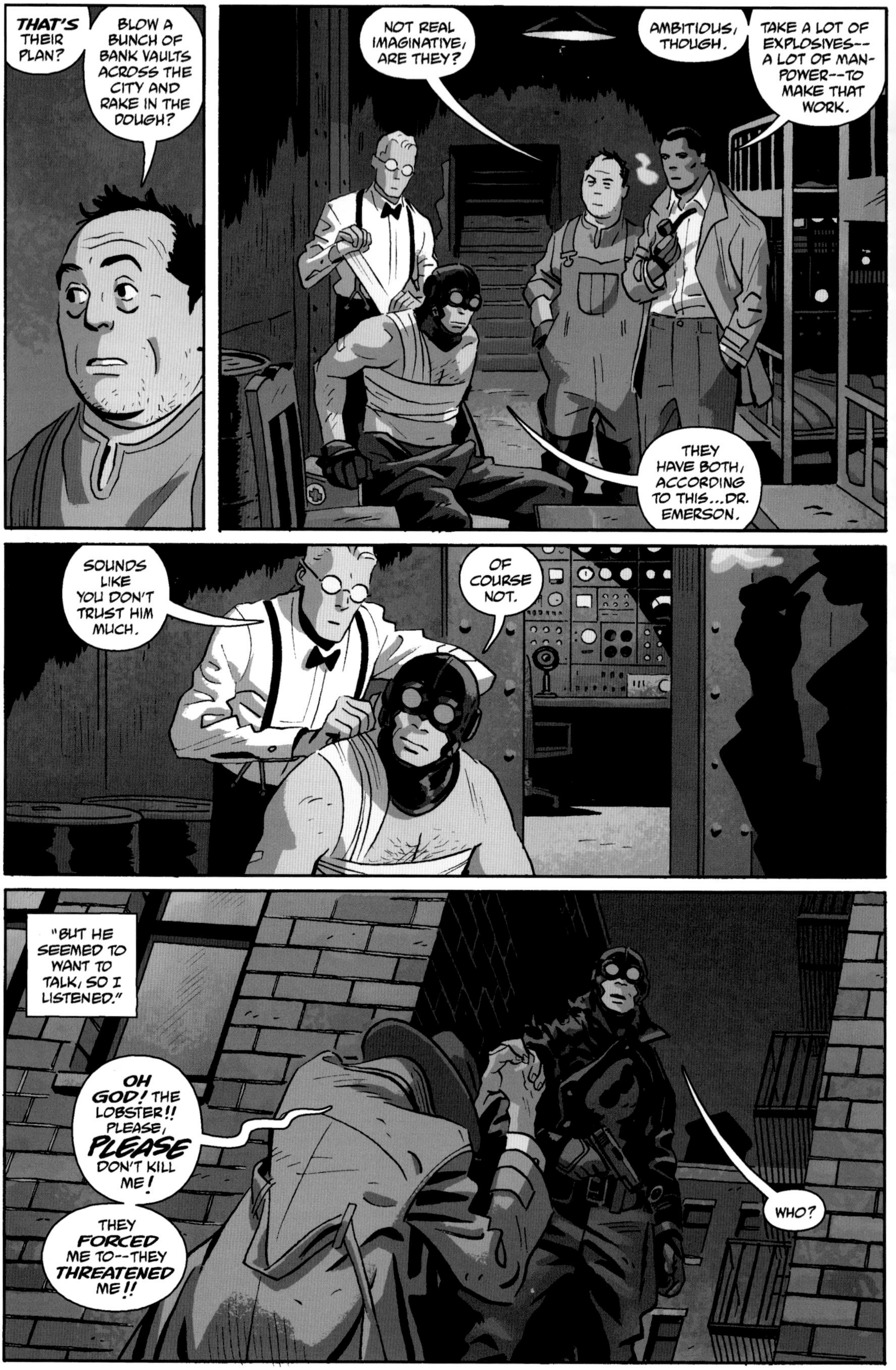
THAT'S THEIR PLAN?
BLOW A BUNCH OF BANK VAULTS ACROSS THE CITY AND RAKE IN THE DOUGH?
NOT REAL IMAGINATIVE, ARE THEY?
AMBITIOUS, THOUGH.
TAKE A LOT OF EXPLOSIVES-- A LOT OF MAN-POWER--TO MAKE THAT WORK.
THEY HAVE BOTH, ACCORDING TO THIS...DR. EMERSON.
SOUNDS LIKE YOU DON'T TRUST HIM MUCH.
OF COURSE NOT.
"BUT HE SEEMED TO WANT TO TALK, SO I LISTENED."
OH GOD! THE LOBSTER!! PLEASE, PLEASE DON'T KILL ME!
THEY FORCED ME TO--THEY THREATENED ME!!
WHO?

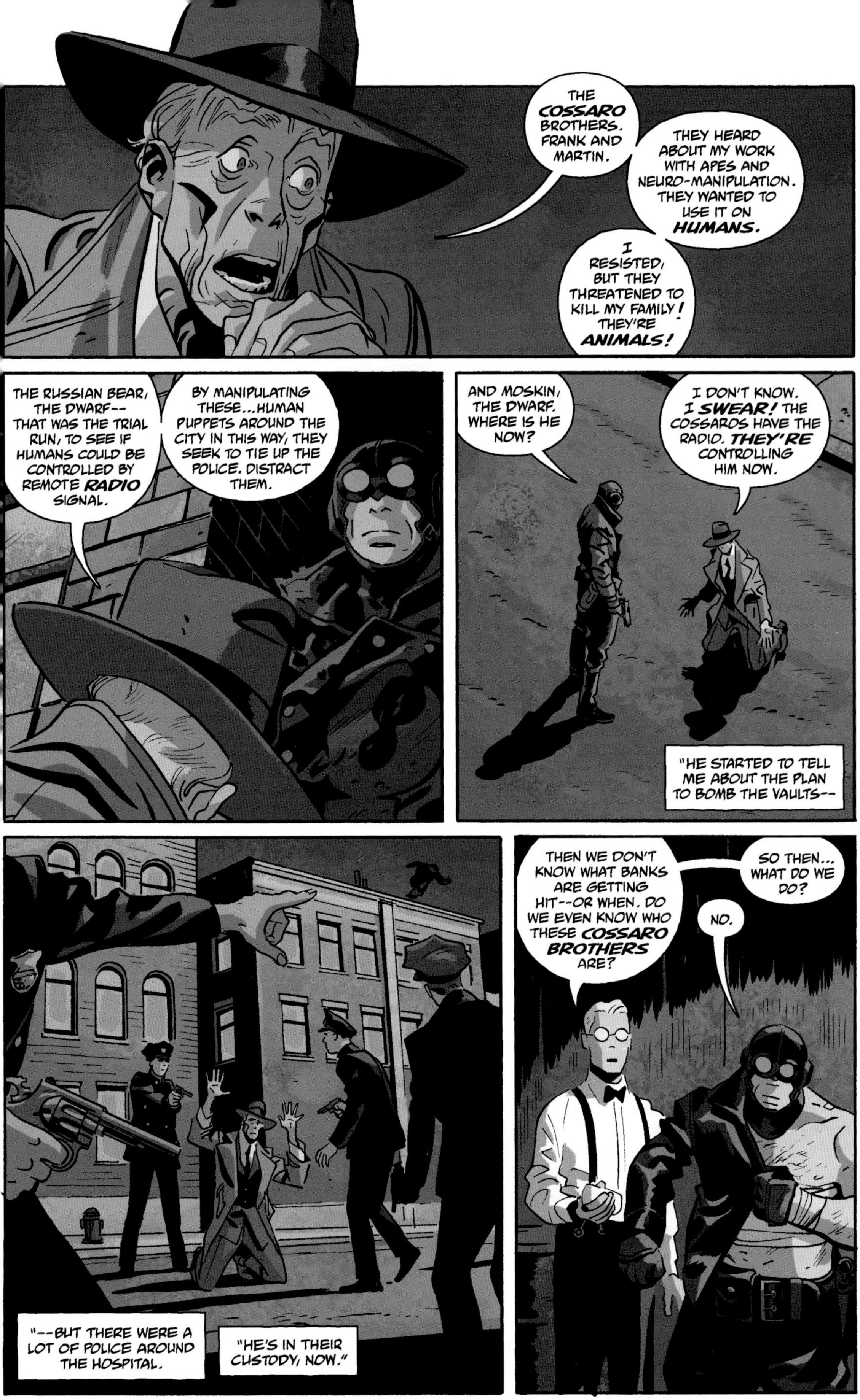
THE COSSARO BROTHERS. FRANK AND MARTIN.
THEY HEARD ABOUT MY WORK WITH APES AND NEURO-MANIPULATION. THEY WANTED TO USE IT ON HUMANS.
I RESISTED, BUT THEY THREATENED TO KILL MY FAMILY! THEY'RE ANIMALS!
THE RUSSIAN BEAR, THE DWARF-- THAT WAS THE TRIAL RUN, TO SEE IF HUMANS COULD BE CONTROLLED BY REMOTE RADIO SIGNAL.
BY MANIPULATING THESE...HUMAN PUPPETS AROUND THE CITY IN THIS WAY, THEY SEEK TO TIE UP THE POLICE. DISTRACT THEM.
AND MOSKIN, THE DWARF. WHERE IS HE NOW?
I DON'T KNOW. I SWEAR! THE COSSAROS HAVE THE RADIO. THEY'RE CONTROLLING HIM NOW.
"HE STARTED TO TELL ME ABOUT THE PLAN TO BOMB THE VAULTS--
"--BUT THERE WERE A LOT OF POLICE AROUND THE HOSPITAL.
"HE'S IN THEIR CUSTODY, NOW."
THEN WE DON'T KNOW WHAT BANKS ARE GETTING HIT--OR WHEN. DO WE EVEN KNOW WHO THESE COSSARO BROTHERS ARE?
NO.
SO THEN... WHAT DO WE DO?

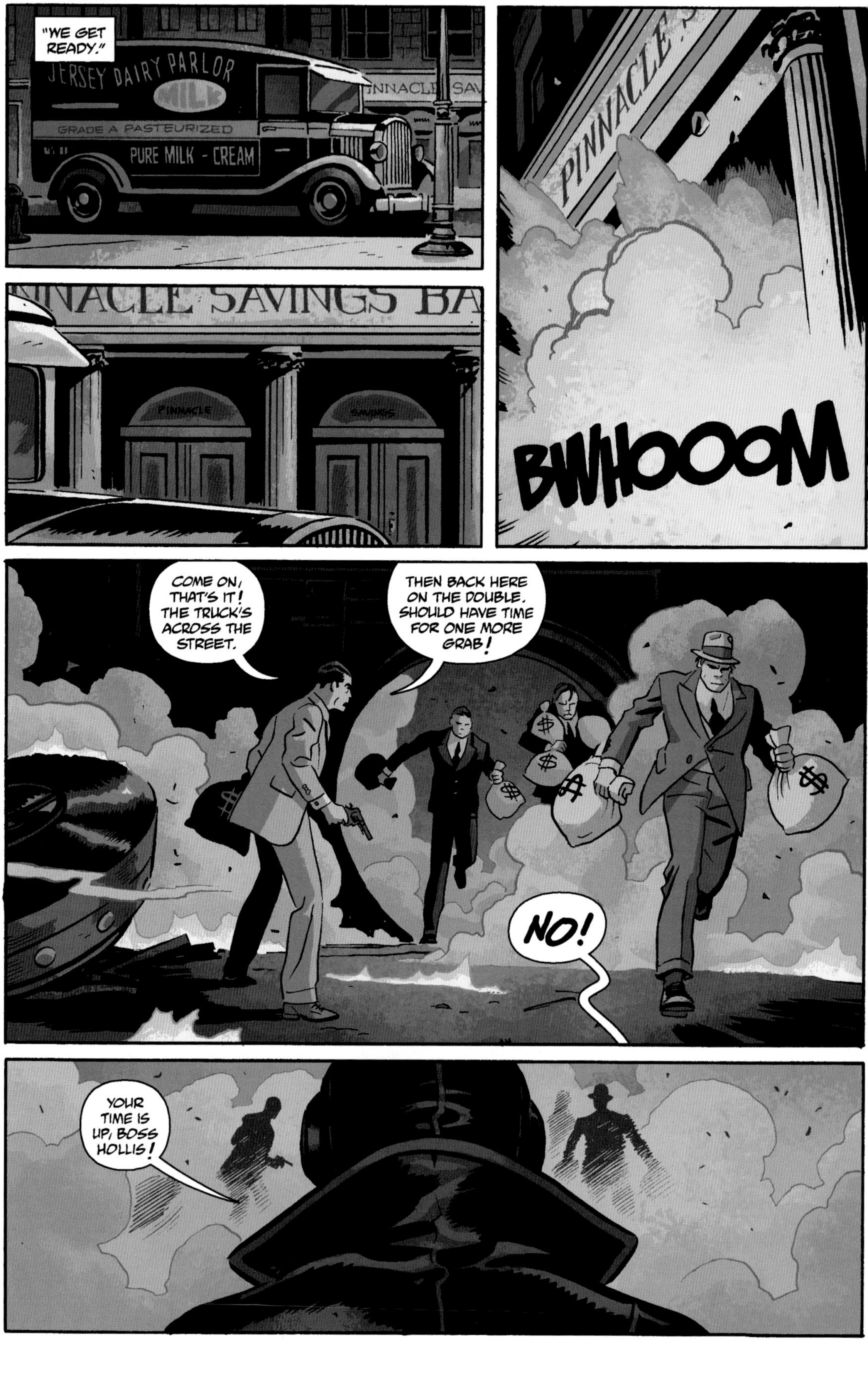
"WE GET READY."
JERSEY DAIRY PARLOR
MILK
GRADE A PASTEURIZED
PURE MILK - CREAM
PINNACLE SAV
PINNACLE S
INNACLE SAVINGS BA
PINNACLE
SAVINGS
BWHOOOM
COME ON, THAT'S IT! THE TRUCK'S ACROSS THE STREET.
THEN BACK HERE ON THE DOUBLE. SHOULD HAVE TIME FOR ONE MORE GRAB!
NO!
YOUR TIME IS UP, BOSS HOLLIS!

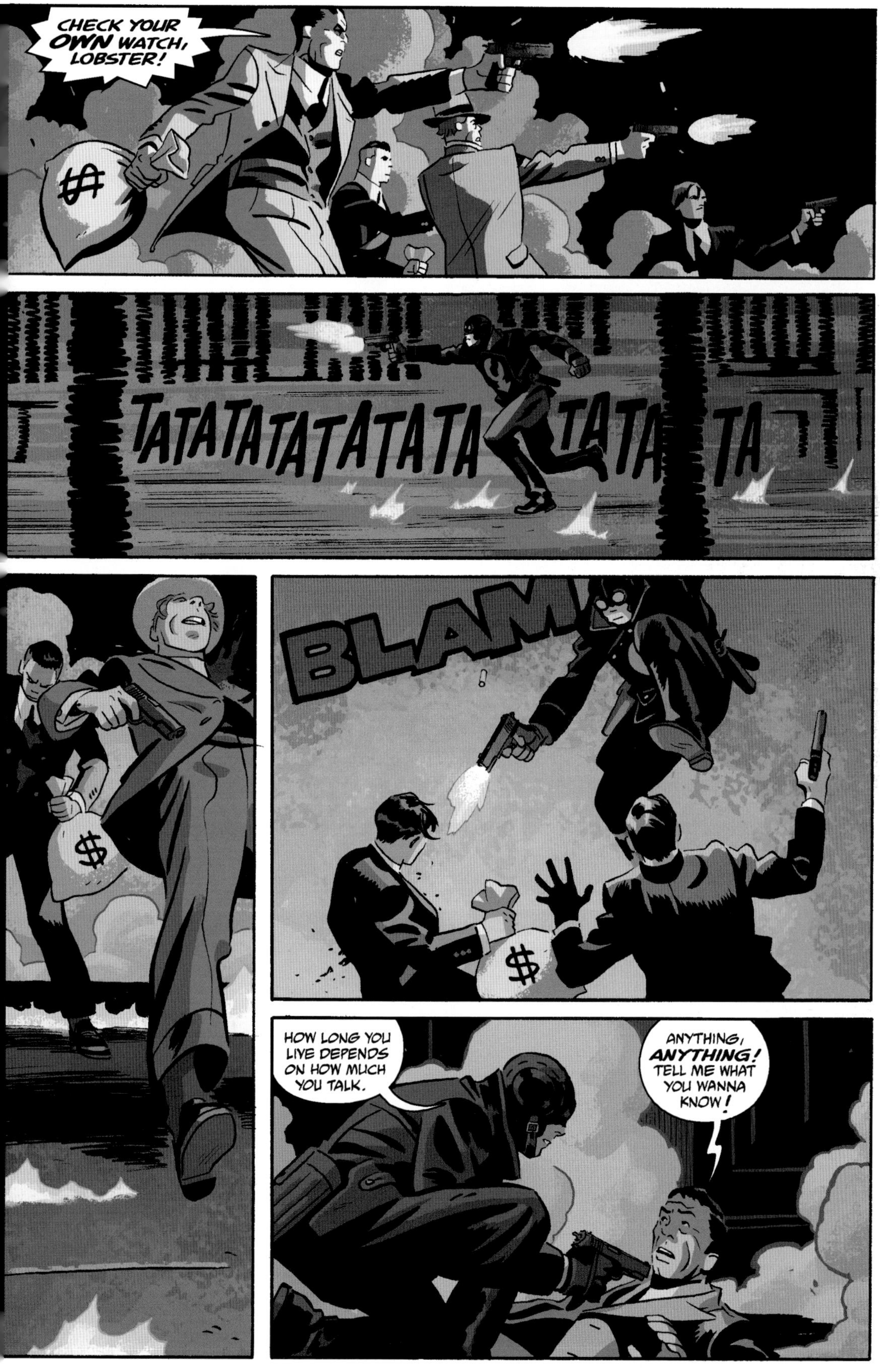
CHECK YOUR OWN WATCH, LOBSTER!
TATATATATATATA TATA TA
BLAM
HOW LONG YOU LIVE DEPENDS ON HOW MUCH YOU TALK.
ANYTHING, ANYTHING! TELL ME WHAT YOU WANNA KNOW!

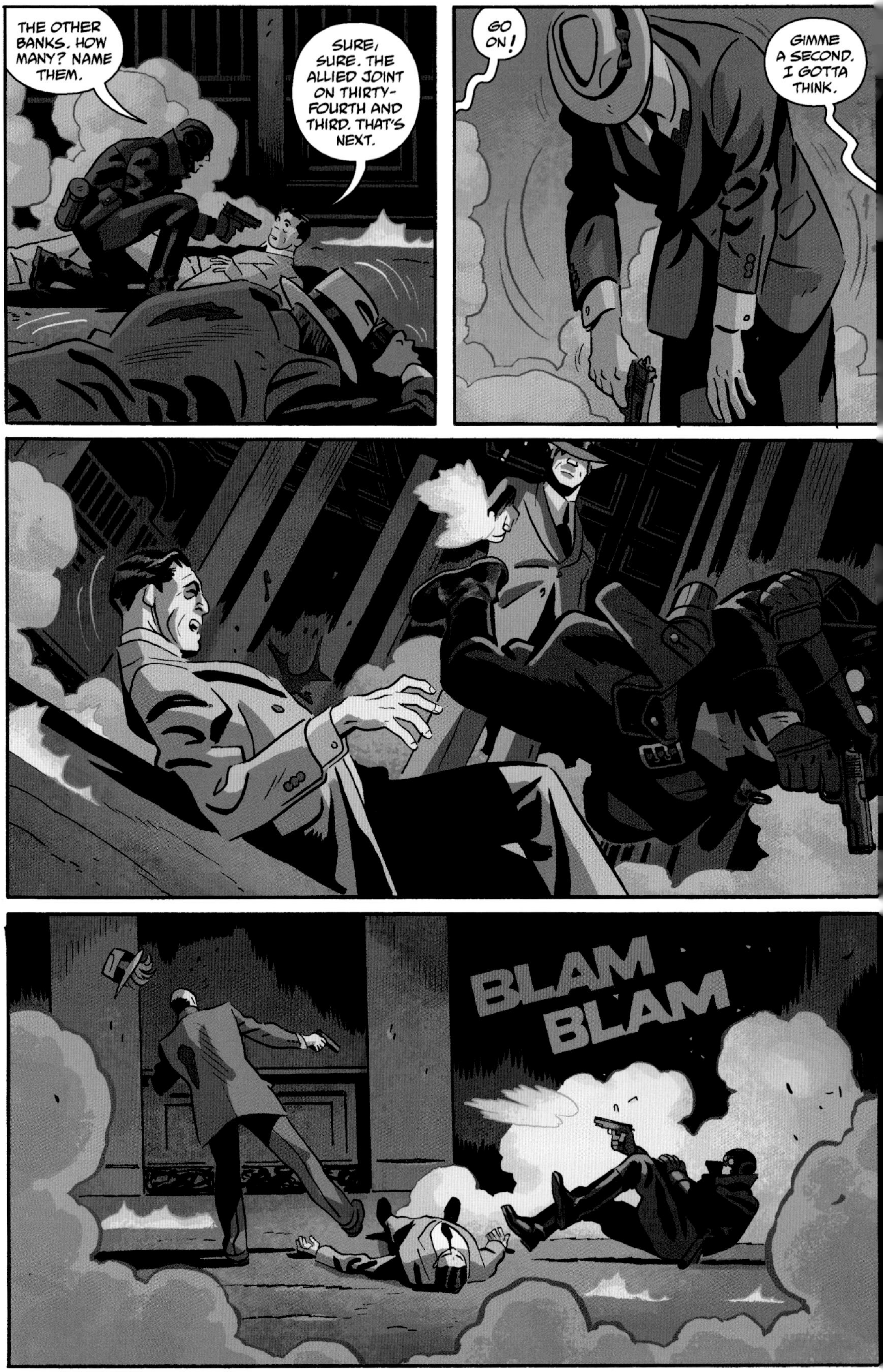
THE OTHER BANKS. HOW MANY? NAME THEM.
SURE, SURE. THE ALLIED JOINT ON THIRTY-FOURTH AND THIRD. THAT'S NEXT.
GO ON!
GIMME A SECOND. I GOTTA THINK.
BLAM
BLAM

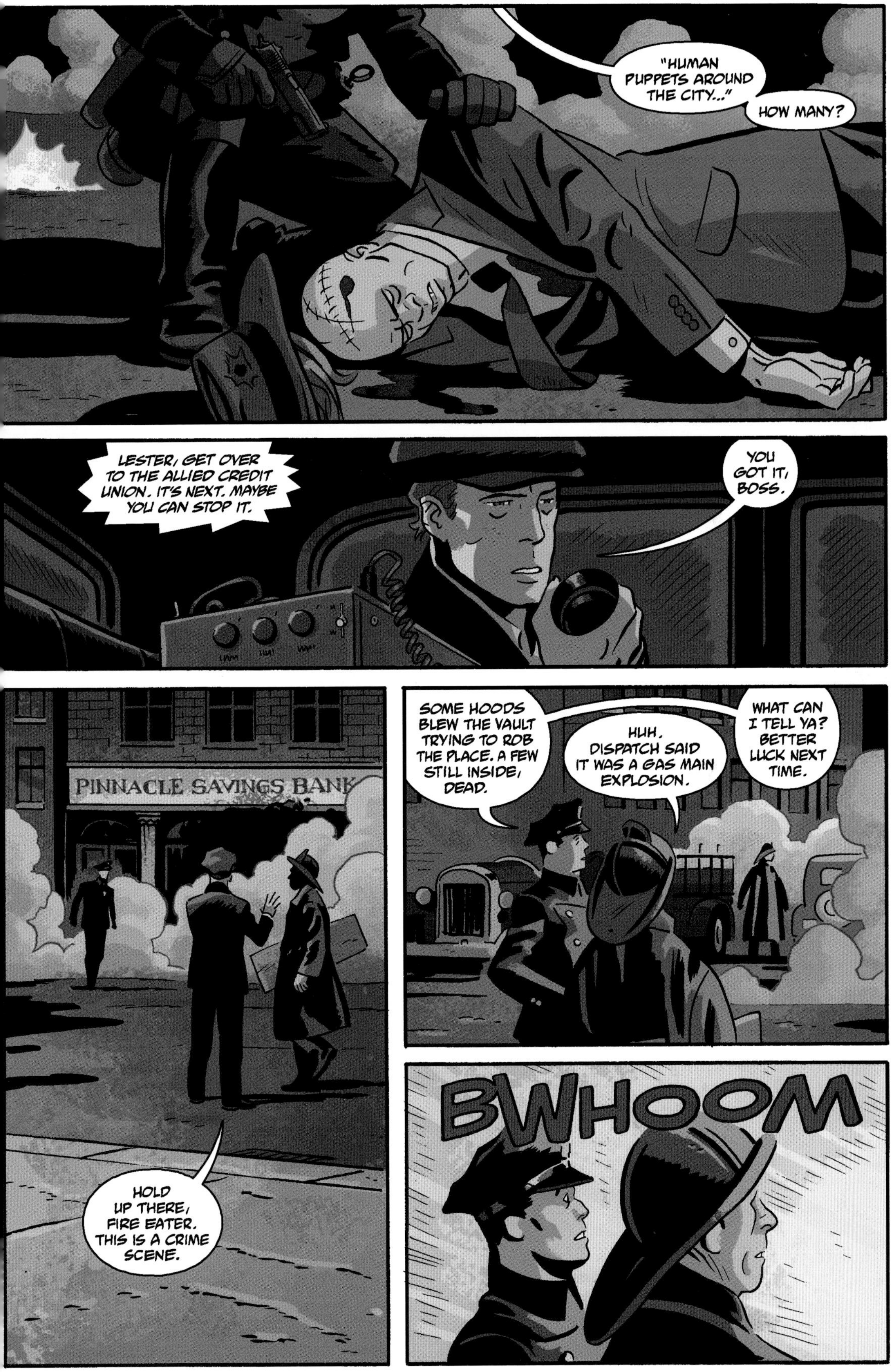
"HUMAN PUPPETS AROUND THE CITY..."
HOW MANY?
LESTER, GET OVER TO THE ALLIED CREDIT UNION. IT'S NEXT. MAYBE YOU CAN STOP IT.
YOU GOT IT, BOSS.
PINNACLE SAVINGS BANK
HOLD UP THERE, FIRE EATER. THIS IS A CRIME SCENE.
SOME HOODS BLEW THE VAULT TRYING TO ROB THE PLACE. A FEW STILL INSIDE, DEAD.
HUH. DISPATCH SAID IT WAS A GAS MAIN EXPLOSION.
WHAT CAN I TELL YA? BETTER LUCK NEXT TIME.
BWHOOM

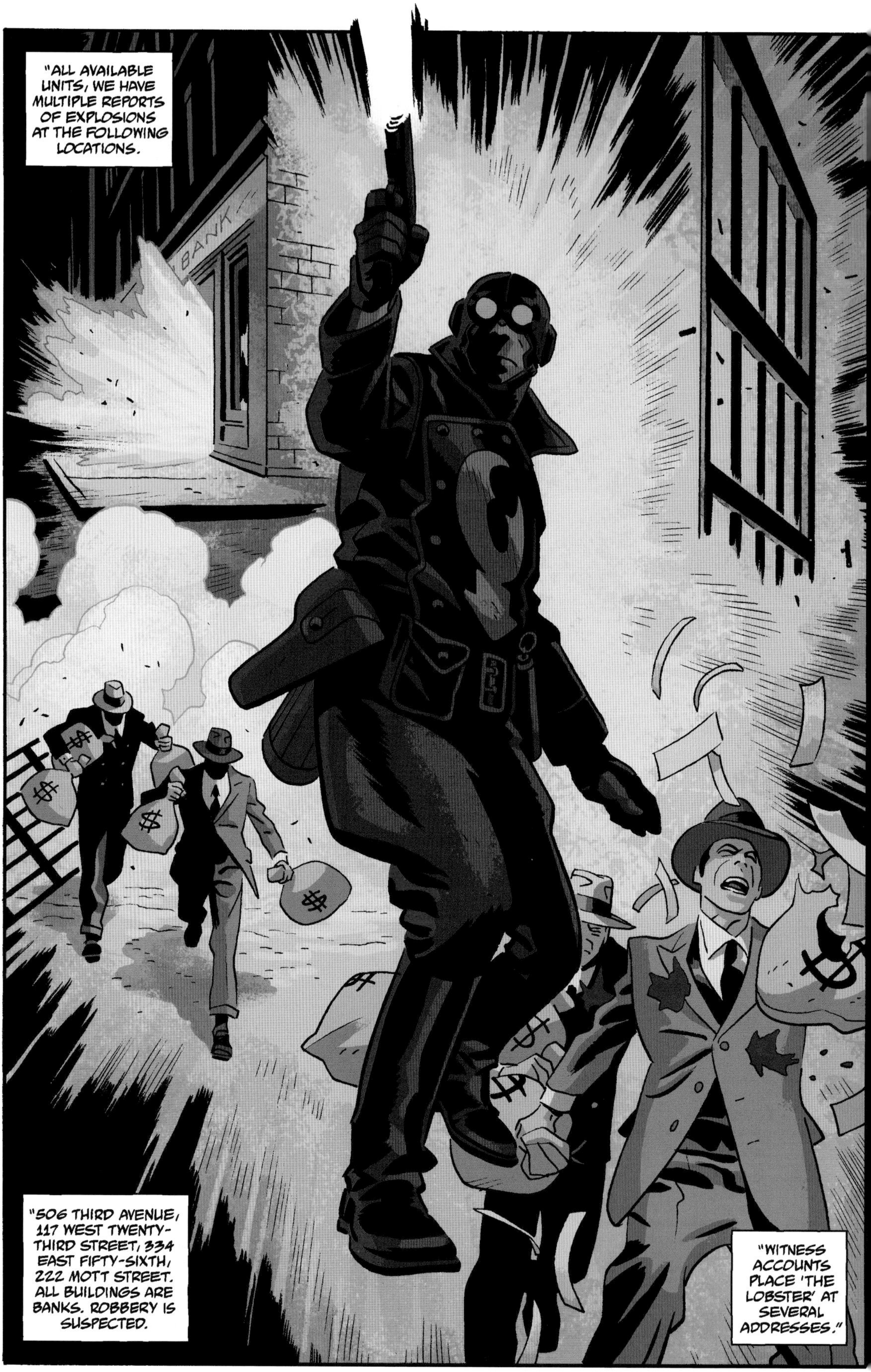
"ALL AVAILABLE UNITS, WE HAVE MULTIPLE REPORTS OF EXPLOSIONS AT THE FOLLOWING LOCATIONS.
BANK
"506 THIRD AVENUE, 117 WEST TWENTY-THIRD STREET, 334 EAST FIFTY-SIXTH, 222 MOTT STREET. ALL BUILDINGS ARE BANKS. ROBBERY IS SUSPECTED.
"WITNESS ACCOUNTS PLACE 'THE LOBSTER' AT SEVERAL ADDRESSES."

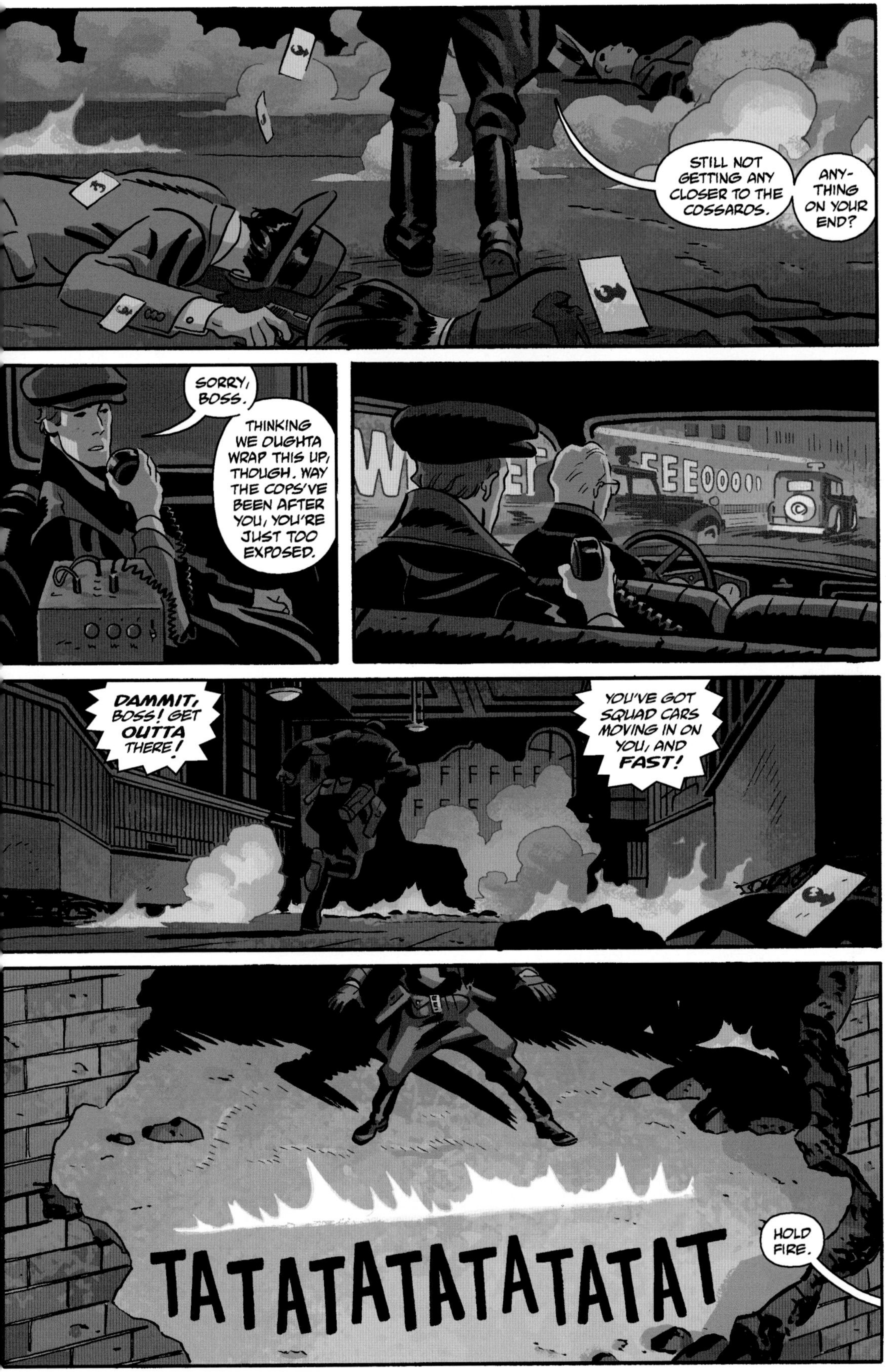
STILL NOT GETTING ANY CLOSER TO THE COSSAROS.
ANY-THING ON YOUR END?
SORRY, BOSS.
THINKING WE OUGHTA WRAP THIS UP, THOUGH. WAY THE COPS'VE BEEN AFTER YOU, YOU'RE JUST TOO EXPOSED.
DAMMIT, BOSS! GET OUTTA THERE!
YOU'VE GOT SQUAD CARS MOVING IN ON YOU, AND FAST!
TATATATATATATATAT
HOLD FIRE.

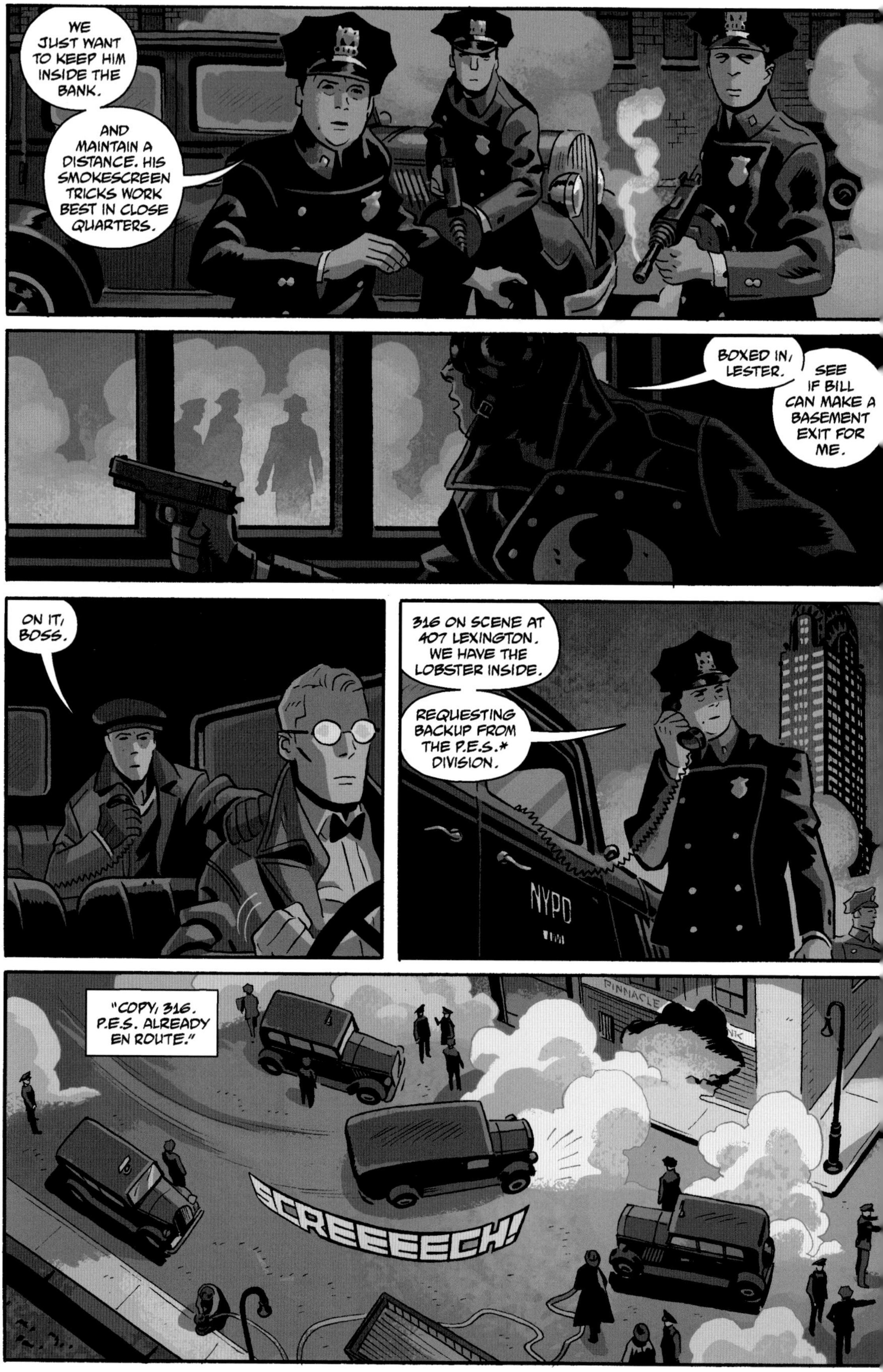

WE JUST WANT TO KEEP HIM INSIDE THE BANK.
AND MAINTAIN A DISTANCE. HIS SMOKESCREEN TRICKS WORK BEST IN CLOSE QUARTERS.
BOXED IN, LESTER.
SEE IF BILL CAN MAKE A BASEMENT EXIT FOR ME.
ON IT, BOSS.
316 ON SCENE AT 407 LEXINGTON. WE HAVE THE LOBSTER INSIDE.
REQUESTING BACKUP FROM THE P.E.S.* DIVISION.
NYPD
"COPY, 316. P.E.S. ALREADY EN ROUTE."
PINNACLE
SCREEEEECH!

*POLICE EMERGENCY SQUAD--1930S SWAT TEA

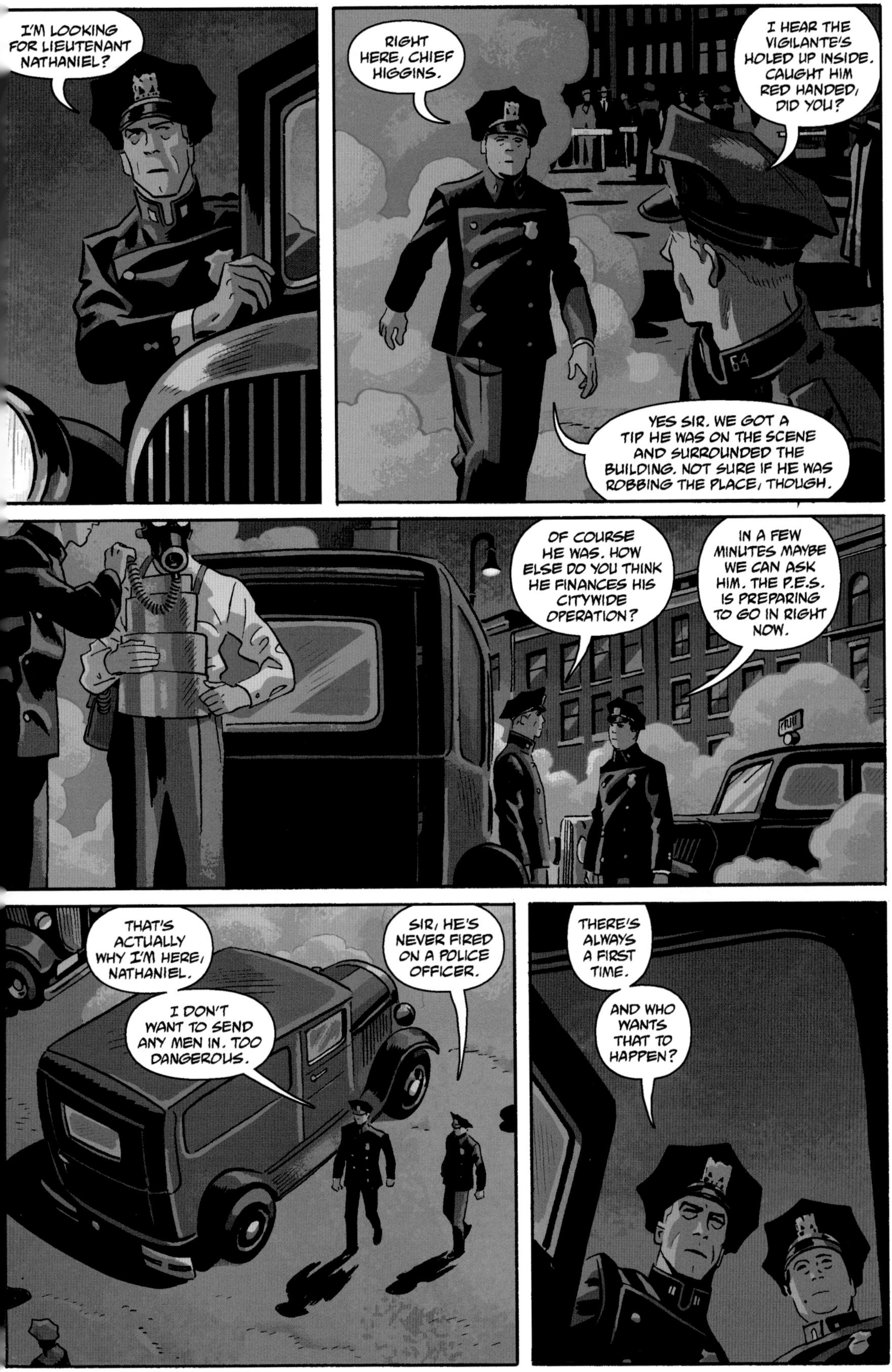
I'M LOOKING FOR LIEUTENANT NATHANIEL?
RIGHT HERE, CHIEF HIGGINS.
I HEAR THE VIGILANTE'S HOLED UP INSIDE. CAUGHT HIM RED HANDED, DID YOU?
YES SIR. WE GOT A TIP HE WAS ON THE SCENE AND SURROUNDED THE BUILDING. NOT SURE IF HE WAS ROBBING THE PLACE, THOUGH.
OF COURSE HE WAS. HOW ELSE DO YOU THINK HE FINANCES HIS CITYWIDE OPERATION?
IN A FEW MINUTES MAYBE WE CAN ASK HIM. THE P.E.S. IS PREPARING TO GO IN RIGHT NOW.
THAT'S ACTUALLY WHY I'M HERE, NATHANIEL.
I DON'T WANT TO SEND ANY MEN IN. TOO DANGEROUS.
SIR, HE'S NEVER FIRED ON A POLICE OFFICER.
THERE'S ALWAYS A FIRST TIME.
AND WHO WANTS THAT TO HAPPEN?

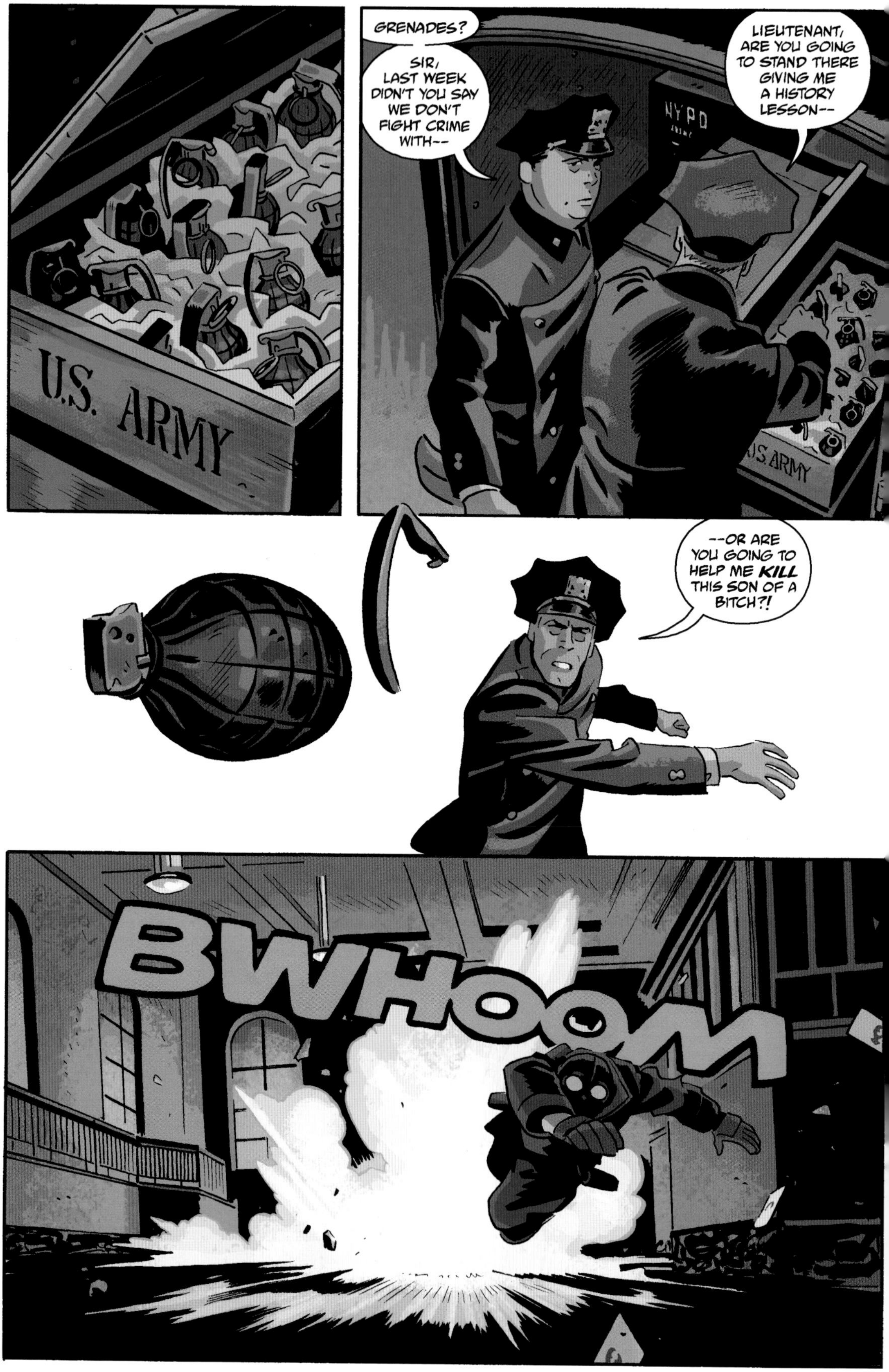
U.S. ARMY
GRENADES?
SIR, LAST WEEK DIDN'T YOU SAY WE DON'T FIGHT CRIME WITH--
LIEUTENANT, ARE YOU GOING TO STAND THERE GIVING ME A HISTORY LESSON--
NYPD
U.S. ARMY
--OR ARE YOU GOING TO HELP ME **KILL** THIS SON OF A BITCH?!
BWHOOM

CHAPTER FOUR

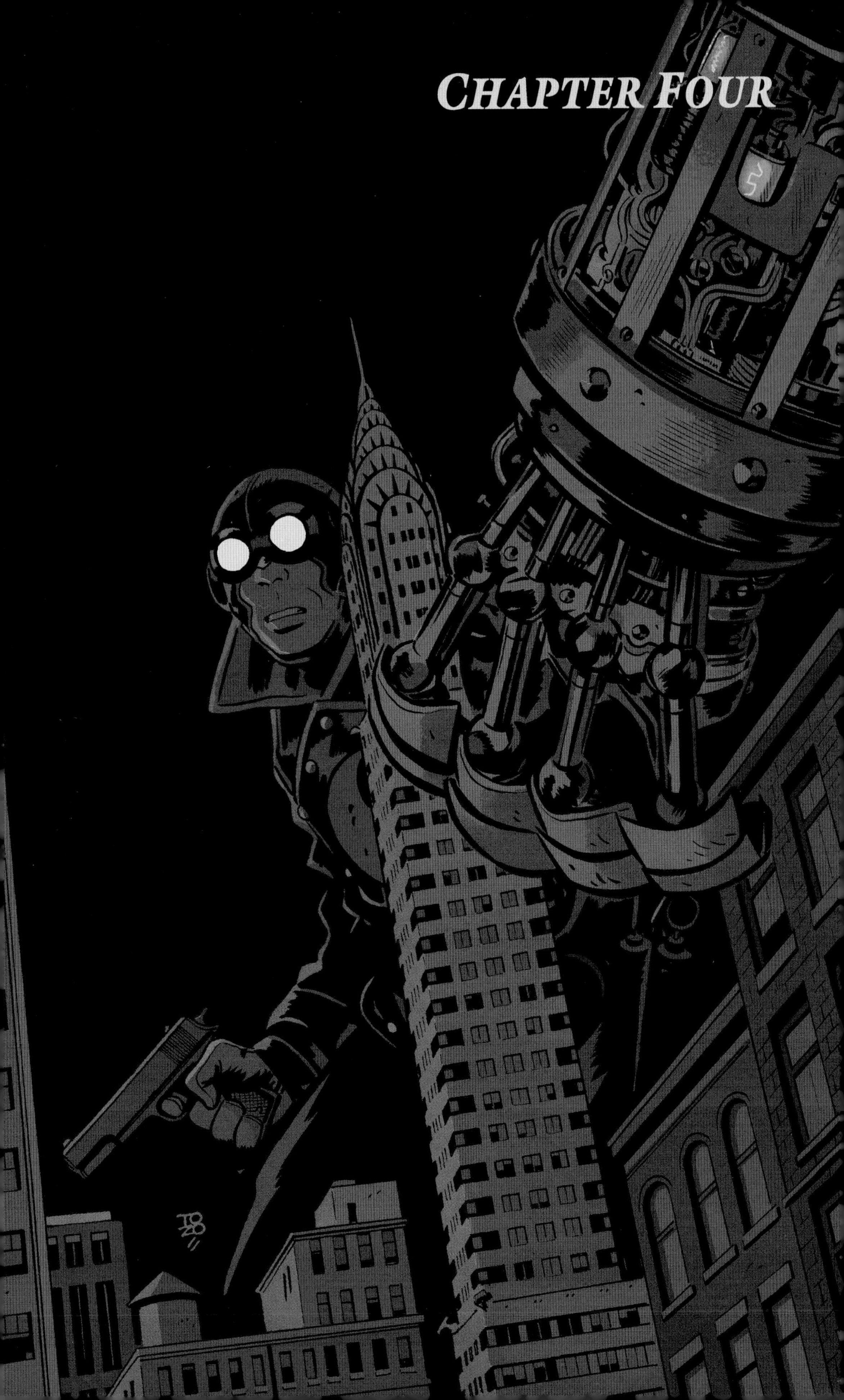

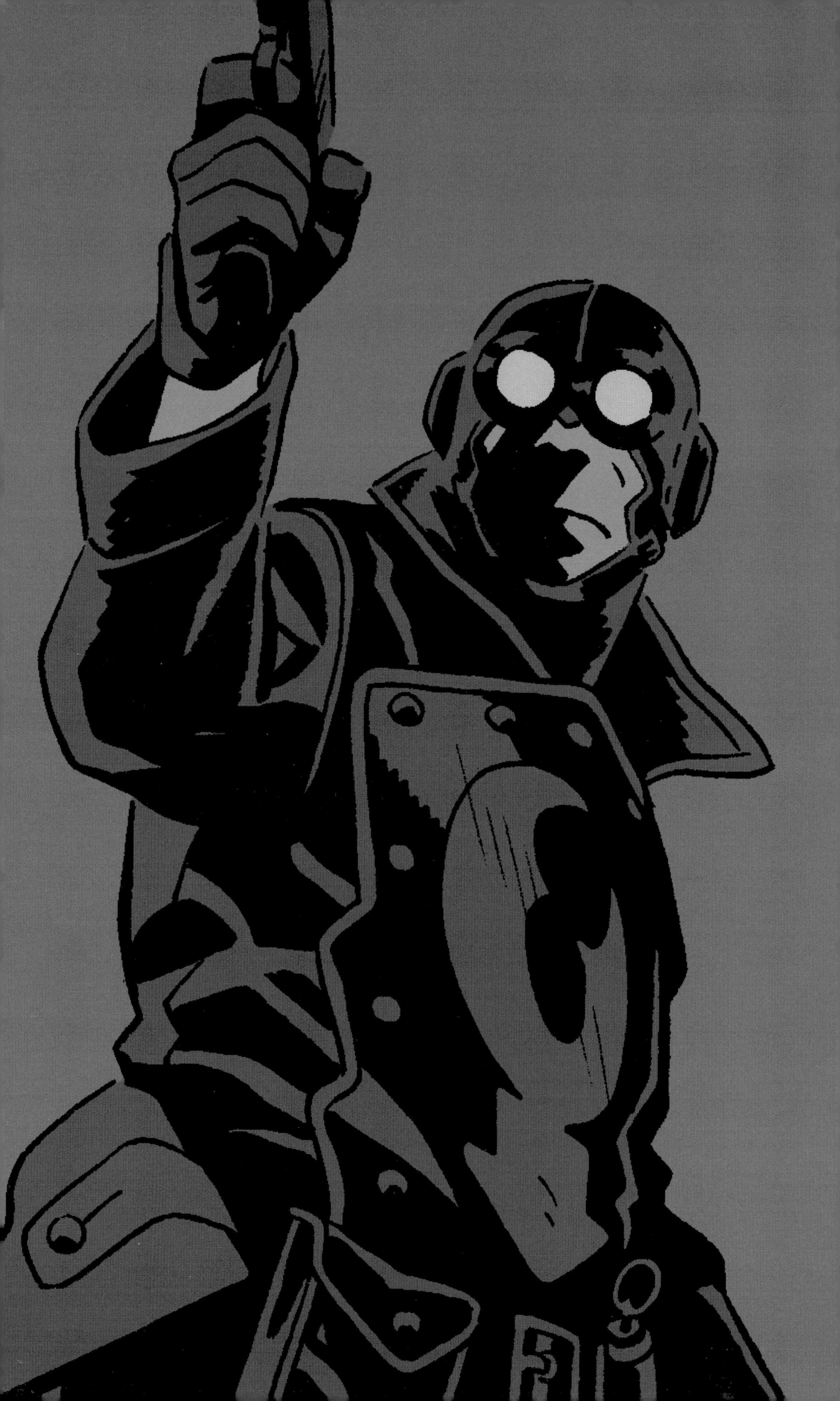

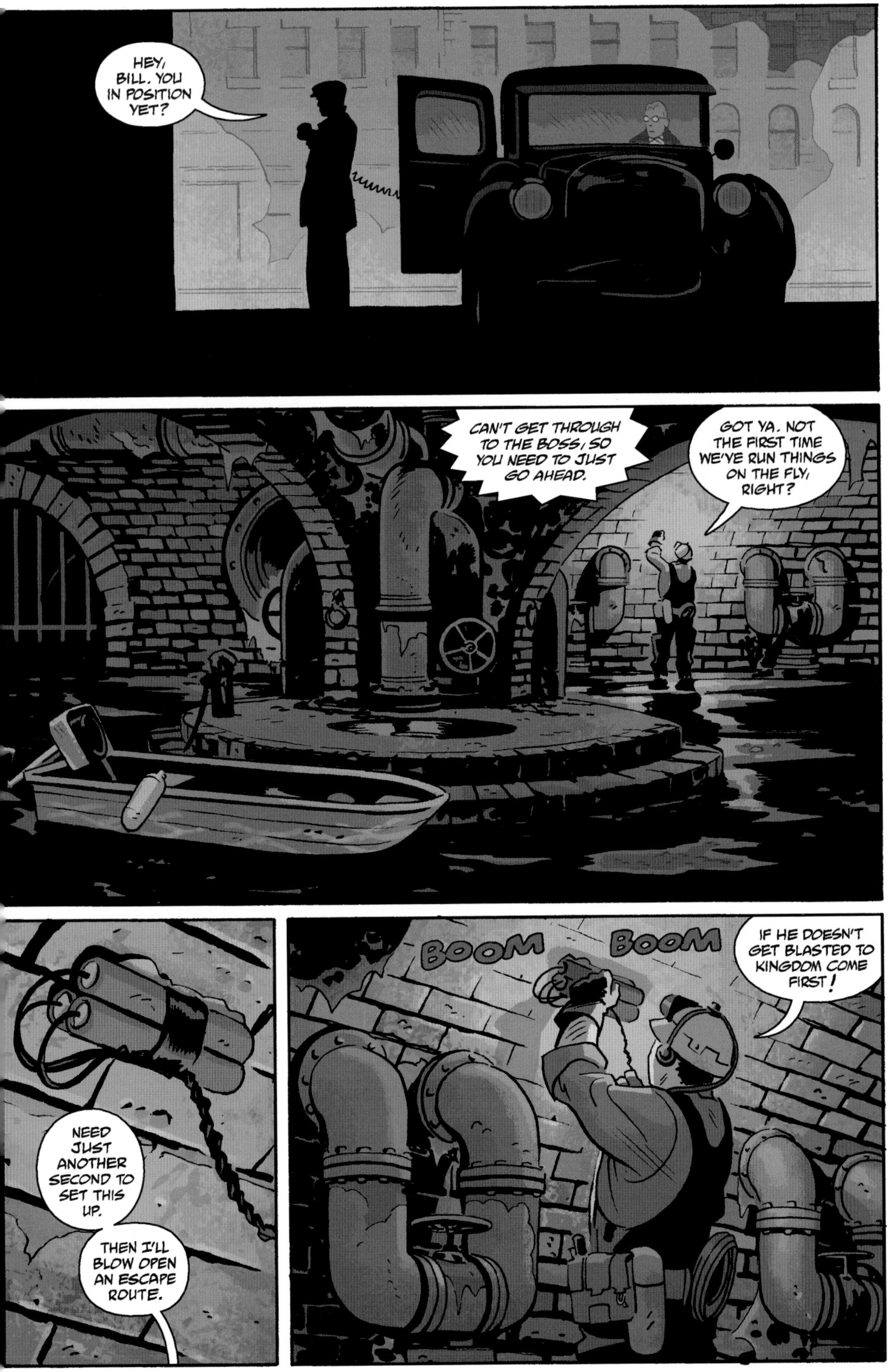
HEY, BILL. YOU IN POSITION YET?
CAN'T GET THROUGH TO THE BOSS, SO YOU NEED TO JUST GO AHEAD.
GOT YA. NOT THE FIRST TIME WE'VE RUN THINGS ON THE FLY, RIGHT?
NEED JUST ANOTHER SECOND TO SET THIS UP.
THEN I'LL BLOW OPEN AN ESCAPE ROUTE.
BOOM
BOOM
IF HE DOESN'T GET BLASTED TO KINGDOM COME FIRST!

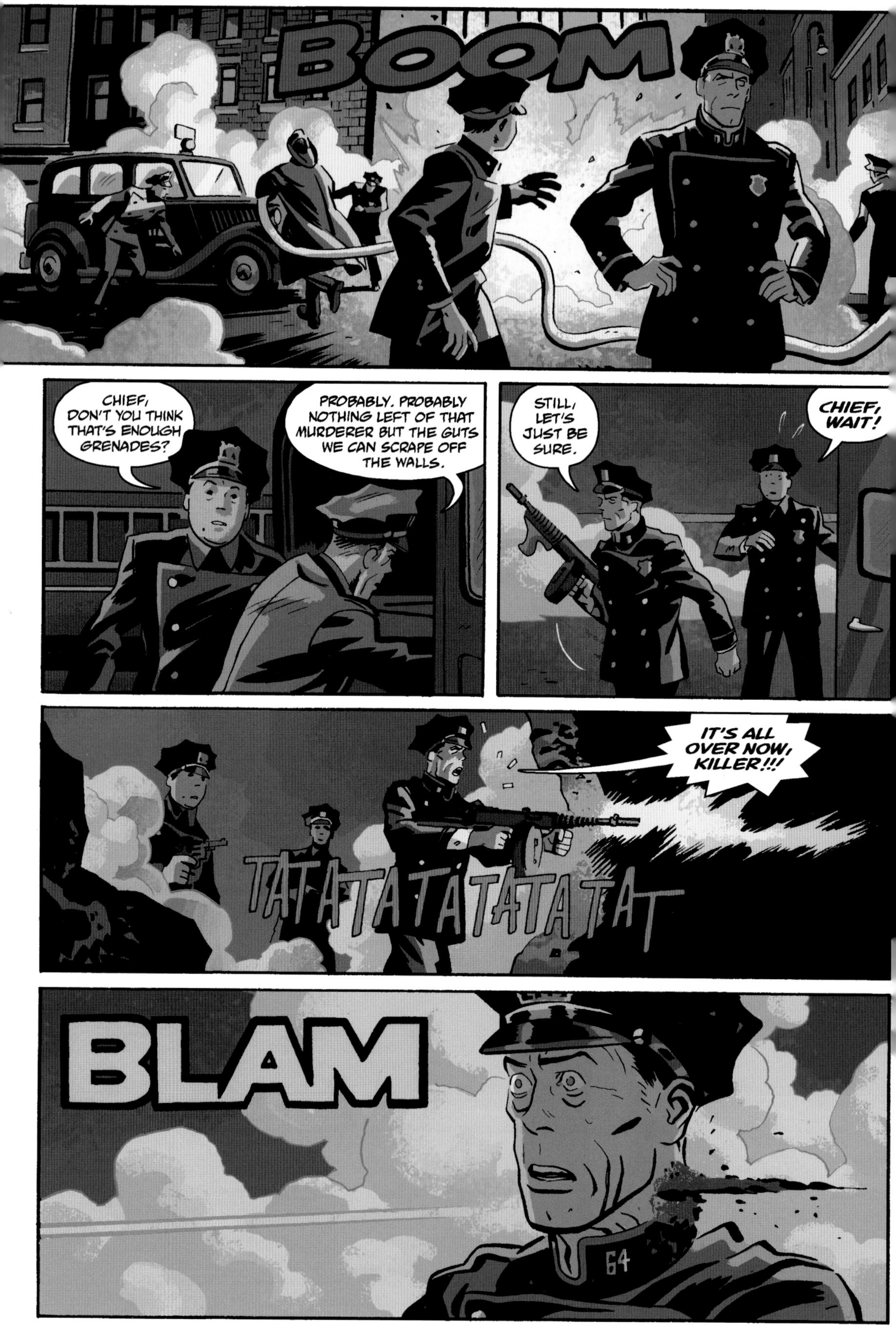
BOOM
CHIEF, DON'T YOU THINK THAT'S ENOUGH GRENADES?
PROBABLY. PROBABLY NOTHING LEFT OF THAT MURDERER BUT THE GUTS WE CAN SCRAPE OFF THE WALLS.
STILL, LET'S JUST BE SURE.
CHIEF, WAIT!
IT'S ALL OVER NOW, KILLER!!!
TATATATATATATATAT
BLAM
64

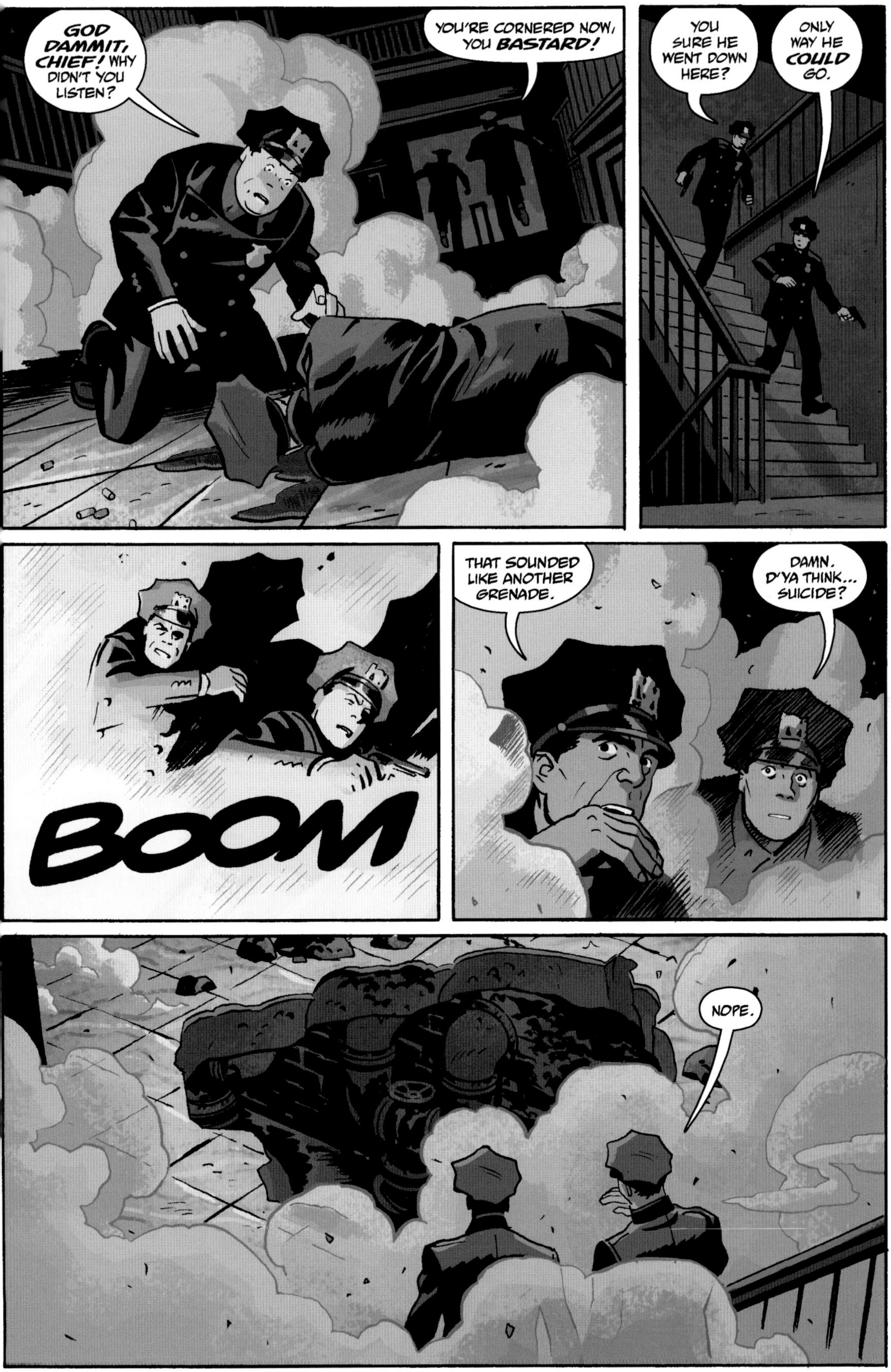
GOD DAMMIT, CHIEF! WHY DIDN'T YOU LISTEN?
YOU'RE CORNERED NOW, YOU BASTARD!
YOU SURE HE WENT DOWN HERE?
ONLY WAY HE COULD GO.
BOOM
THAT SOUNDED LIKE ANOTHER GRENADE.
DAMN. D'YA THINK... SUICIDE?
NOPE.

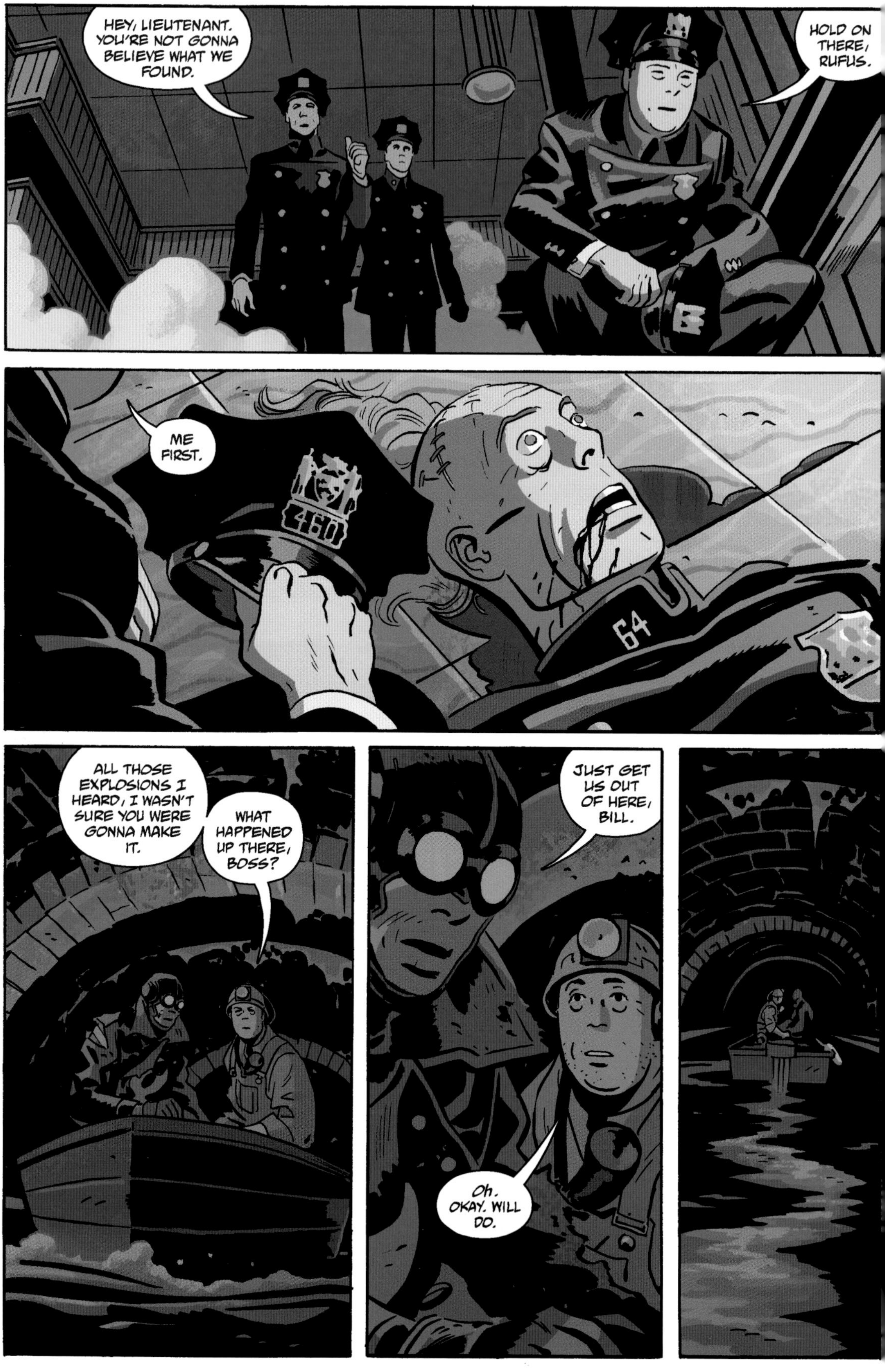

HEY, LIEUTENANT. YOU'RE NOT GONNA BELIEVE WHAT WE FOUND.
HOLD ON THERE, RUFUS.
ME FIRST.
ALL THOSE EXPLOSIONS I HEARD, I WASN'T SURE YOU WERE GONNA MAKE IT.
WHAT HAPPENED UP THERE, BOSS?
JUST GET US OUT OF HERE, BILL.
Oh. OKAY. WILL DO.

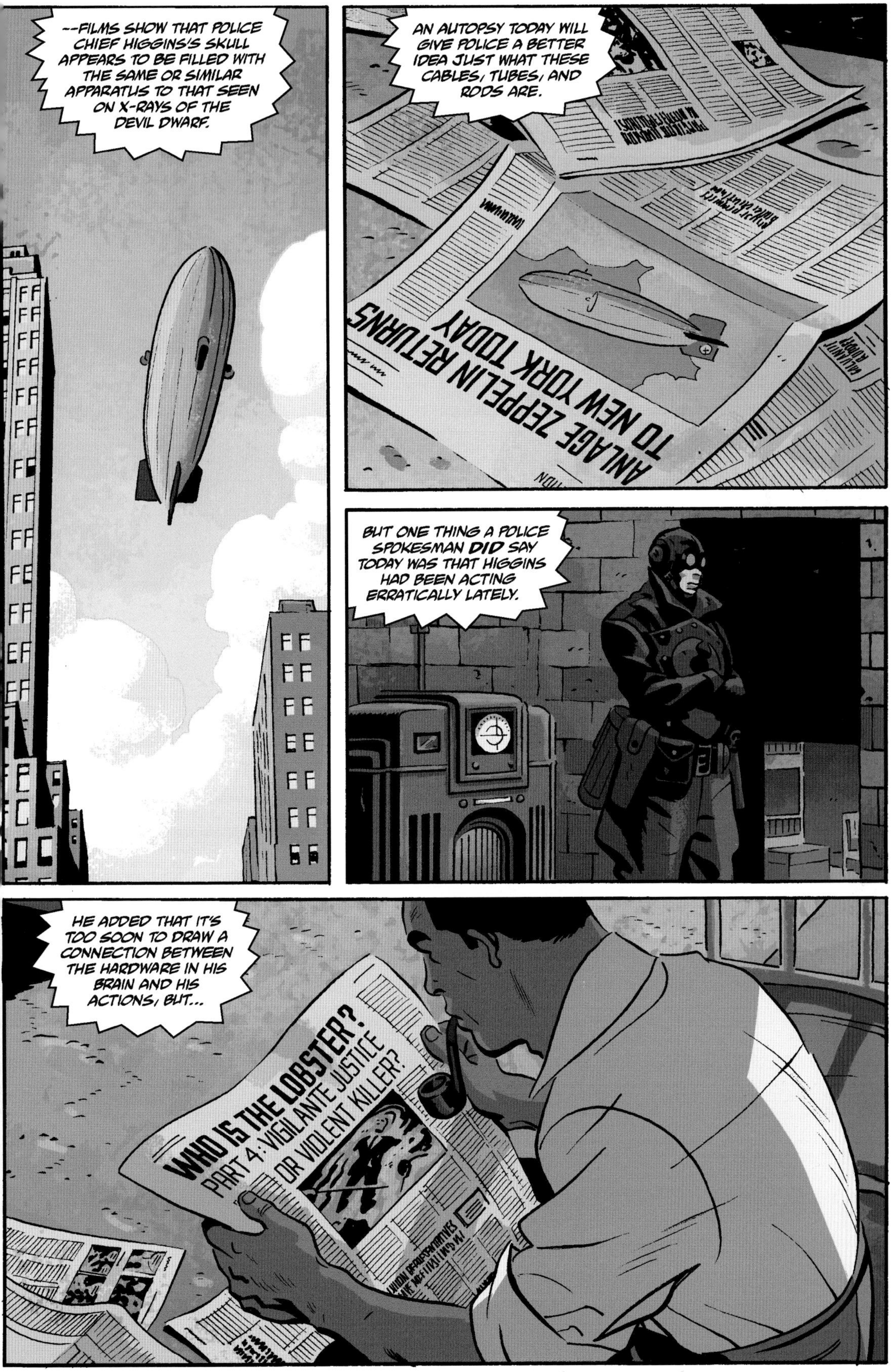
--FILMS SHOW THAT POLICE CHIEF HIGGINS'S SKULL APPEARS TO BE FILLED WITH THE SAME OR SIMILAR APPARATUS TO THAT SEEN ON X-RAYS OF THE DEVIL DWARF.
AN AUTOPSY TODAY WILL GIVE POLICE A BETTER IDEA JUST WHAT THESE CABLES, TUBES, AND RODS ARE.
ANLAGE ZEPPELIN RETURNS TO NEW YORK TODAY
BUT ONE THING A POLICE SPOKESMAN DID SAY TODAY WAS THAT HIGGINS HAD BEEN ACTING ERRATICALLY LATELY.
HE ADDED THAT IT'S TOO SOON TO DRAW A CONNECTION BETWEEN THE HARDWARE IN HIS BRAIN AND HIS ACTIONS, BUT...
WHO IS THE LOBSTER?
PART 4: VIGILANTE JUSTICE OR VIOLENT KILLER?

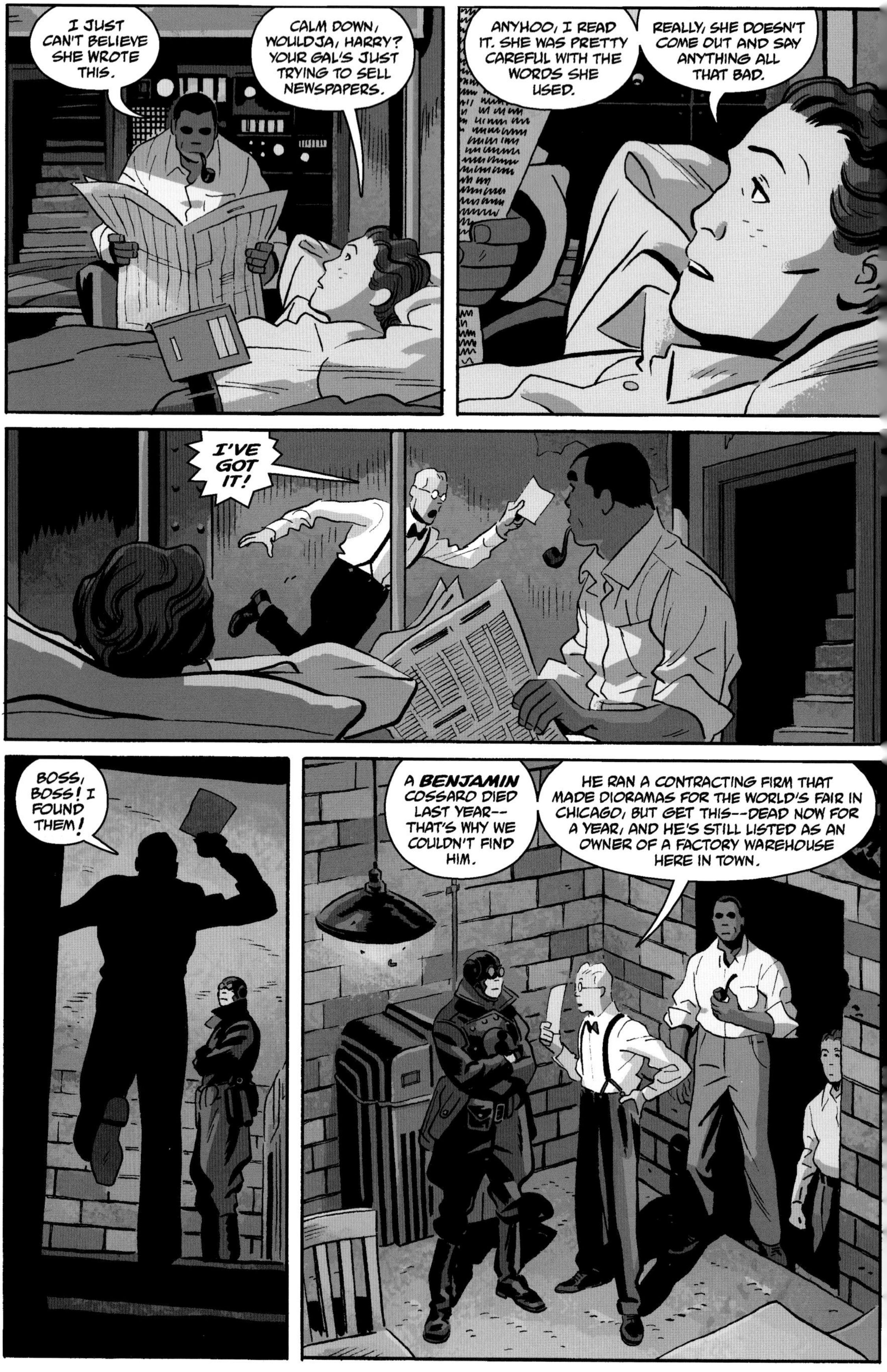
I JUST CAN'T BELIEVE SHE WROTE THIS.
CALM DOWN, WOULDJA, HARRY? YOUR GAL'S JUST TRYING TO SELL NEWSPAPERS.
ANYHOO, I READ IT. SHE WAS PRETTY CAREFUL WITH THE WORDS SHE USED.
REALLY, SHE DOESN'T COME OUT AND SAY ANYTHING ALL THAT BAD.
I'VE GOT IT!
BOSS, BOSS! I FOUND THEM!
A BENJAMIN COSSARO DIED LAST YEAR-- THAT'S WHY WE COULDN'T FIND HIM.
HE RAN A CONTRACTING FIRM THAT MADE DIORAMAS FOR THE WORLD'S FAIR IN CHICAGO, BUT GET THIS--DEAD NOW FOR A YEAR, AND HE'S STILL LISTED AS AN OWNER OF A FACTORY WAREHOUSE HERE IN TOWN.

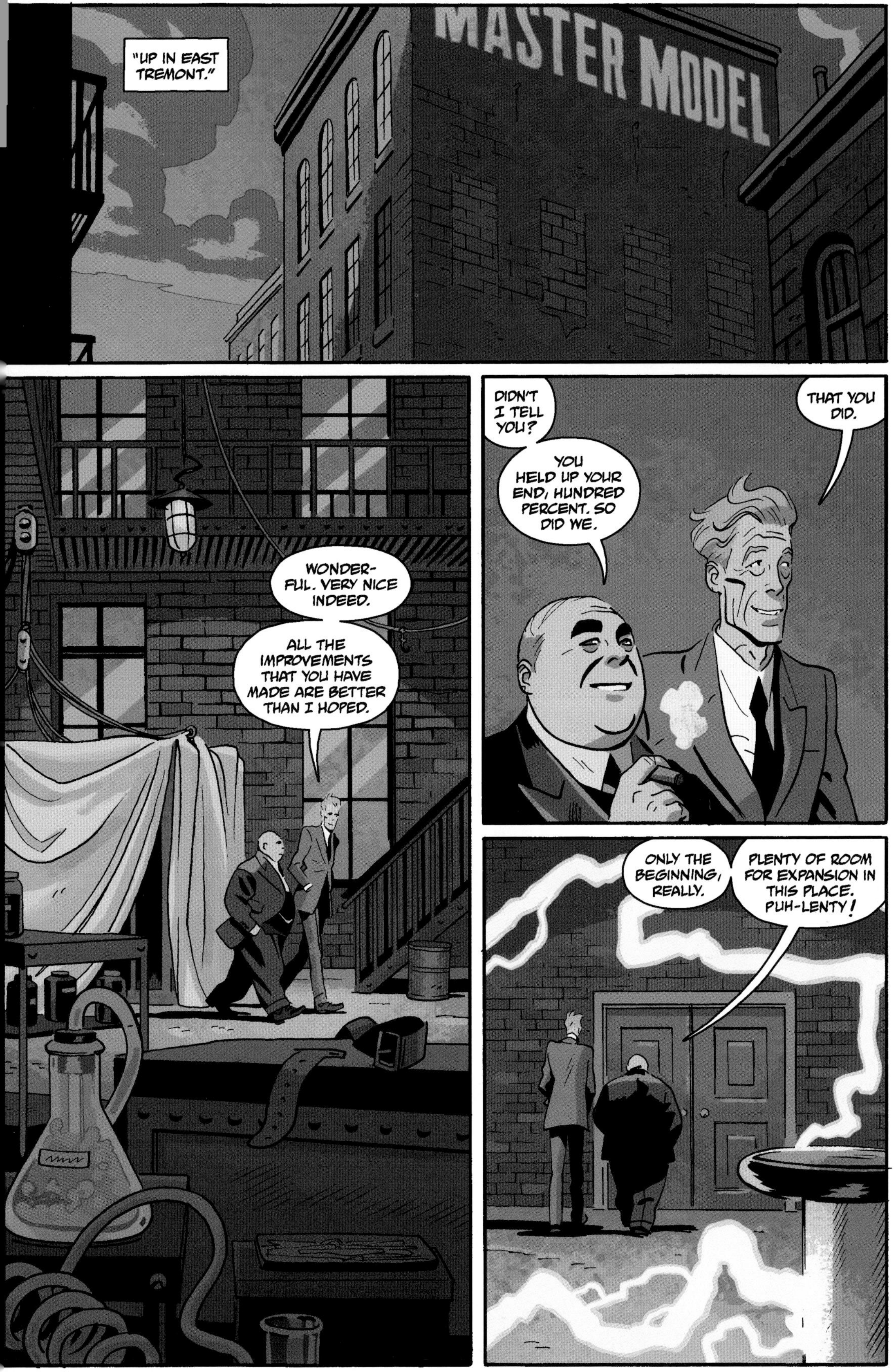
"UP IN EAST TREMONT."
MASTER MODEL
WONDER-FUL. VERY NICE INDEED.
ALL THE IMPROVEMENTS THAT YOU HAVE MADE ARE BETTER THAN I HOPED.
DIDN'T I TELL YOU?
YOU HELD UP YOUR END, HUNDRED PERCENT. SO DID WE.
THAT YOU DID.
ONLY THE BEGINNING, REALLY.
PLENTY OF ROOM FOR EXPANSION IN THIS PLACE. PUH-LENTY!

BUT THIS MODEL OF NEW YORK...I THOUGHT IT WAS IMPORTANT TO YOU.

BECAUSE OUR FATHER DESIGNED IT?

ALL THE MORE REASON TO MOVE IT OUT. IT JUST MAKES ME MAD SEEING IT.

AH, YES. YOUR FATHER. IF ONLY I HAD MADE HIS ACQUAINTANCE EARLIER.

I THINK I WOULD HAVE SERVED HIM BETTER THAN POOR, DELUDED ERIK ANDRES.

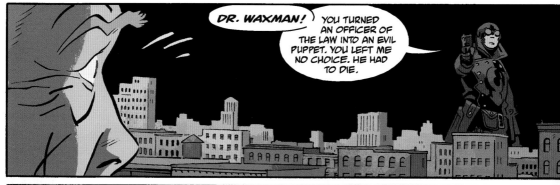

DR. WAXMAN!

YOU TURNED AN OFFICER OF THE LAW INTO AN EVIL PUPPET. YOU LEFT ME NO CHOICE. HE HAD TO DIE.

AND SO DO YOU!

BLAM
BLAM
BLAM

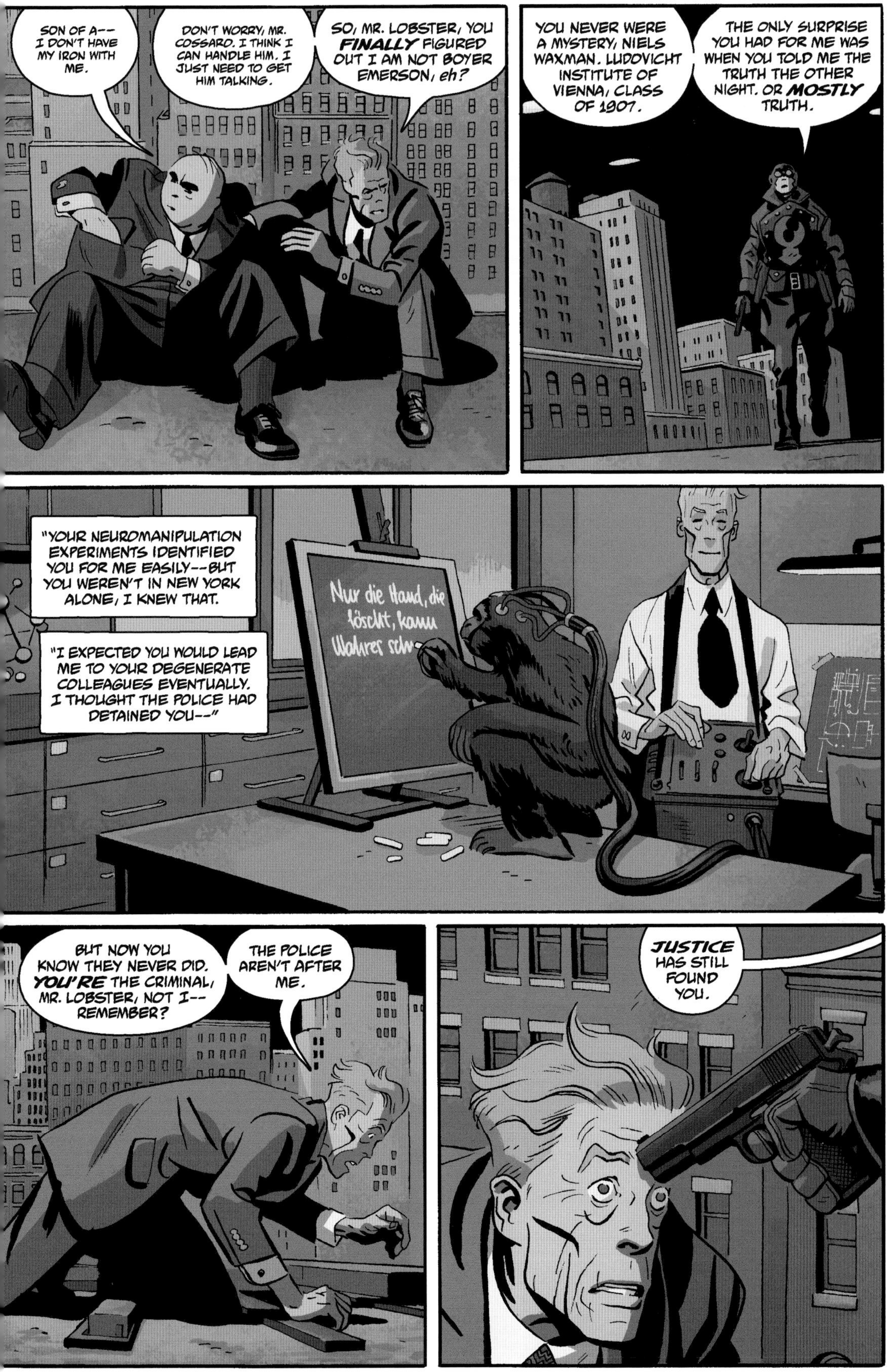
SON OF A-- I DON'T HAVE MY IRON WITH ME.
DON'T WORRY, MR. COSSARO. I THINK I CAN HANDLE HIM. I JUST NEED TO GET HIM TALKING.
SO, MR. LOBSTER, YOU FINALLY FIGURED OUT I AM NOT BOYER EMERSON, eh?
YOU NEVER WERE A MYSTERY, NIELS WAXMAN. LUDOVICHT INSTITUTE OF VIENNA, CLASS OF 1907.
THE ONLY SURPRISE YOU HAD FOR ME WAS WHEN YOU TOLD ME THE TRUTH THE OTHER NIGHT. OR MOSTLY TRUTH.
"YOUR NEUROMANIPULATION EXPERIMENTS IDENTIFIED YOU FOR ME EASILY--BUT YOU WEREN'T IN NEW YORK ALONE, I KNEW THAT.
Nur die Hand, die löscht, kann Wahres sch
"I EXPECTED YOU WOULD LEAD ME TO YOUR DEGENERATE COLLEAGUES EVENTUALLY. I THOUGHT THE POLICE HAD DETAINED YOU--"
BUT NOW YOU KNOW THEY NEVER DID. YOU'RE THE CRIMINAL, MR. LOBSTER, NOT I-- REMEMBER?
THE POLICE AREN'T AFTER ME.
JUSTICE HAS STILL FOUND YOU.

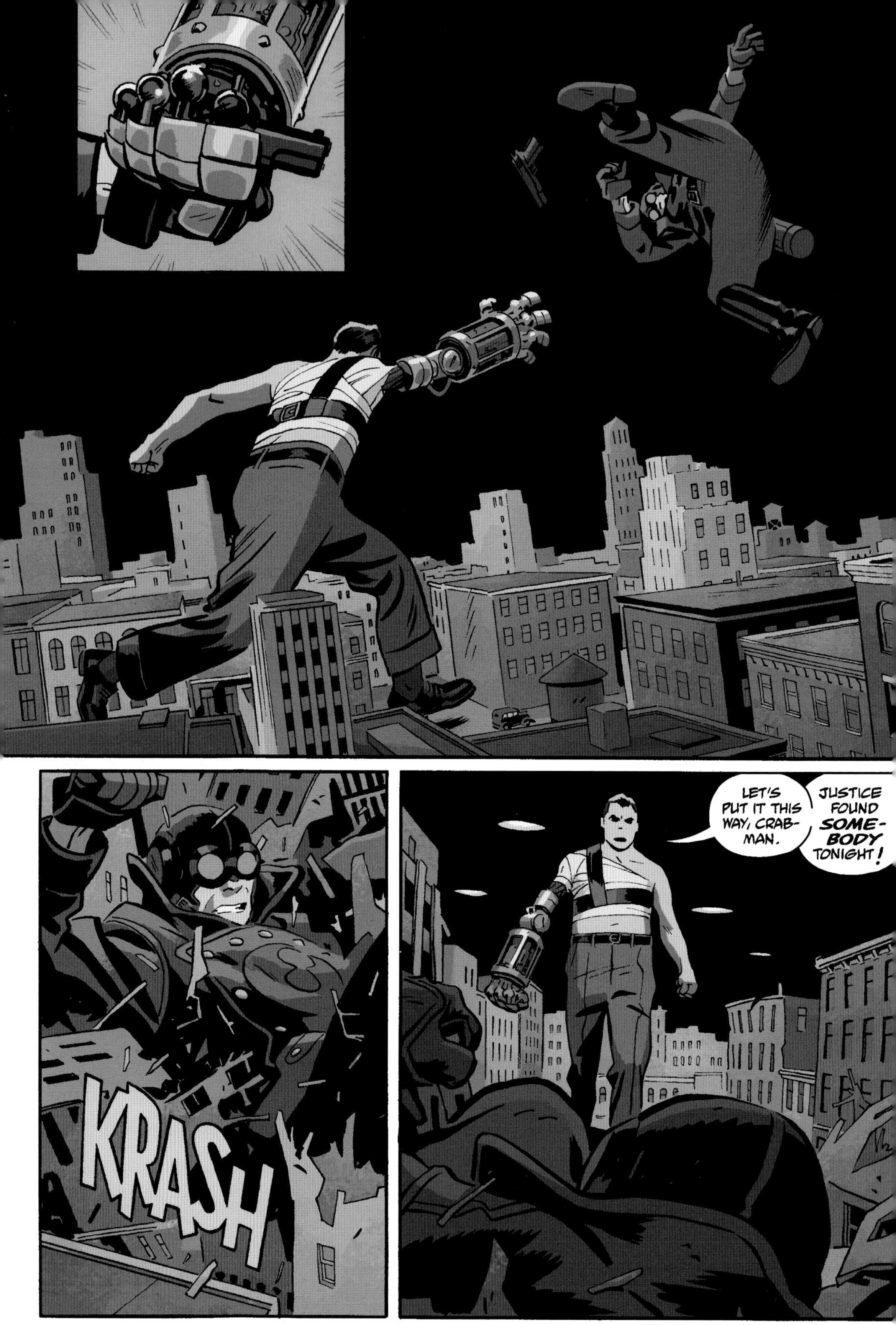
KRASH
LET'S PUT IT THIS WAY, CRAB-MAN.
JUSTICE FOUND SOME-BODY TONIGHT!

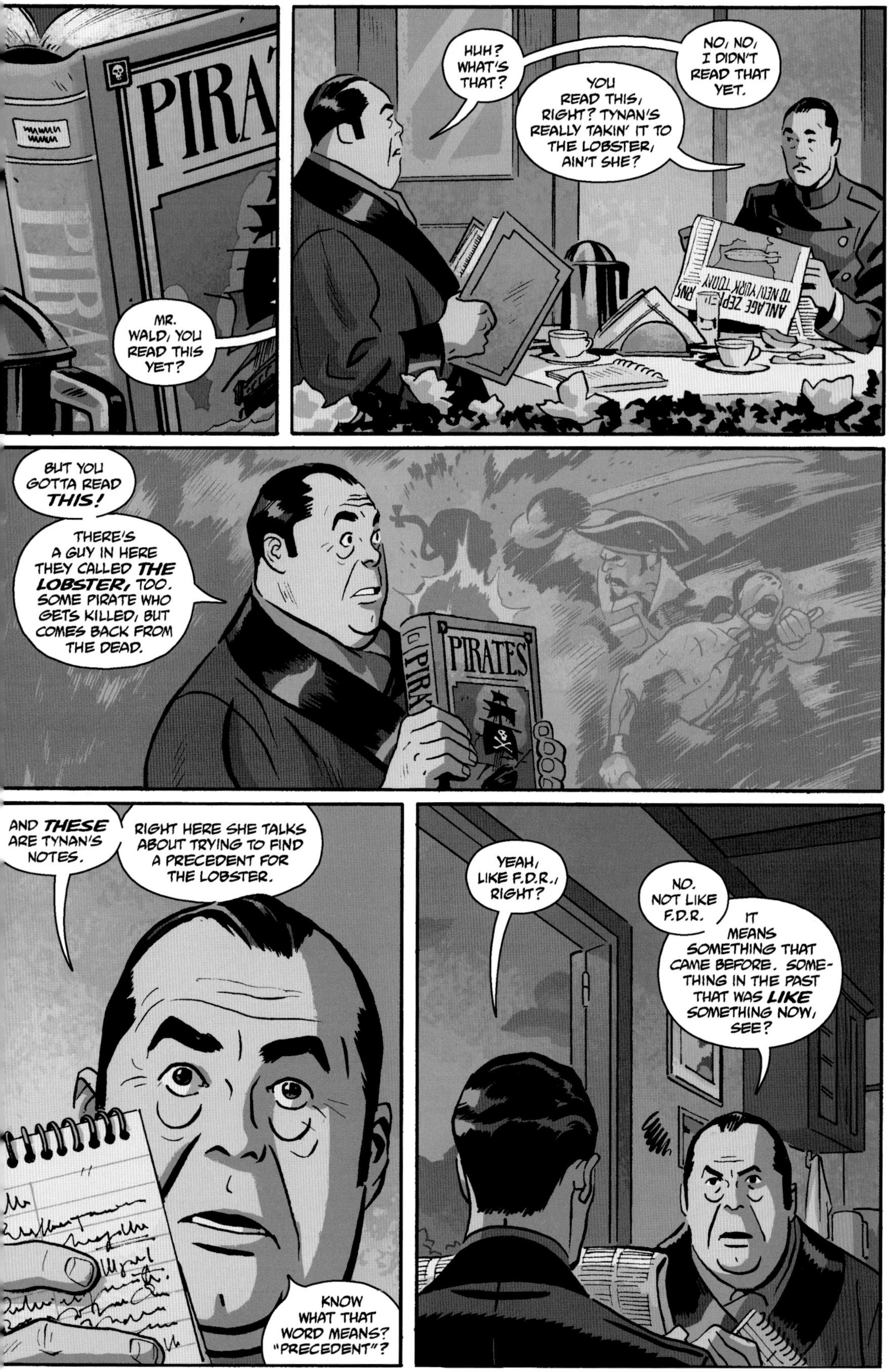
MR. WALD, YOU READ THIS YET?
HUH? WHAT'S THAT?
YOU READ THIS, RIGHT? TYNAN'S REALLY TAKIN' IT TO THE LOBSTER, AIN'T SHE?
NO, NO, I DIDN'T READ THAT YET.
BUT YOU GOTTA READ *THIS!*
THERE'S A GUY IN HERE THEY CALLED *THE LOBSTER,* TOO. SOME PIRATE WHO GETS KILLED, BUT COMES BACK FROM THE DEAD.
PIRATES
AND *THESE* ARE TYNAN'S NOTES.
RIGHT HERE SHE TALKS ABOUT TRYING TO FIND A PRECEDENT FOR THE LOBSTER.
KNOW WHAT THAT WORD MEANS? "PRECEDENT"?
YEAH, LIKE F.D.R., RIGHT?
NO. NOT LIKE F.D.R.
IT MEANS SOMETHING THAT CAME BEFORE. SOME-THING IN THE PAST THAT WAS *LIKE* SOMETHING NOW, SEE?

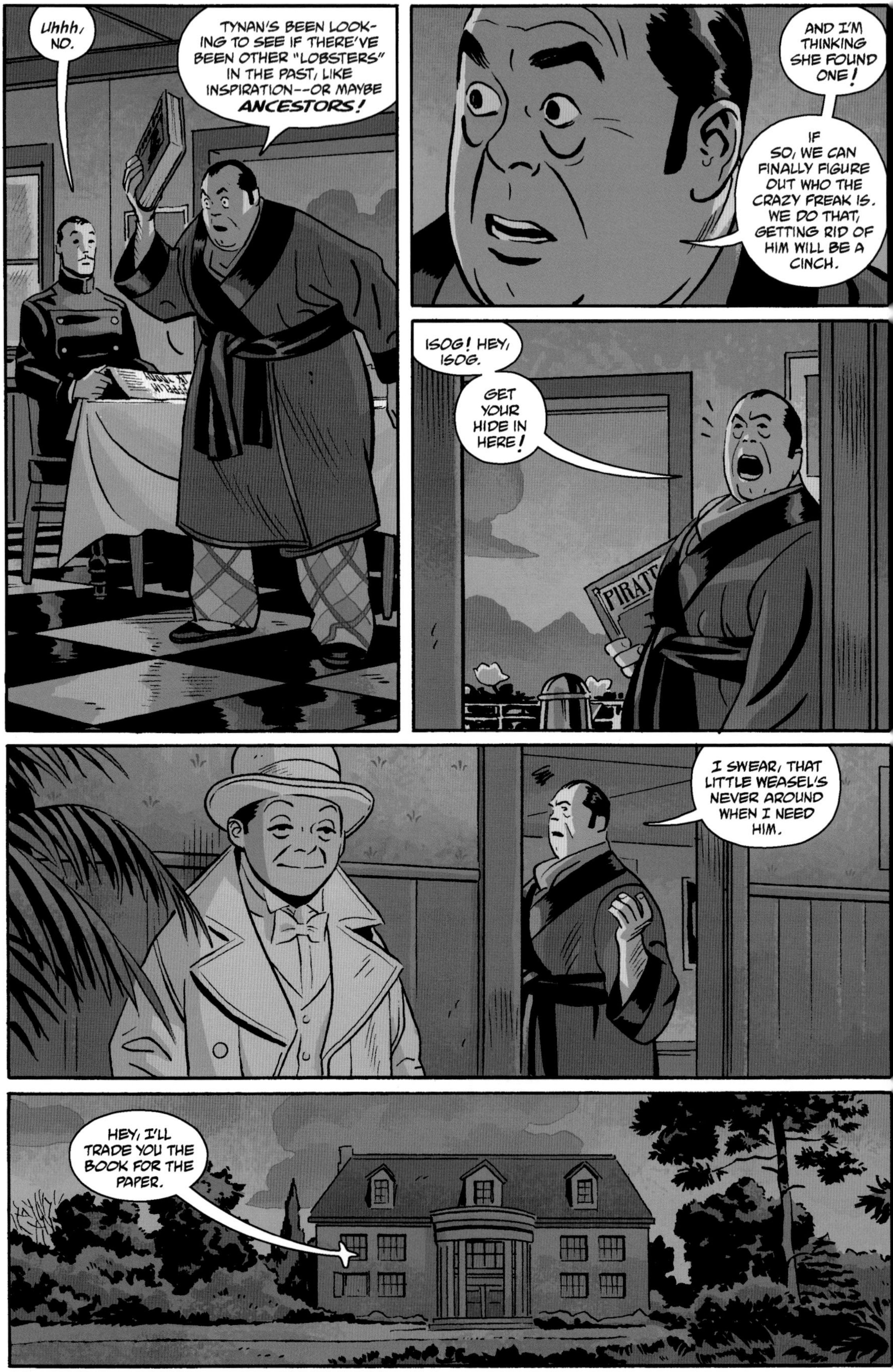
Uhhh, NO.
TYNAN'S BEEN LOOKING TO SEE IF THERE'VE BEEN OTHER "LOBSTERS" IN THE PAST, LIKE INSPIRATION--OR MAYBE ANCESTORS!
AND I'M THINKING SHE FOUND ONE!
IF SO, WE CAN FINALLY FIGURE OUT WHO THE CRAZY FREAK IS. WE DO THAT, GETTING RID OF HIM WILL BE A CINCH.
ISOG! HEY, ISOG.
GET YOUR HIDE IN HERE!
PIRATE
I SWEAR, THAT LITTLE WEASEL'S NEVER AROUND WHEN I NEED HIM.
HEY, I'LL TRADE YOU THE BOOK FOR THE PAPER.

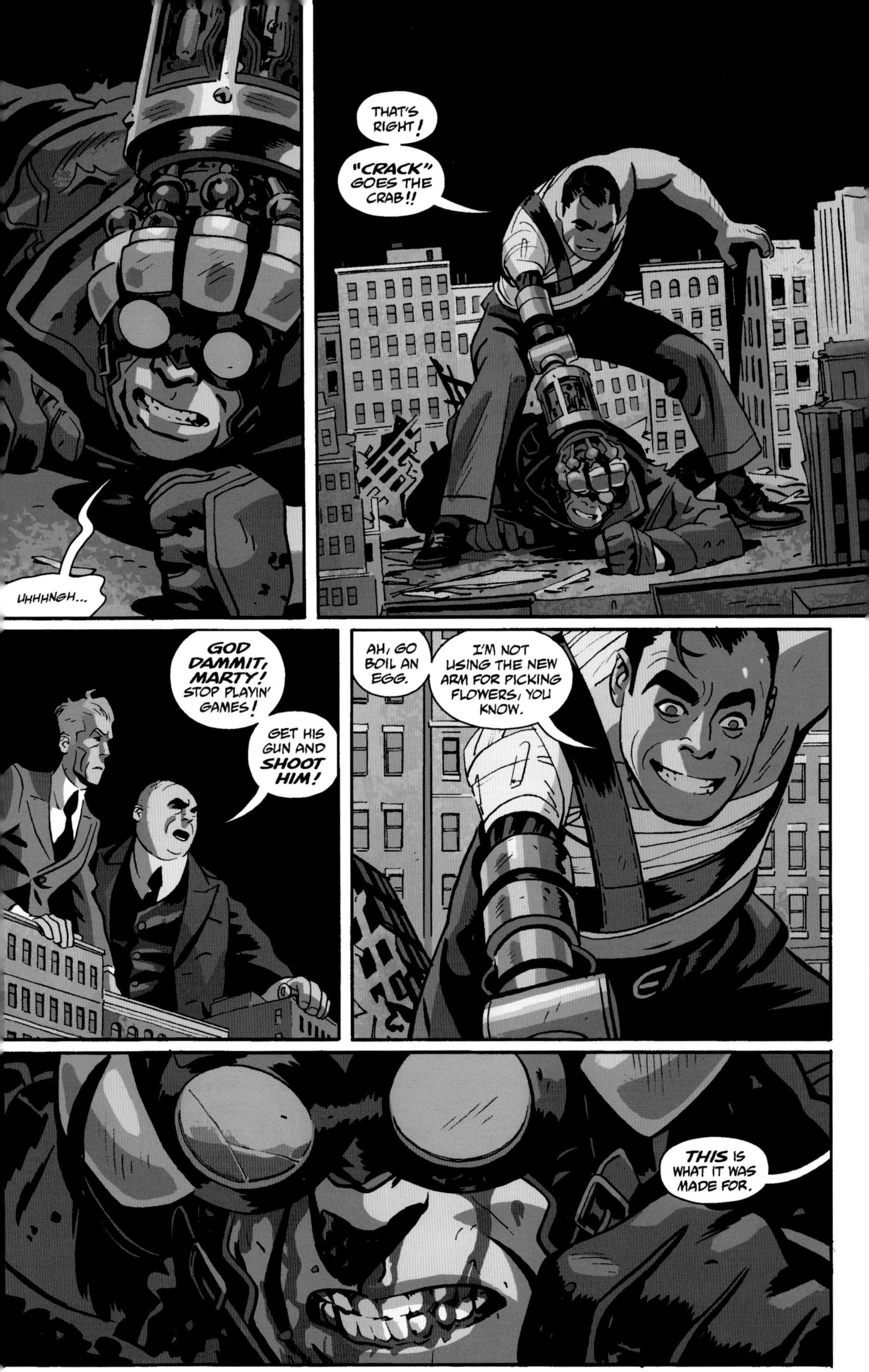
UHHHNGH...
THAT'S RIGHT!
"CRACK" GOES THE CRAB!!
GOD DAMMIT, MARTY! STOP PLAYIN' GAMES!
GET HIS GUN AND SHOOT HIM!
AH, GO BOIL AN EGG.
I'M NOT USING THE NEW ARM FOR PICKING FLOWERS, YOU KNOW.
THIS IS WHAT IT WAS MADE FOR.

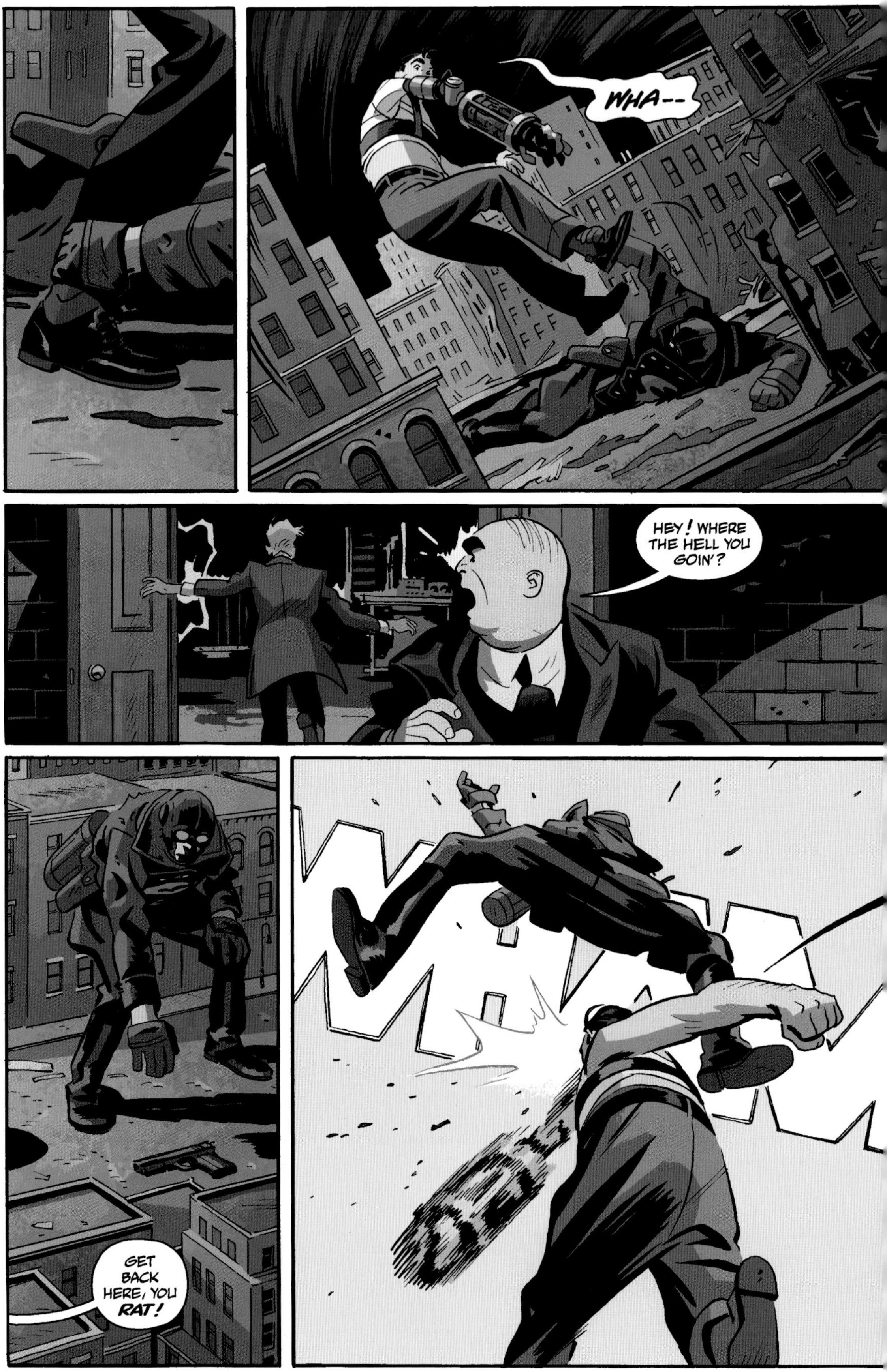
WHA--
HEY! WHERE THE HELL YOU GOIN'?
GET BACK HERE, YOU RAT!

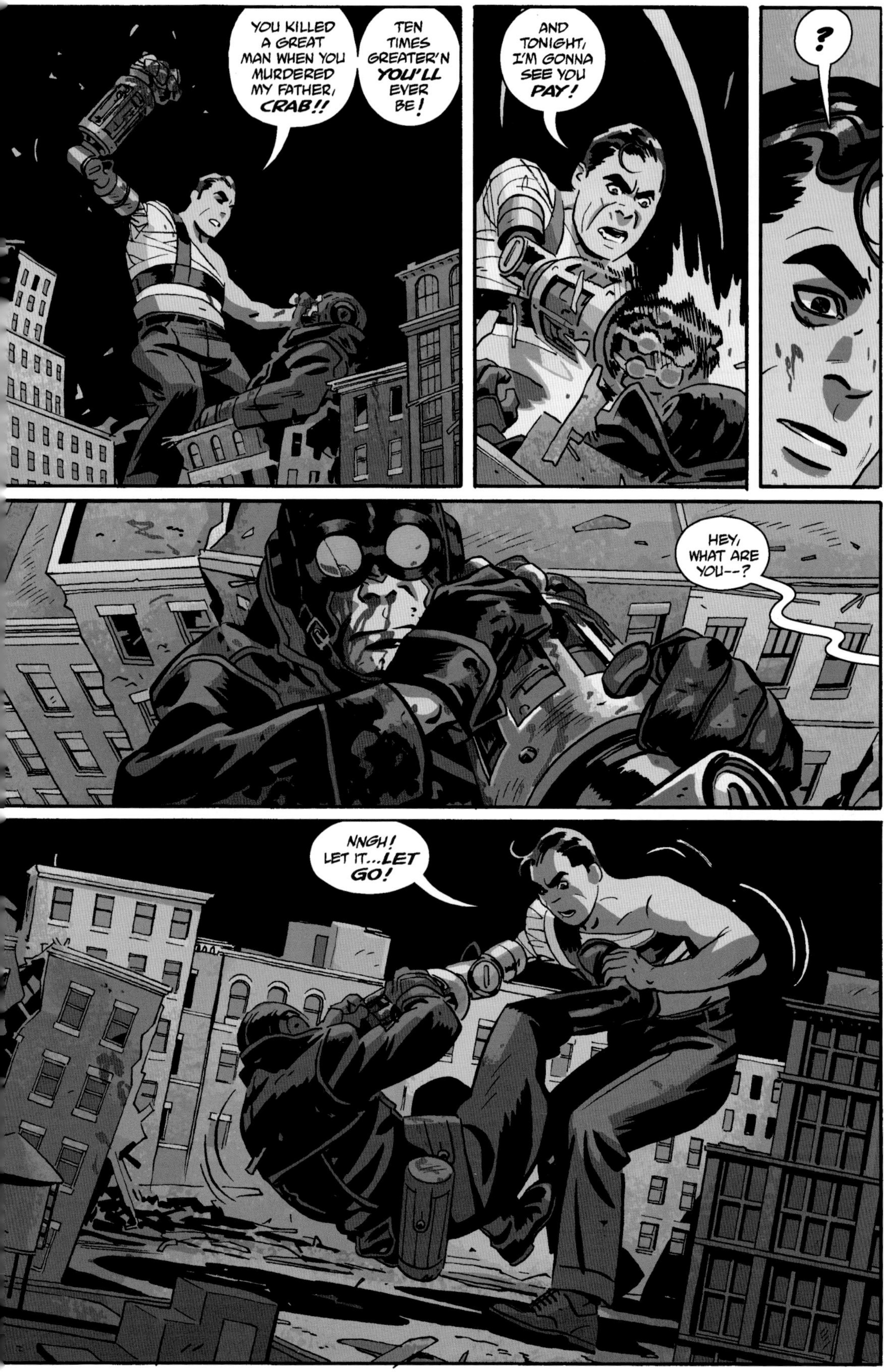
YOU KILLED A GREAT MAN WHEN YOU MURDERED MY FATHER, CRAB!!
TEN TIMES GREATER'N YOU'LL EVER BE!
AND TONIGHT, I'M GONNA SEE YOU PAY!
?
HEY, WHAT ARE YOU--?
NNGH! LET IT...LET GO!

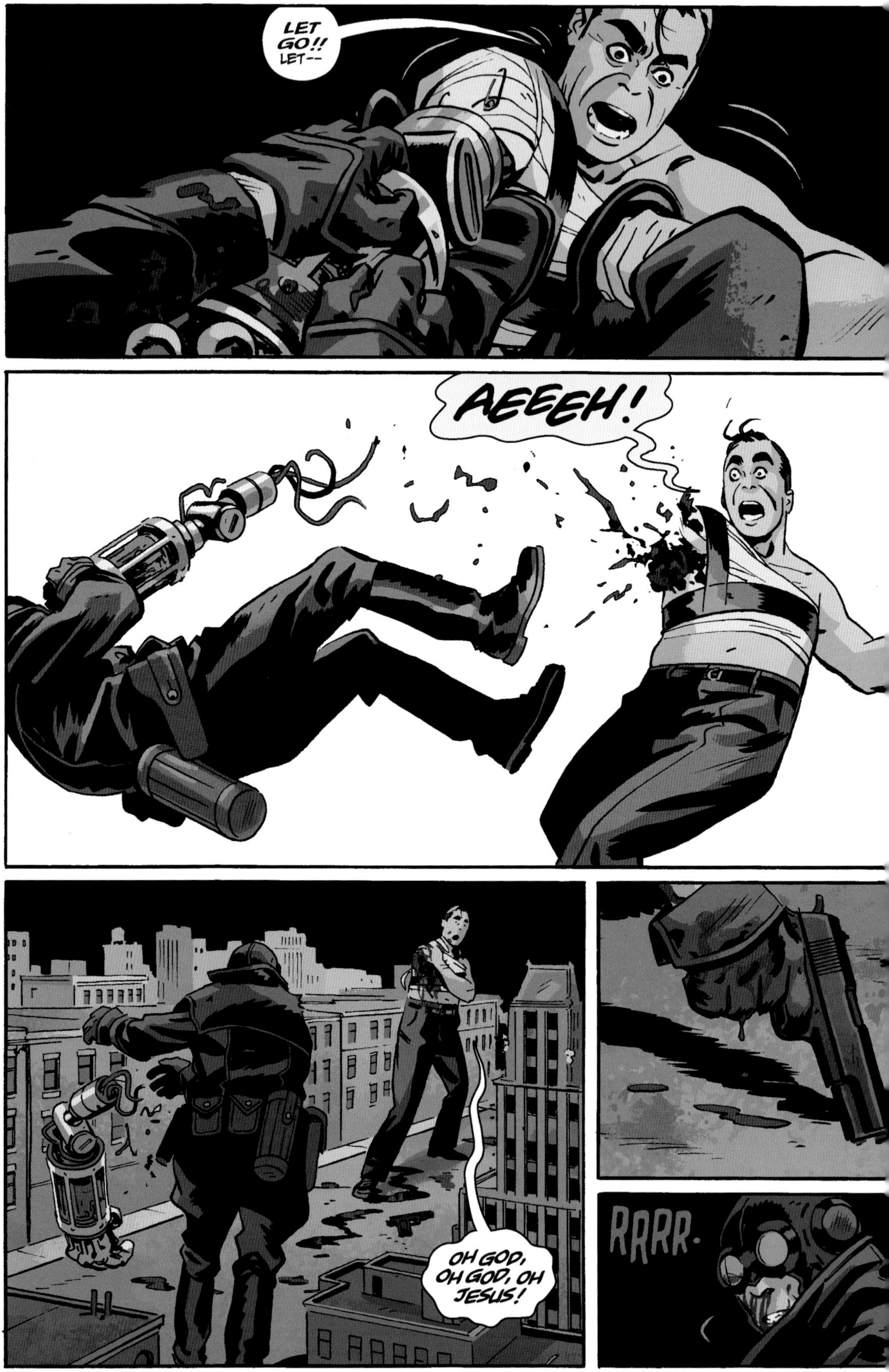
LET GO!! LET--
AEEEH!
OH GOD, OH GOD, OH JESUS!
RRRR.

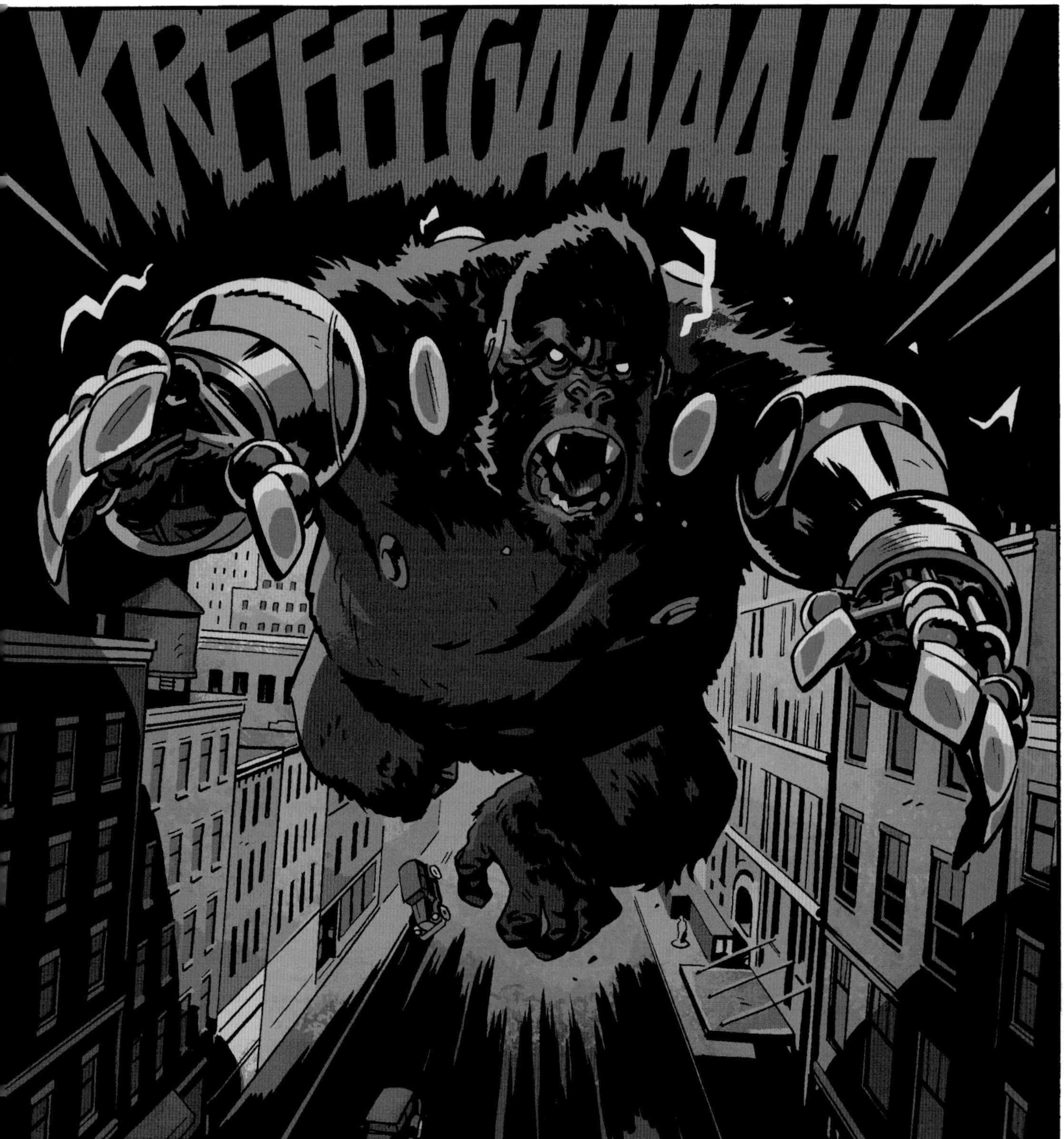
KREEEGAAAAHH

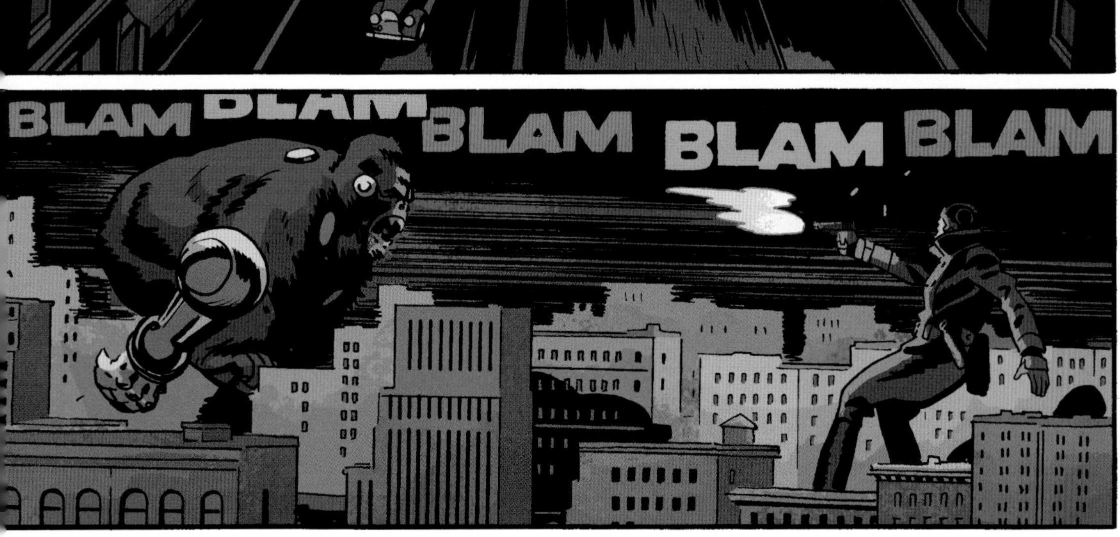
BLAM BLAM BLAM BLAM BLAM

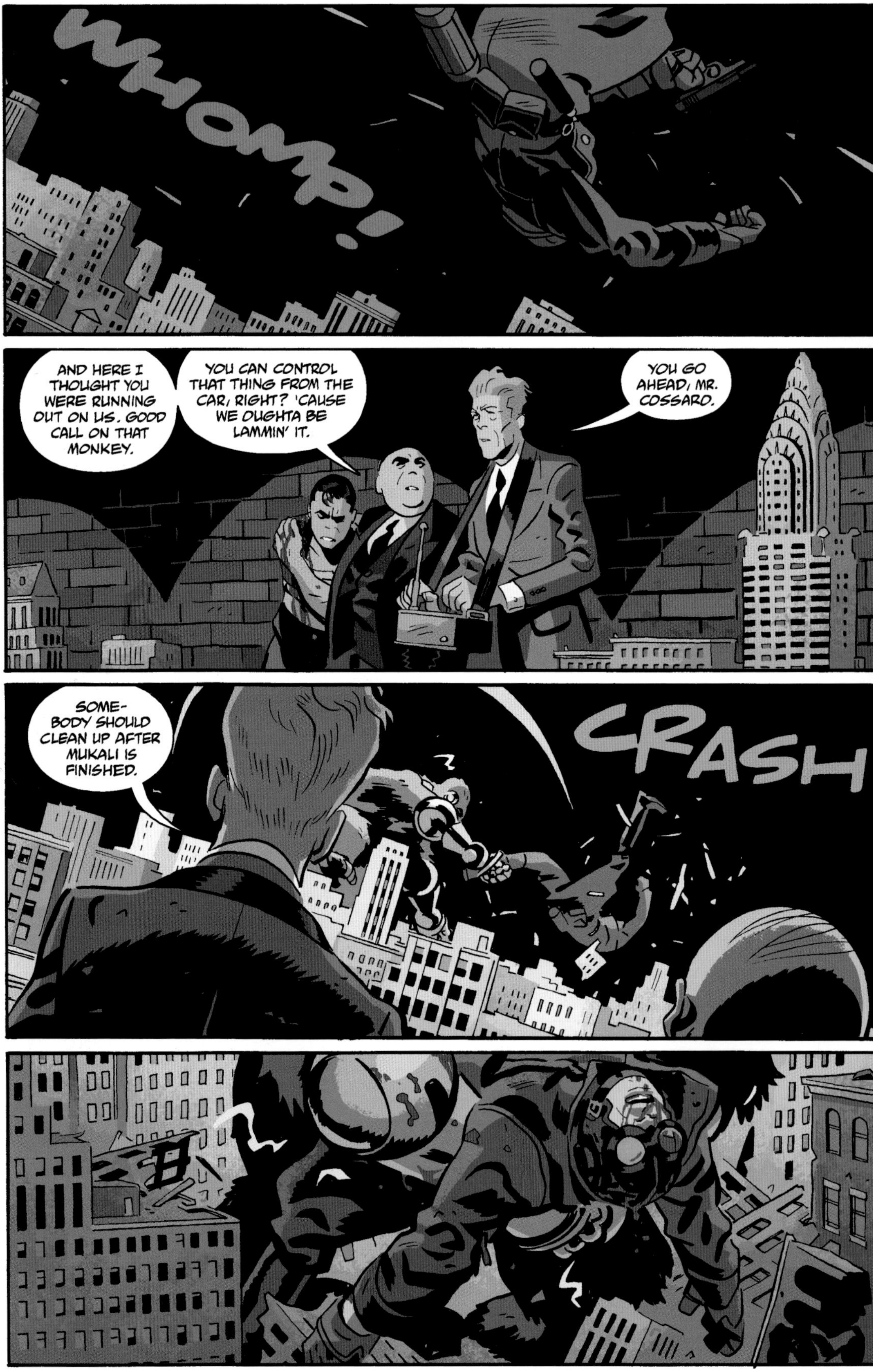
WHOMP!
AND HERE I THOUGHT YOU WERE RUNNING OUT ON US. GOOD CALL ON THAT MONKEY.
YOU CAN CONTROL THAT THING FROM THE CAR, RIGHT? 'CAUSE WE OUGHTA BE LAMMIN' IT.
YOU GO AHEAD, MR. COSSARO.
SOME-BODY SHOULD CLEAN UP AFTER MUKALI IS FINISHED.
CRASH

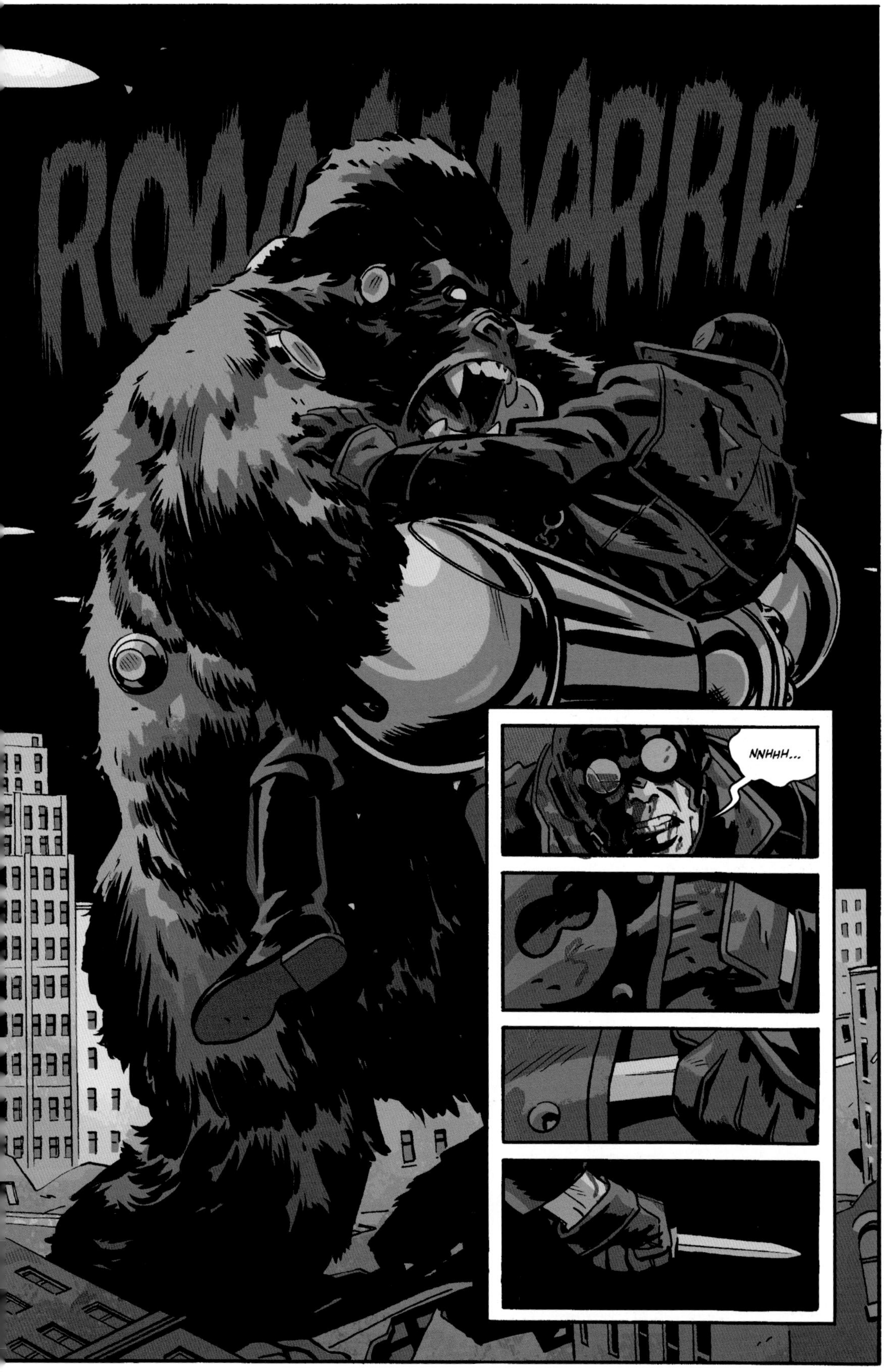
ROAAAAARRR
NNHHH...

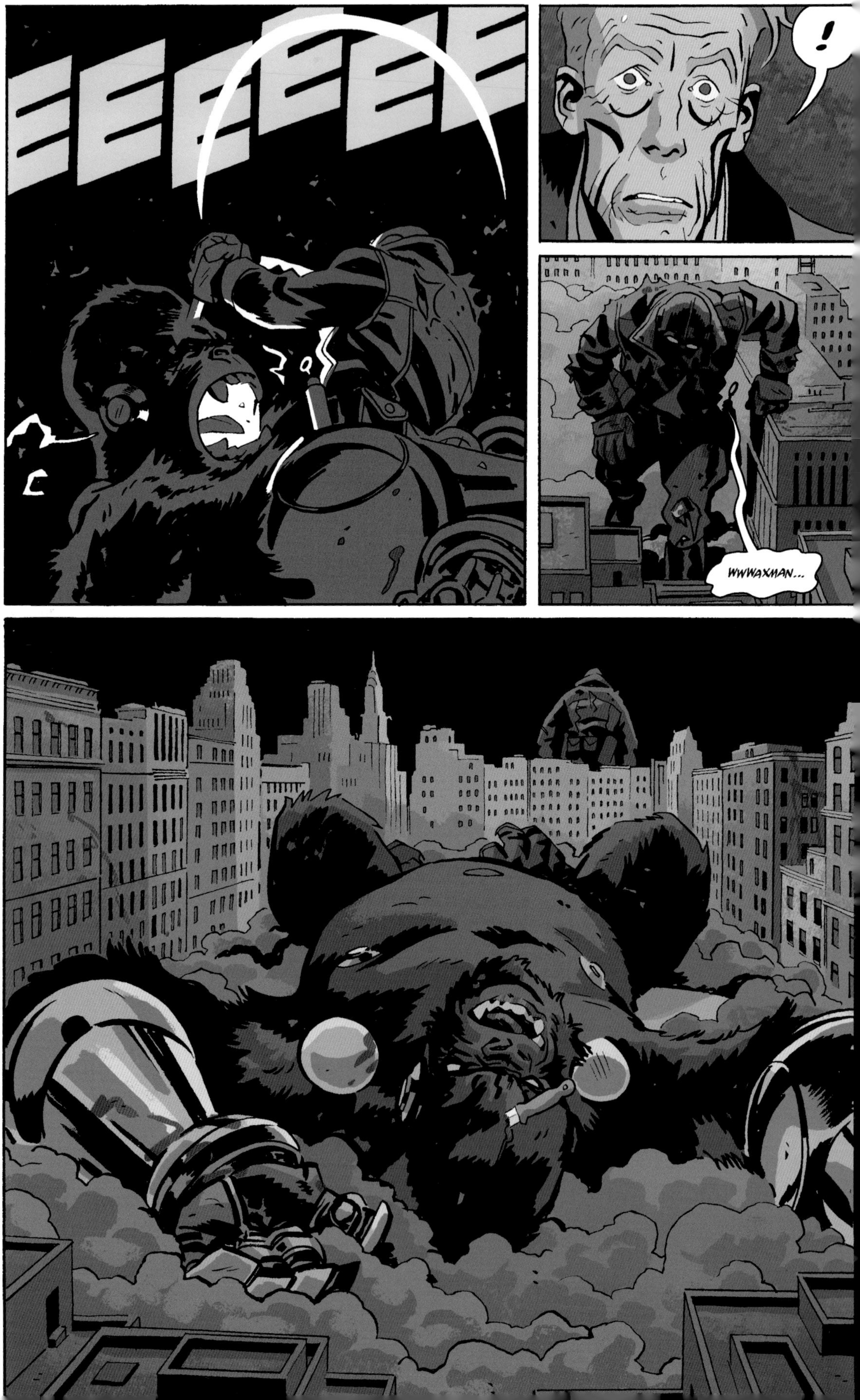
EEEEEEE
!
WWWAXMAN...

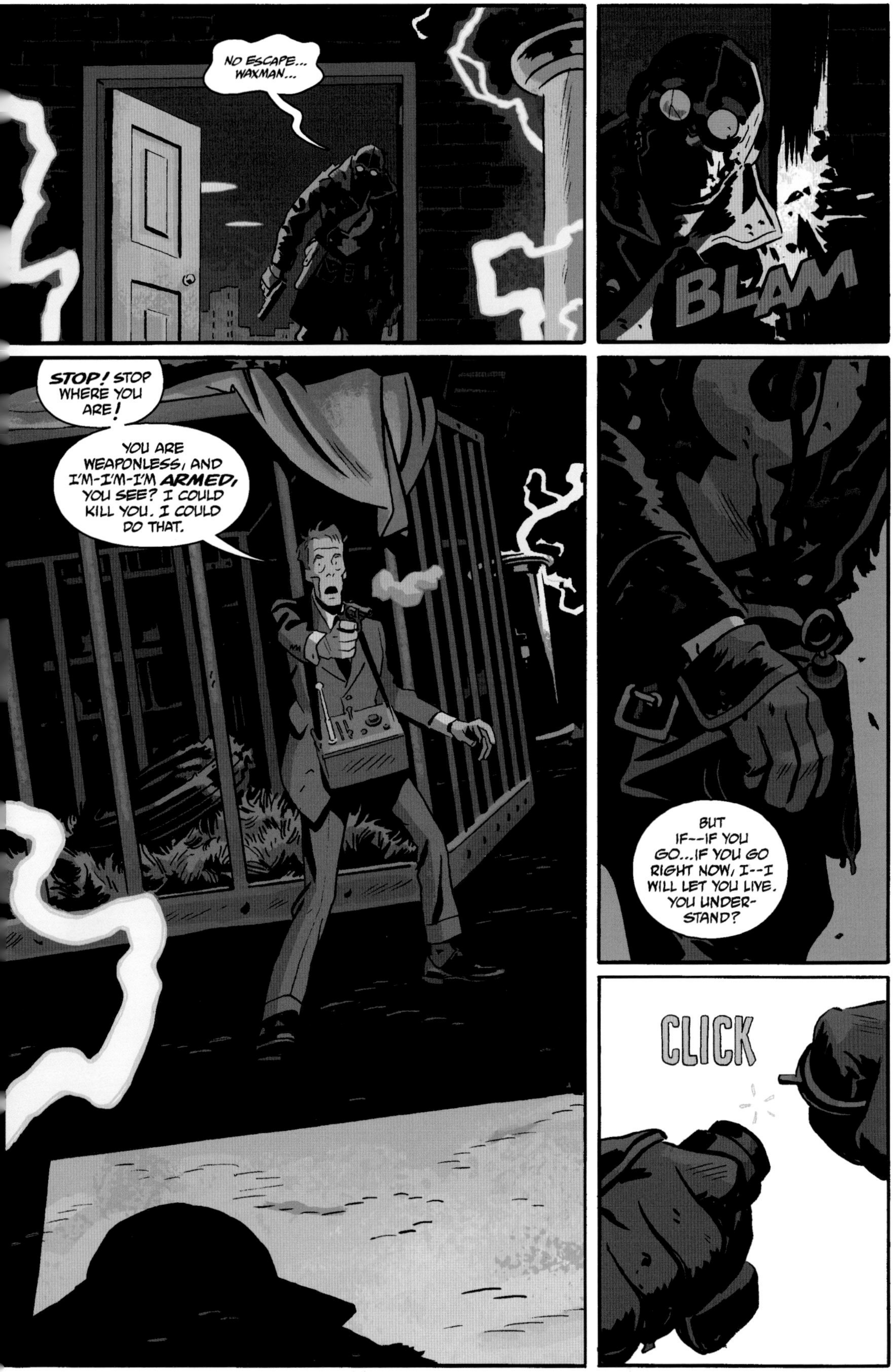
NO ESCAPE... WAXMAN...
BLAM
STOP! STOP WHERE YOU ARE!
YOU ARE WEAPONLESS, AND I'M-I'M-I'M ARMED, YOU SEE? I COULD KILL YOU. I COULD DO THAT.
BUT IF--IF YOU GO...IF YOU GO RIGHT NOW, I--I WILL LET YOU LIVE. YOU UNDER-STAND?
CLICK

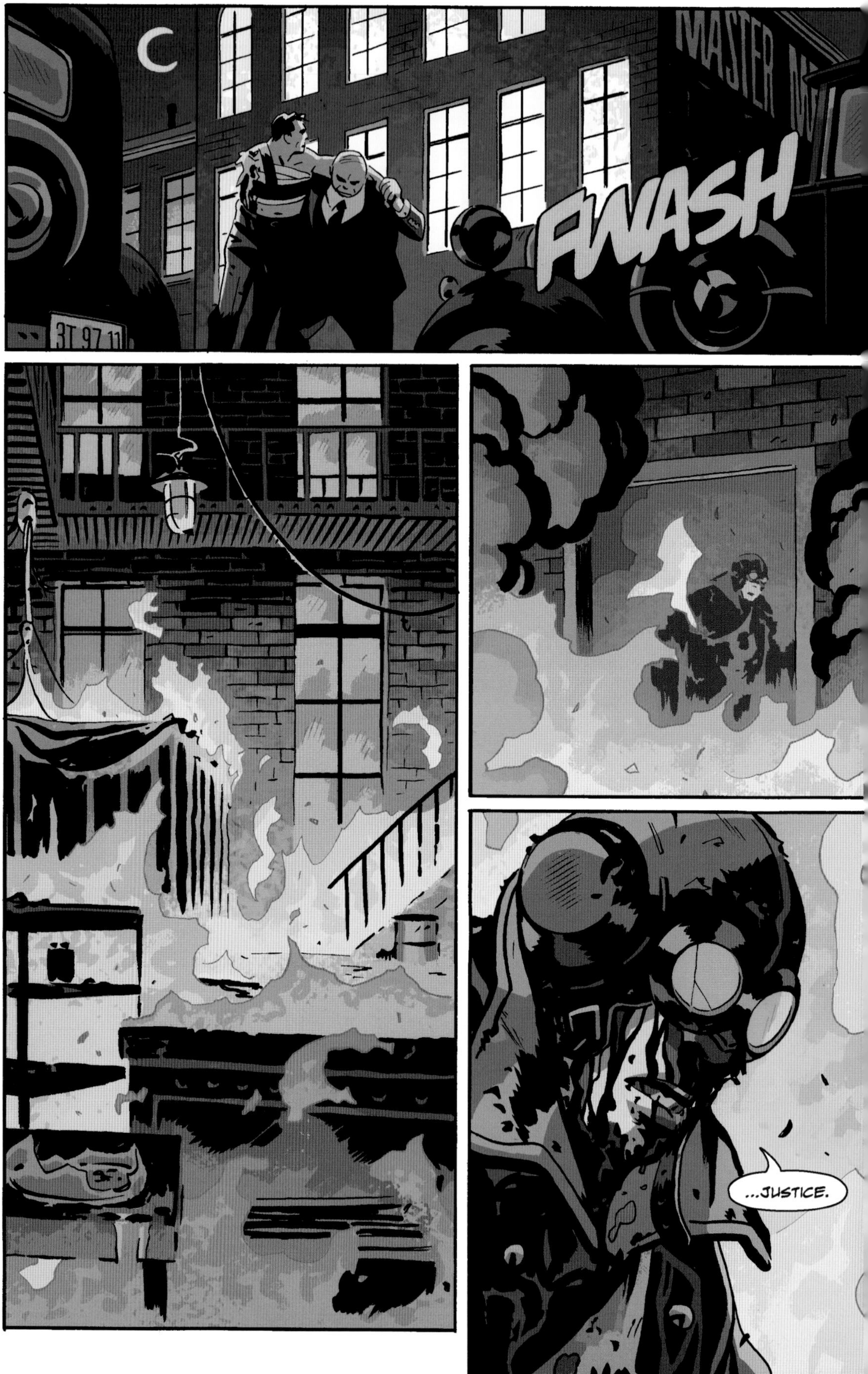
MASTER
FWASH
3T 97 11
...JUSTICE.

CHAPTER FIVE

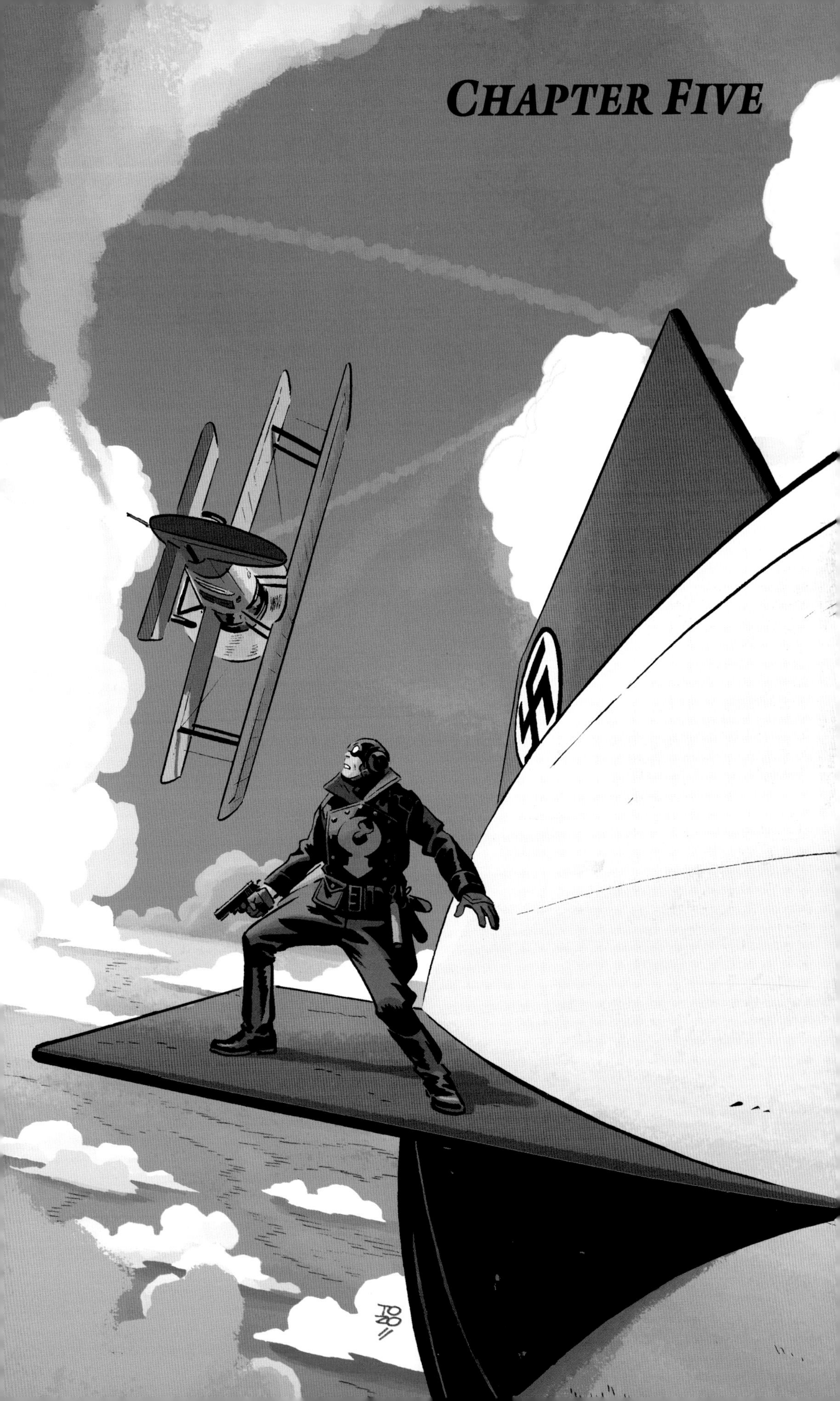

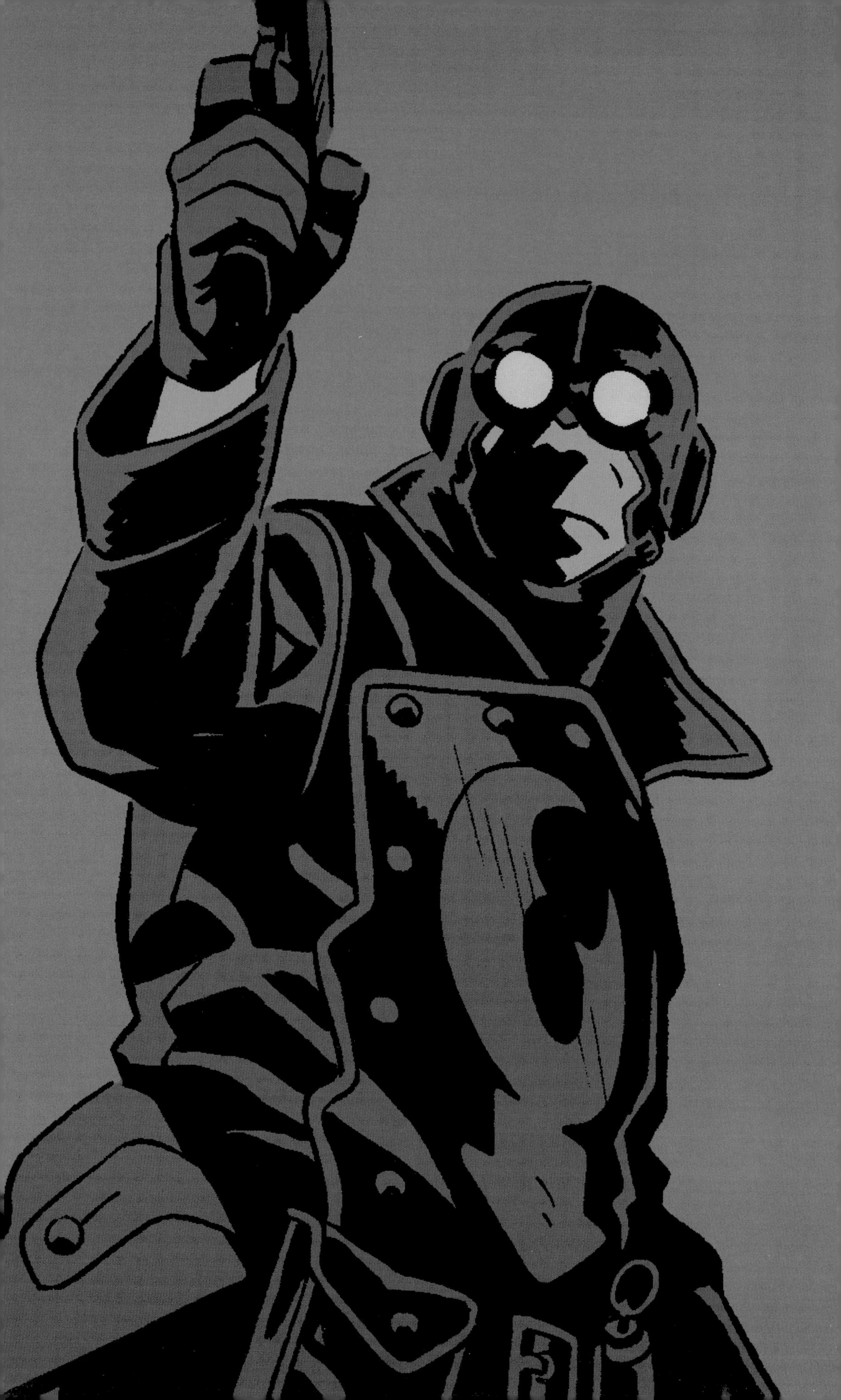

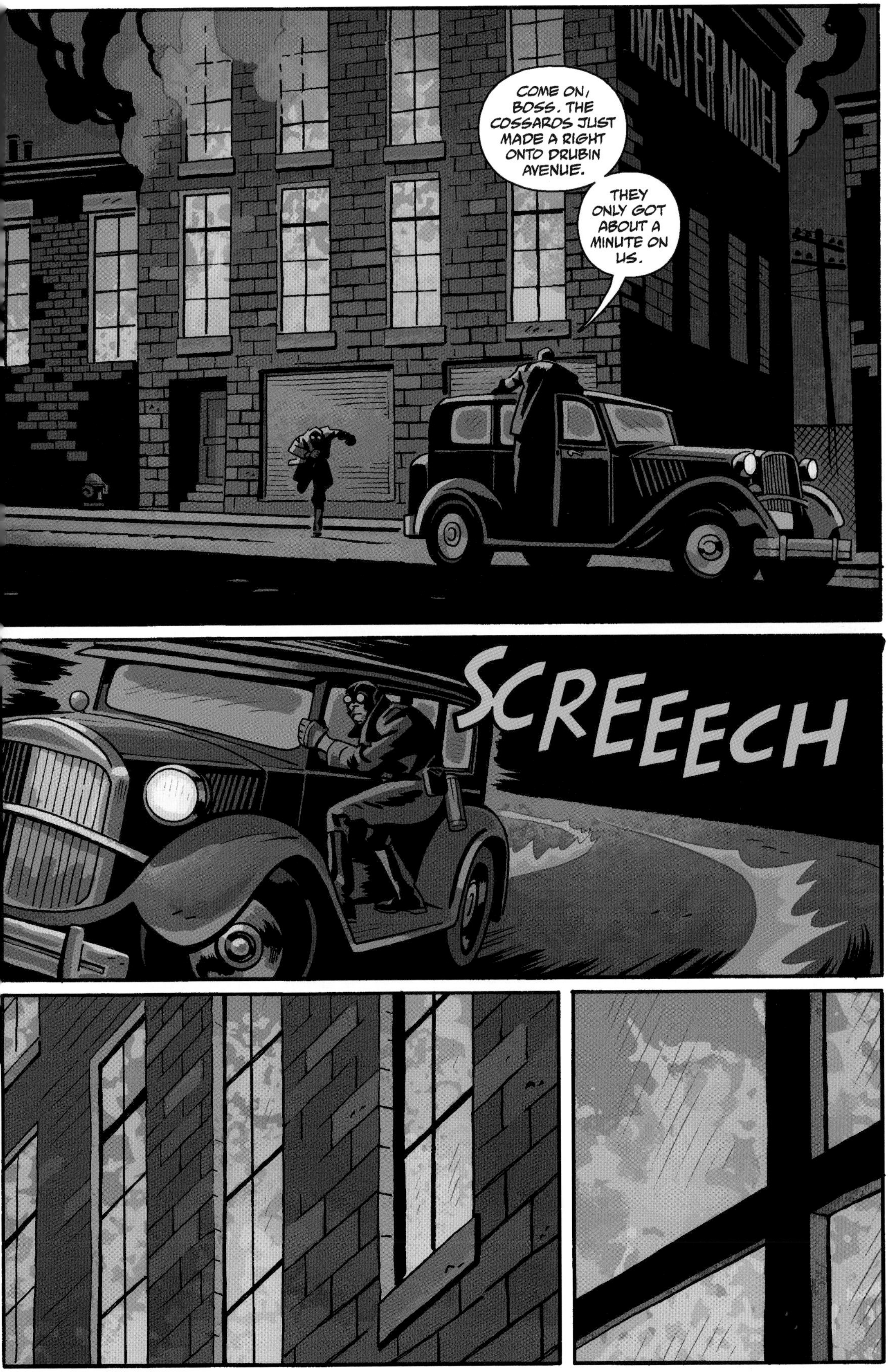
MASTER MODEL
COME ON, BOSS. THE COSSAROS JUST MADE A RIGHT ONTO DRUBIN AVENUE.
THEY ONLY GOT ABOUT A MINUTE ON US.
SCREEECH

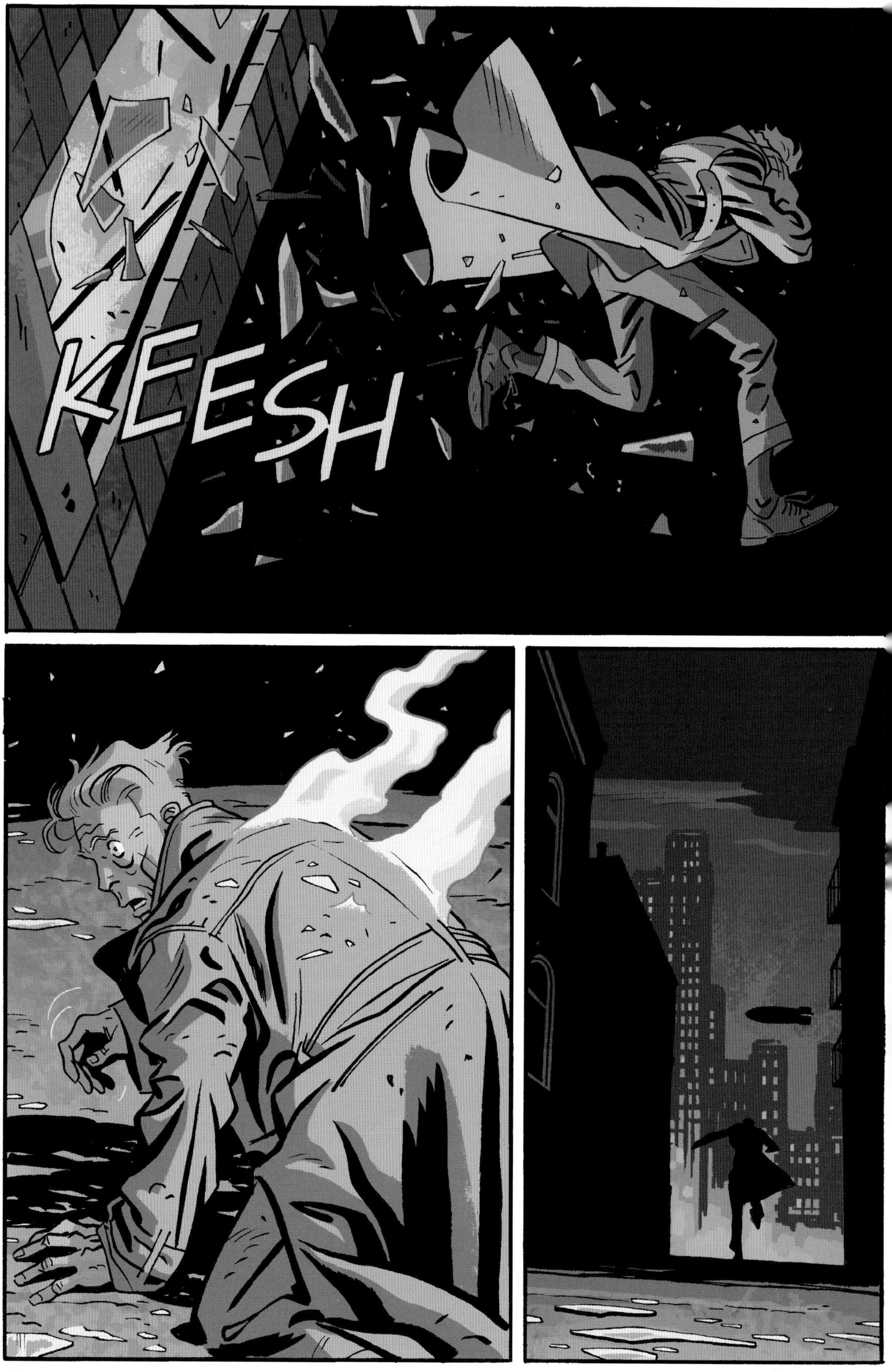
KEESH

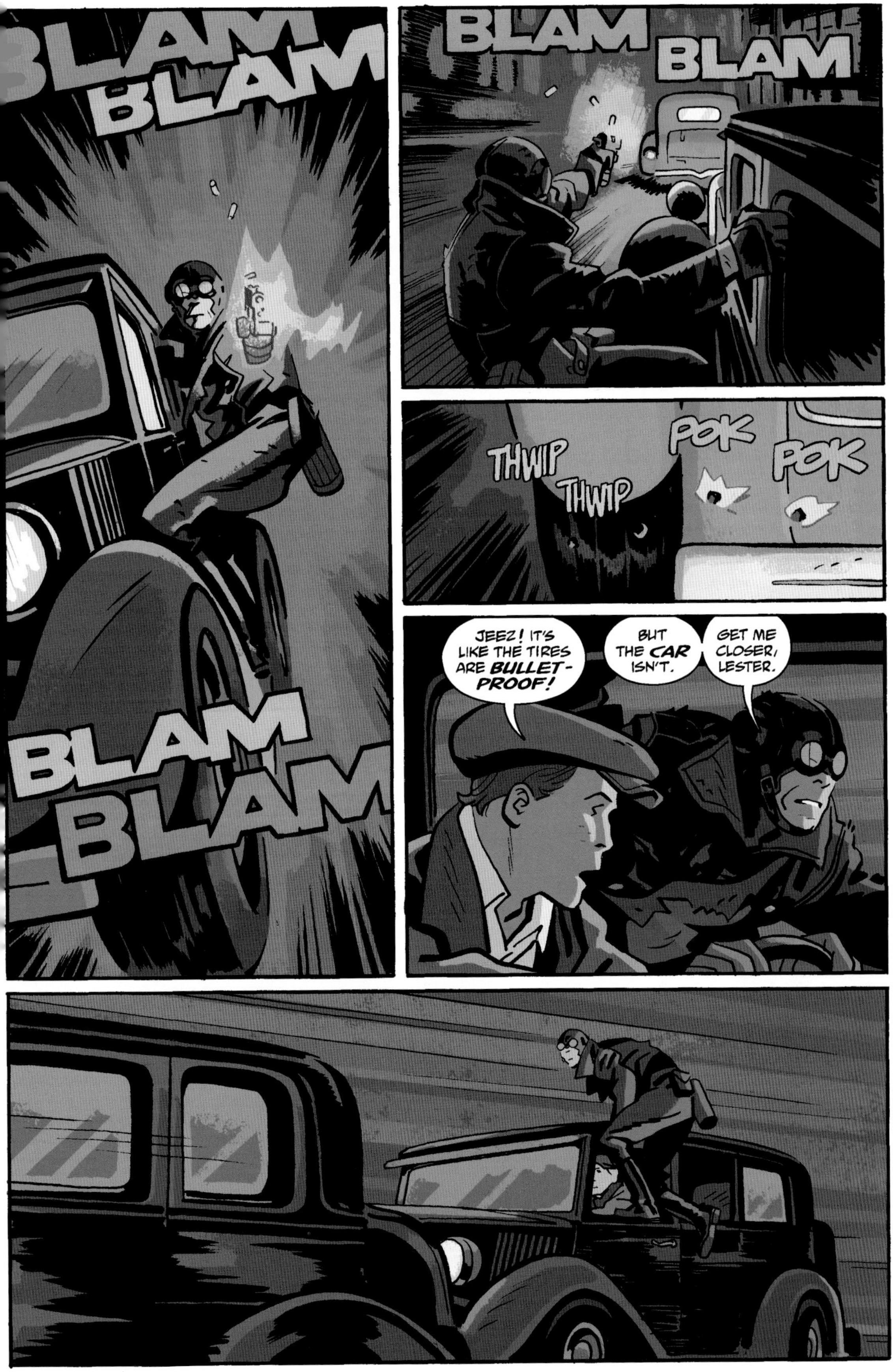
BLAM
BLAM
BLAM
BLAM
BLAM
BLAM
THWIP
THWIP
POK
POK
JEEZ! IT'S LIKE THE TIRES ARE BULLET-PROOF!
BUT THE CAR ISN'T.
GET ME CLOSER, LESTER.

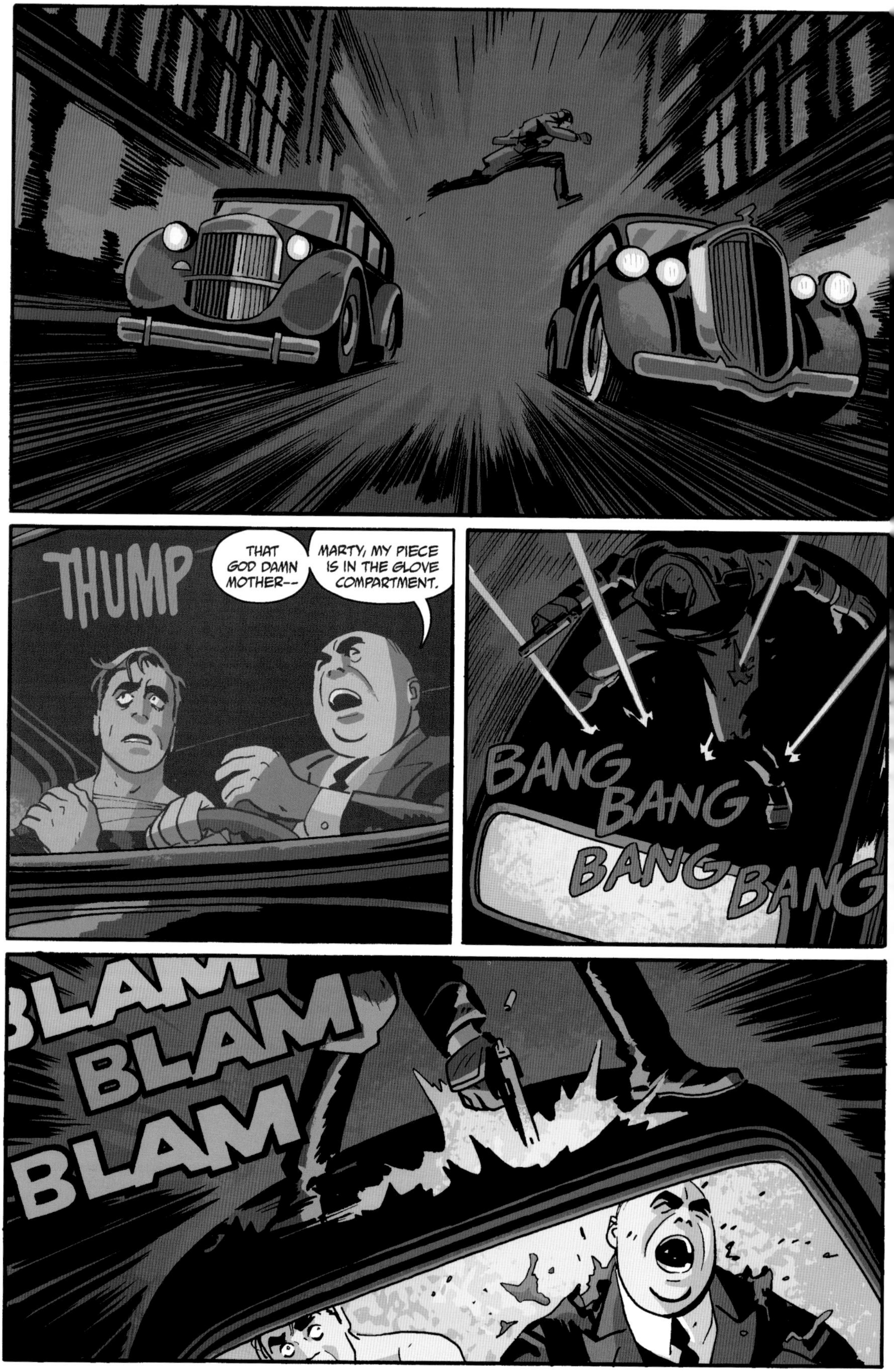
THUMP
THAT GOD DAMN MOTHER--
MARTY, MY PIECE IS IN THE GLOVE COMPARTMENT.
BANG BANG BANG BANG
BLAM BLAM BLAM BLAM

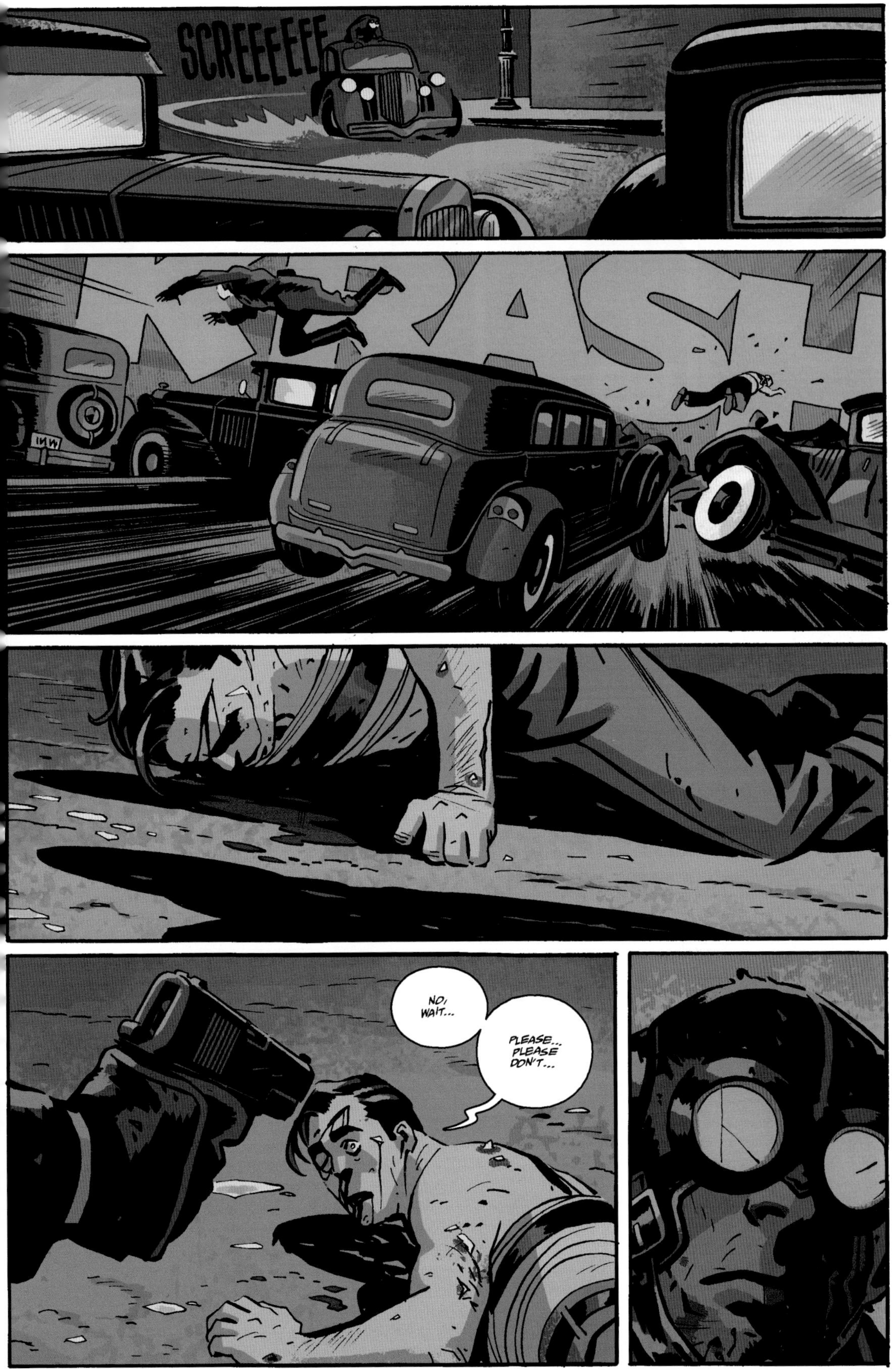
SCREEEEEEE
NO, WAIT...
PLEASE... PLEASE DON'T...

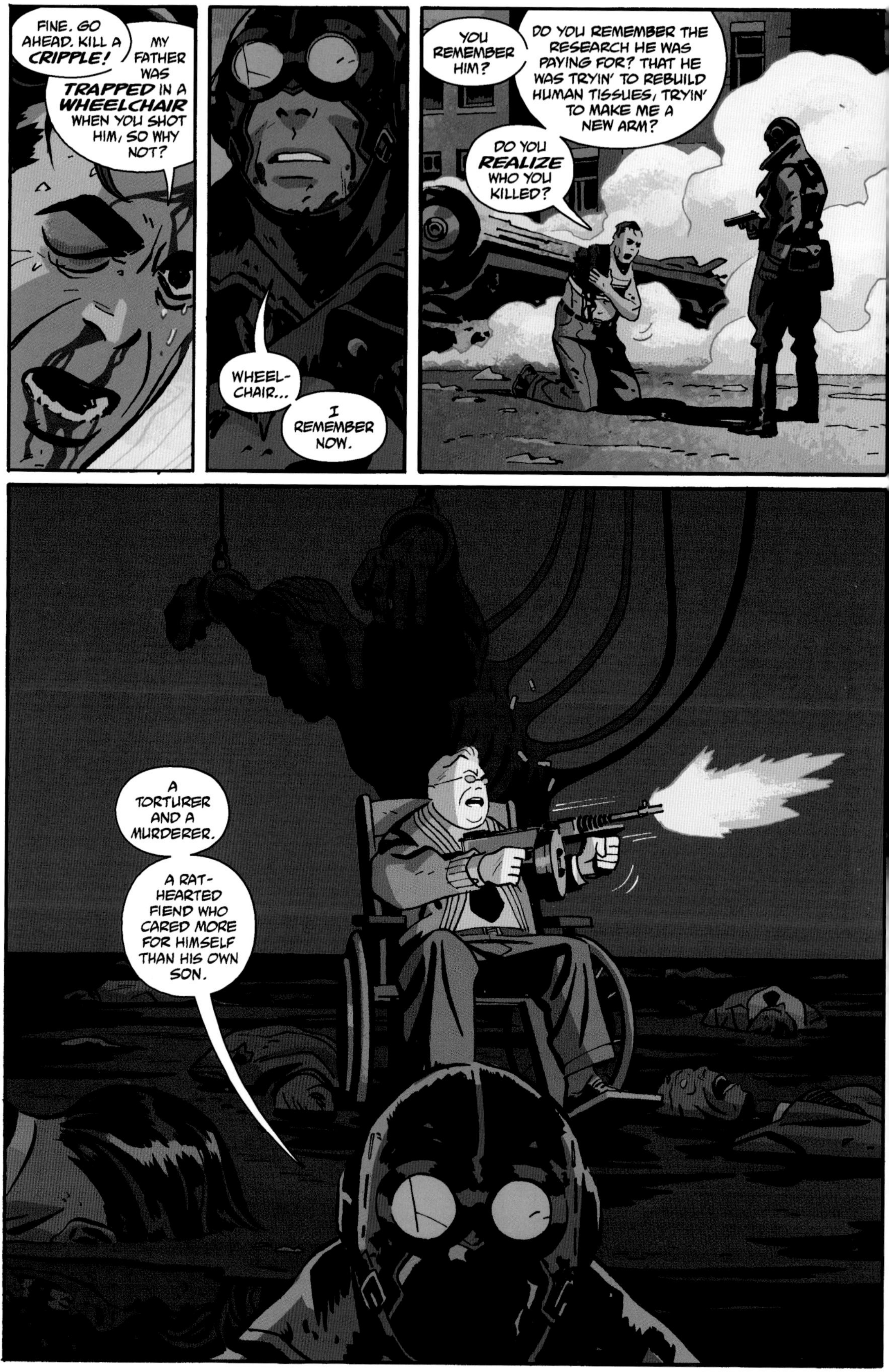
FINE. GO AHEAD. KILL A *CRIPPLE!*
MY FATHER WAS *TRAPPED* IN A *WHEELCHAIR* WHEN YOU SHOT HIM, SO WHY NOT?
WHEEL-CHAIR...
I REMEMBER NOW.
YOU REMEMBER HIM?
DO YOU REMEMBER THE RESEARCH HE WAS PAYING FOR? THAT HE WAS TRYIN' TO REBUILD HUMAN TISSUES, TRYIN' TO MAKE ME A NEW ARM?
DO YOU *REALIZE* WHO YOU KILLED?
A TORTURER AND A MURDERER.
A RAT-HEARTED FIEND WHO CARED MORE FOR HIMSELF THAN HIS OWN SON.

"LIKE YOU AND YOUR BROTHER, A *PREDATOR* FEEDING ON THIS CITY.

"BUT IT'S *MY* CITY.

"AND I'M ALWAYS WATCHING.

"I'LL ALWAYS PROTECT MY CITY.

"SO THAT THE INNOCENT DON'T HAVE TO BE AFRAID."

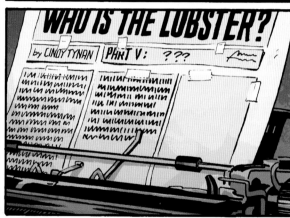

WHO IS THE LUBSTER?

by CINDY TYNAN | PART V: ???

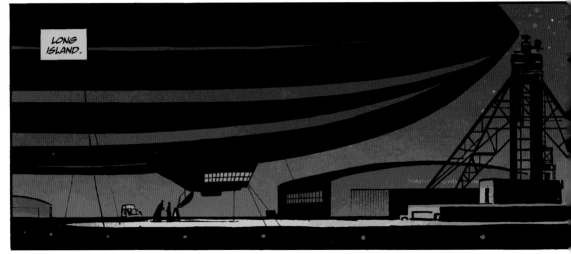

LONG ISLAND.

PASS-PORT?

YES, YES. HERE. ONLY PLEASE HURRY.

RELAX, MISTER. PLENTY OF TICKETS LEFT.

THE GARTBERG ZEPPELIN COMING TO THE STATES WAS A BIG DEAL, BUT NOBODY WANTS TO FLY *INTO* GERMANY THESE DAYS.

AT LAST I CAN RELAX.

THIS IS FOR THE BEST. THE GERMANS, I THINK, WILL BETTER APPRECIATE MY TALENTS.

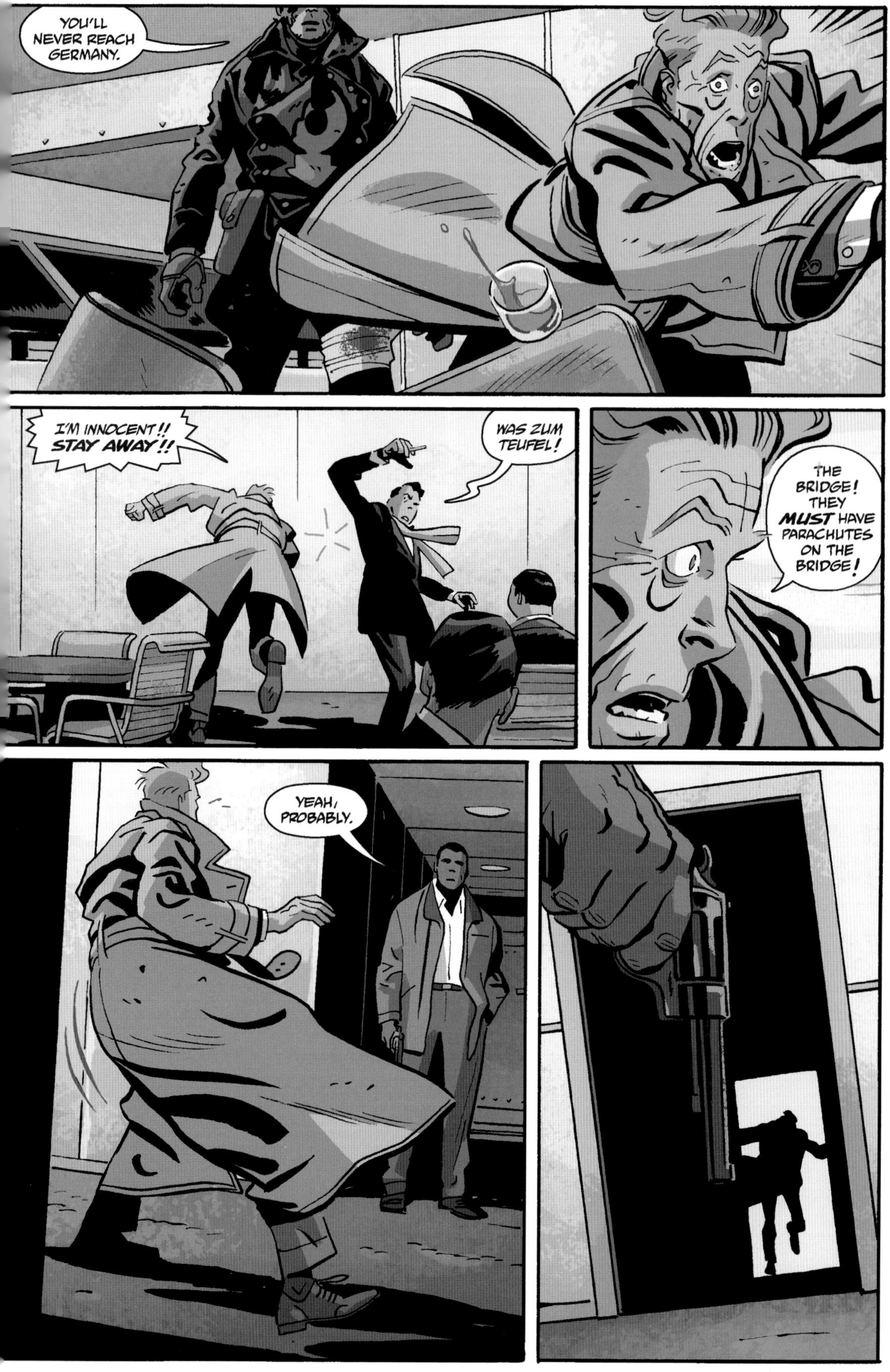
YOU'LL NEVER REACH GERMANY.
I'M INNOCENT!! STAY AWAY!!
WAS ZUM TEUFEL!
THE BRIDGE! THEY MUST HAVE PARACHUTES ON THE BRIDGE!
YEAH, PROBABLY.

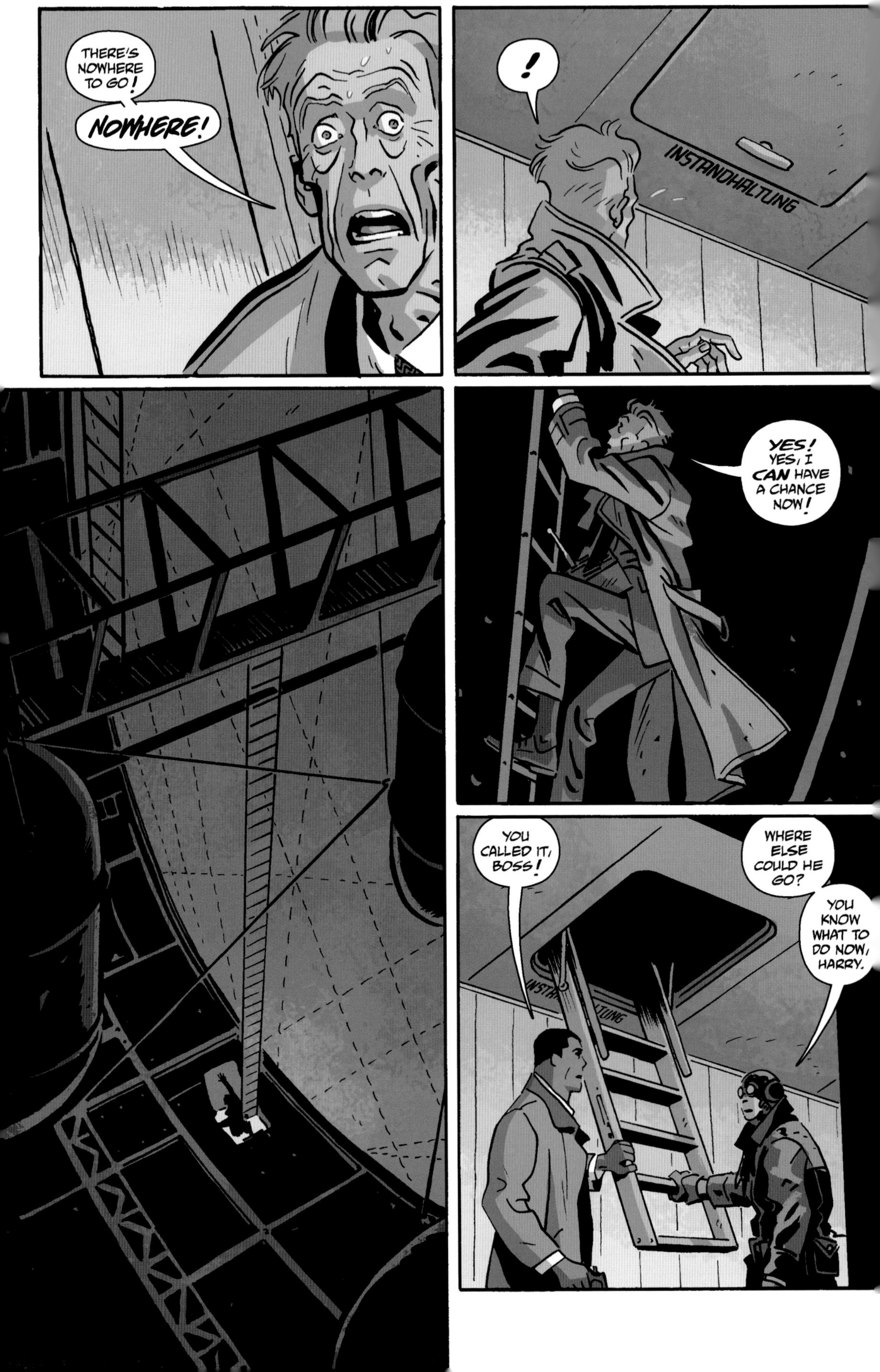
THERE'S NOWHERE TO GO!
NOWHERE!
!
INSTANDHALTUNG
YES! YES, I CAN HAVE A CHANCE NOW!
YOU CALLED IT, BOSS!
WHERE ELSE COULD HE GO?
YOU KNOW WHAT TO DO NOW, HARRY.

THERE SHE GOES. LOOK AT THE *SIZE* OF THAT THING.

YOU LOOK AT IT. I GOT WORK TO DO.

THERE YOU GO AGAIN. WHATTA YOU GOT AGAINST THE GERMANS, ANYWAY?

WORLD WAR ONE, FOR STARTERS. REMEMBER HOW MUCH FUN THAT WAS?

AND THIS HITLER GUY, YOU ASK ME, HE'S JUST ANOTHER--

HEY, WHAT THE HELL IS THAT?

RRRRRRRRRR

VROOOOOOOM!

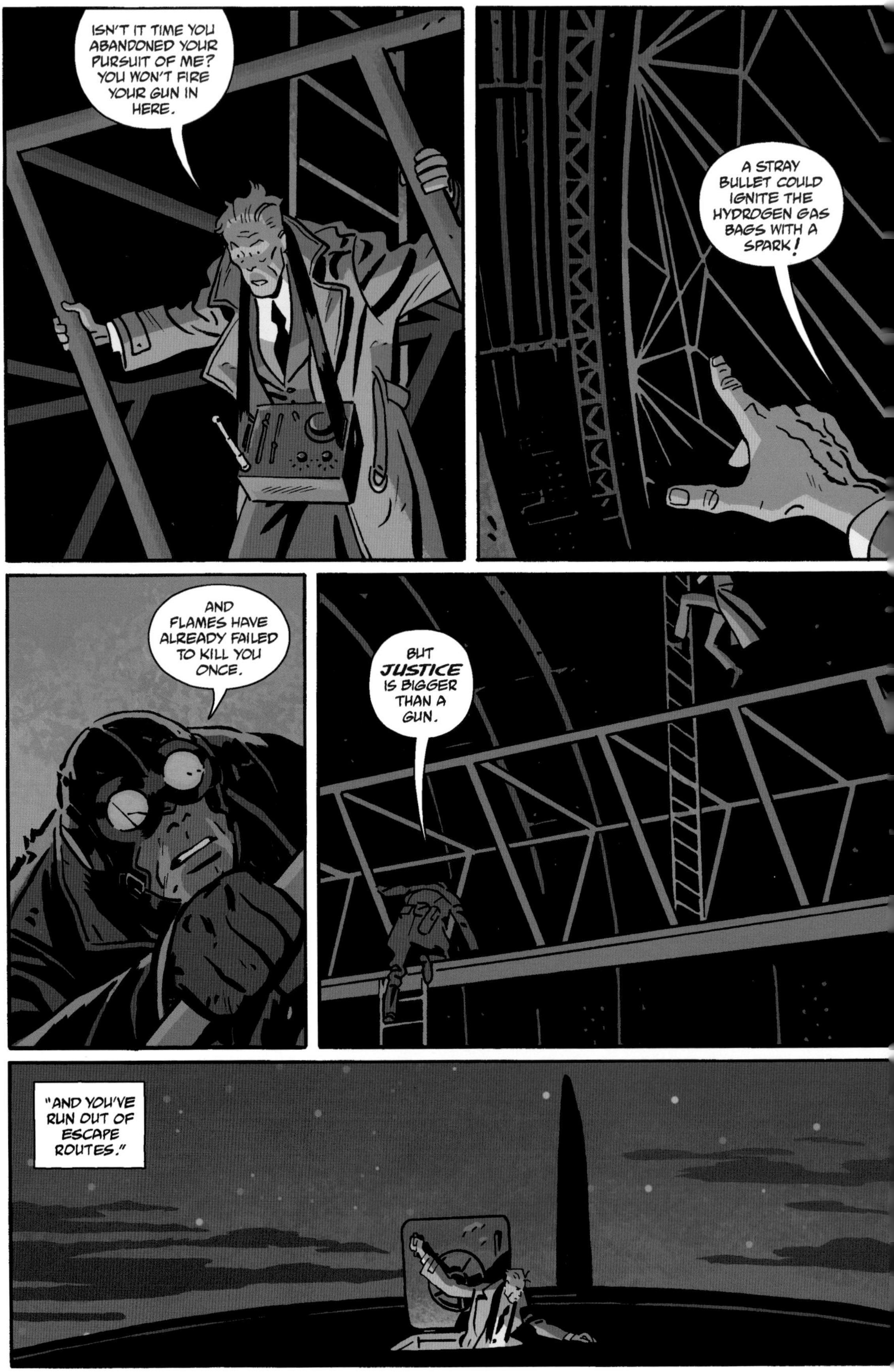
ISN'T IT TIME YOU ABANDONED YOUR PURSUIT OF ME? YOU WON'T FIRE YOUR GUN IN HERE.
A STRAY BULLET COULD IGNITE THE HYDROGEN GAS BAGS WITH A SPARK!
AND FLAMES HAVE ALREADY FAILED TO KILL YOU ONCE.
BUT JUSTICE IS BIGGER THAN A GUN.
"AND YOU'VE RUN OUT OF ESCAPE ROUTES."

DEAD END.

REALLY? WHAT ABOUT MY HISTORY HAS EVER SHOWN ME TO BE STUPID?

SMART MEN DIE TOO, WAXMAN.

VROOOOOOOM

HA HA HA. RADIO TRANSMISSION, LOBSTER MAN! UP HERE, NOTHING CAN INTERFERE WITH IT!

"AND THAT PLANE'S PILOT IS MY RECEIVER-- LEWIS MOSKIN. HE'S WAITING FOR HIS ORDERS."

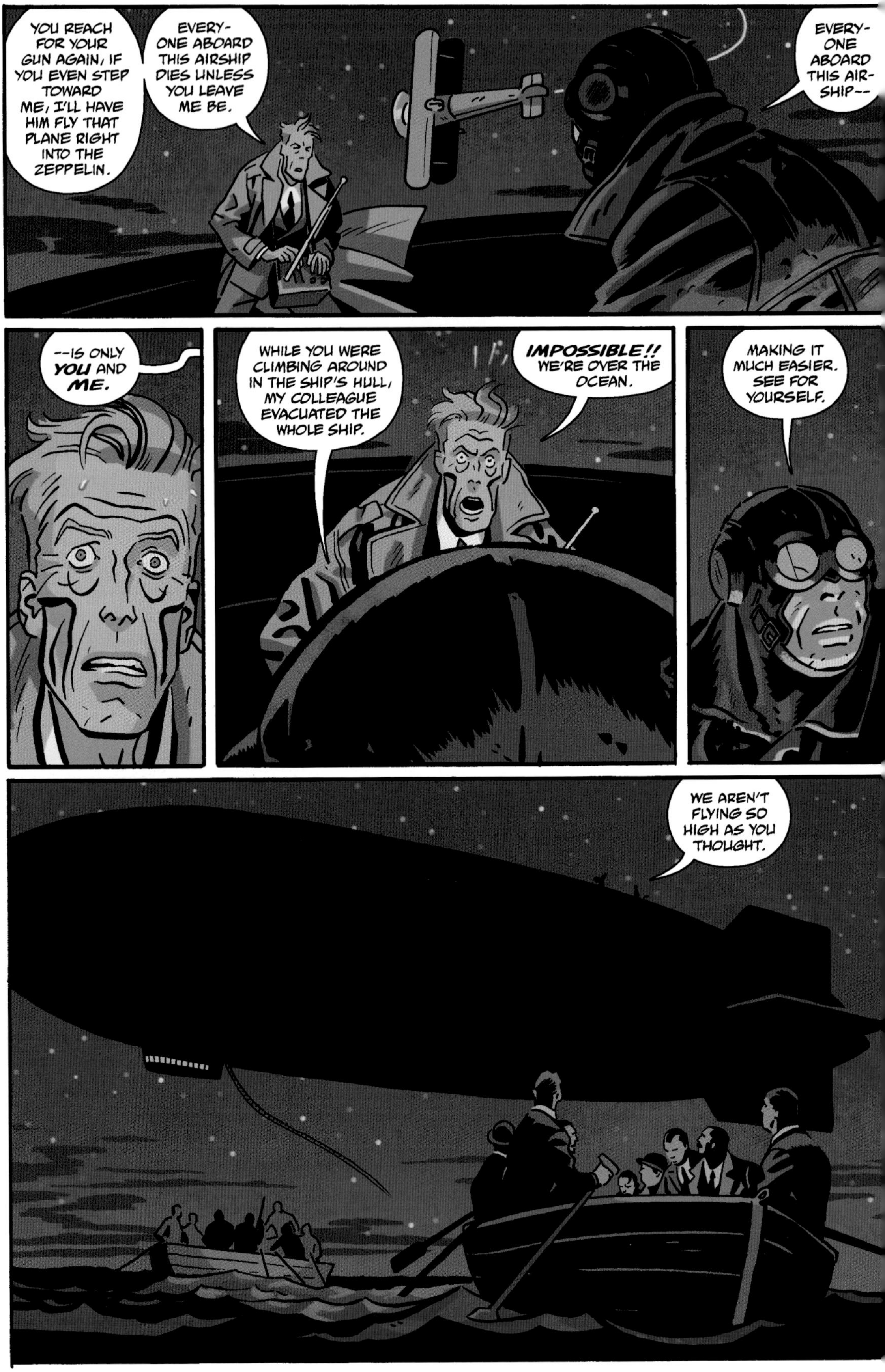
YOU REACH FOR YOUR GUN AGAIN, IF YOU EVEN STEP TOWARD ME, I'LL HAVE HIM FLY THAT PLANE RIGHT INTO THE ZEPPELIN.
EVERY-ONE ABOARD THIS AIRSHIP DIES UNLESS YOU LEAVE ME BE.
EVERY-ONE ABOARD THIS AIR-SHIP--
--IS ONLY YOU AND ME.
WHILE YOU WERE CLIMBING AROUND IN THE SHIP'S HULL, MY COLLEAGUE EVACUATED THE WHOLE SHIP.
IMPOSSIBLE!! WE'RE OVER THE OCEAN.
MAKING IT MUCH EASIER. SEE FOR YOURSELF.
WE AREN'T FLYING SO HIGH AS YOU THOUGHT.

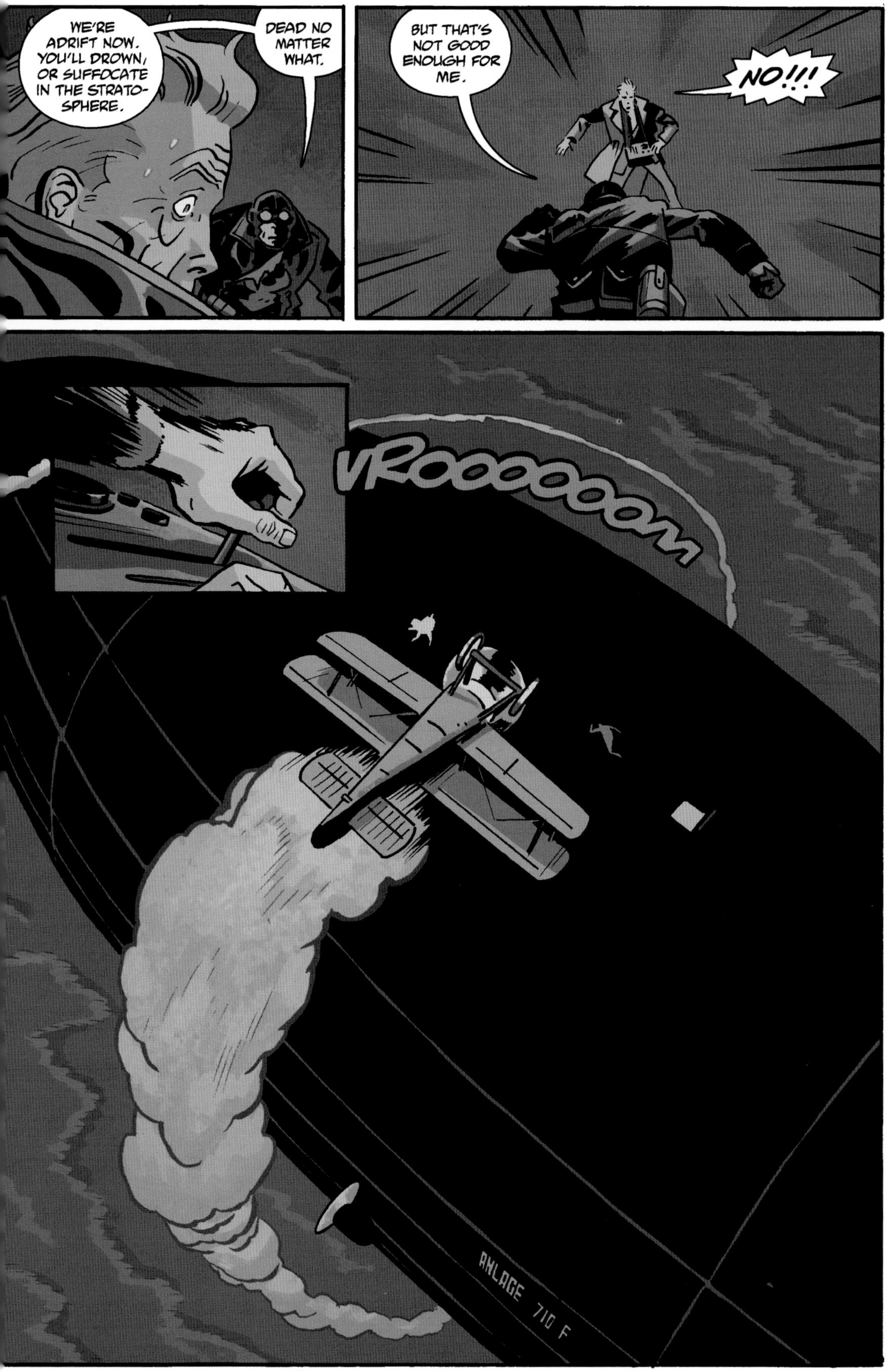
WE'RE ADRIFT NOW. YOU'LL DROWN, OR SUFFOCATE IN THE STRATO-SPHERE.
DEAD NO MATTER WHAT.
BUT THAT'S NOT GOOD ENOUGH FOR ME.
NO!!!
VROOOOOOOM
ANLAGE 710 F

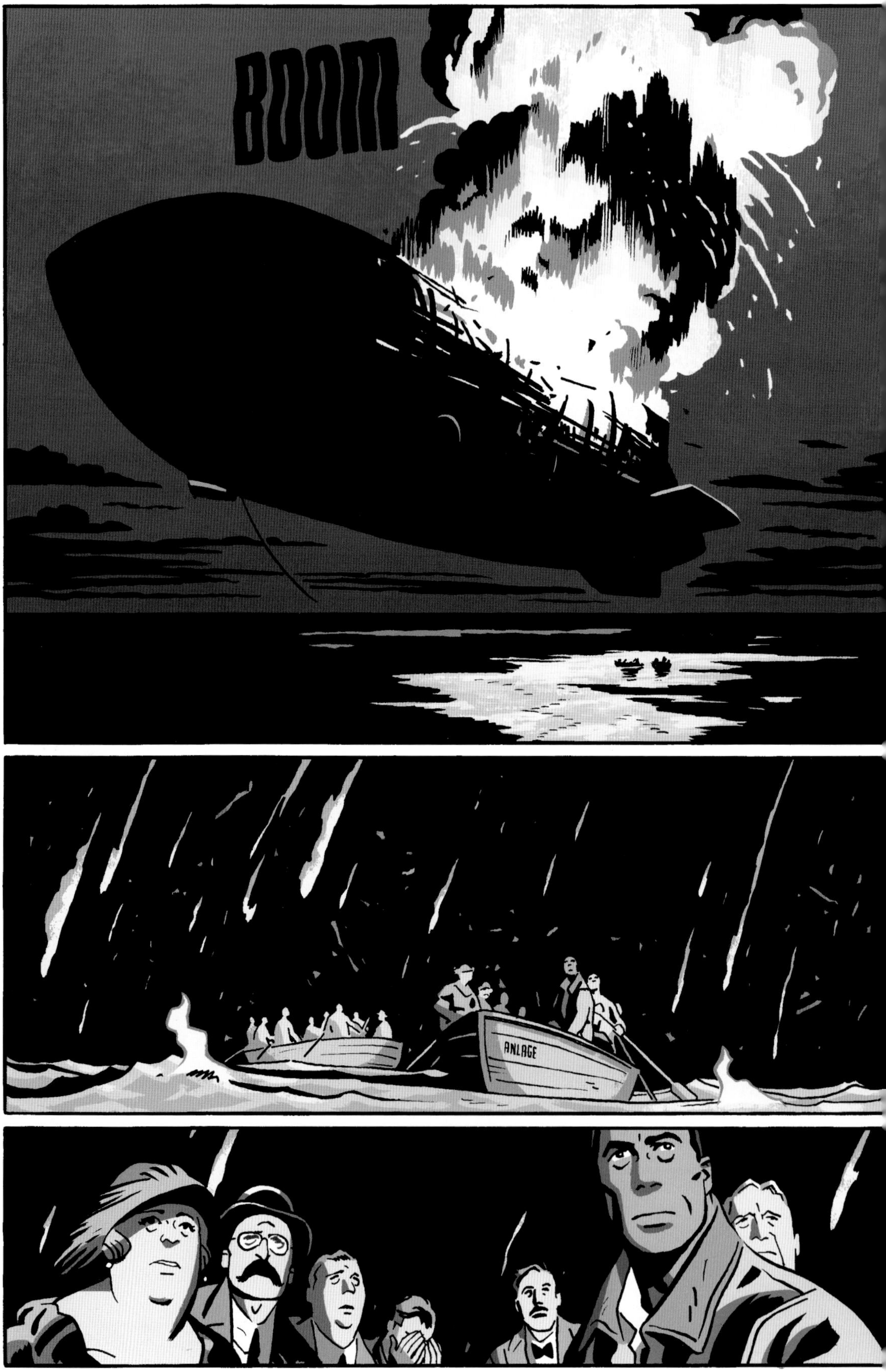
BOOM
ANLAGE

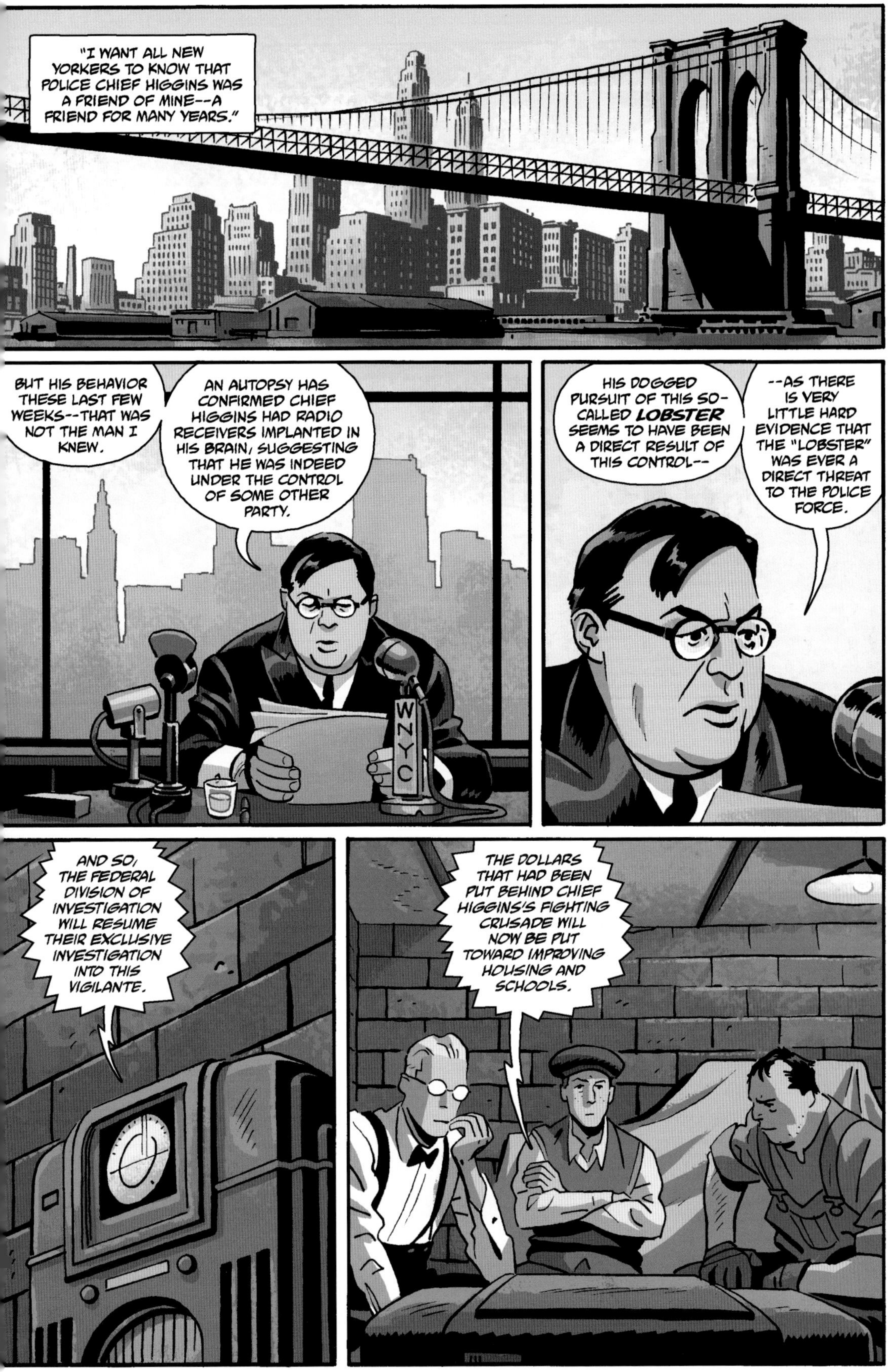
"I WANT ALL NEW YORKERS TO KNOW THAT POLICE CHIEF HIGGINS WAS A FRIEND OF MINE--A FRIEND FOR MANY YEARS."
BUT HIS BEHAVIOR THESE LAST FEW WEEKS--THAT WAS NOT THE MAN I KNEW.
AN AUTOPSY HAS CONFIRMED CHIEF HIGGINS HAD RADIO RECEIVERS IMPLANTED IN HIS BRAIN, SUGGESTING THAT HE WAS INDEED UNDER THE CONTROL OF SOME OTHER PARTY.
WNYC
HIS DOGGED PURSUIT OF THIS SO-CALLED LOBSTER SEEMS TO HAVE BEEN A DIRECT RESULT OF THIS CONTROL--
--AS THERE IS VERY LITTLE HARD EVIDENCE THAT THE "LOBSTER" WAS EVER A DIRECT THREAT TO THE POLICE FORCE.
AND SO, THE FEDERAL DIVISION OF INVESTIGATION WILL RESUME THEIR EXCLUSIVE INVESTIGATION INTO THIS VIGILANTE.
THE DOLLARS THAT HAD BEEN PUT BEHIND CHIEF HIGGINS'S FIGHTING CRUSADE WILL NOW BE PUT TOWARD IMPROVING HOUSING AND SCHOOLS.

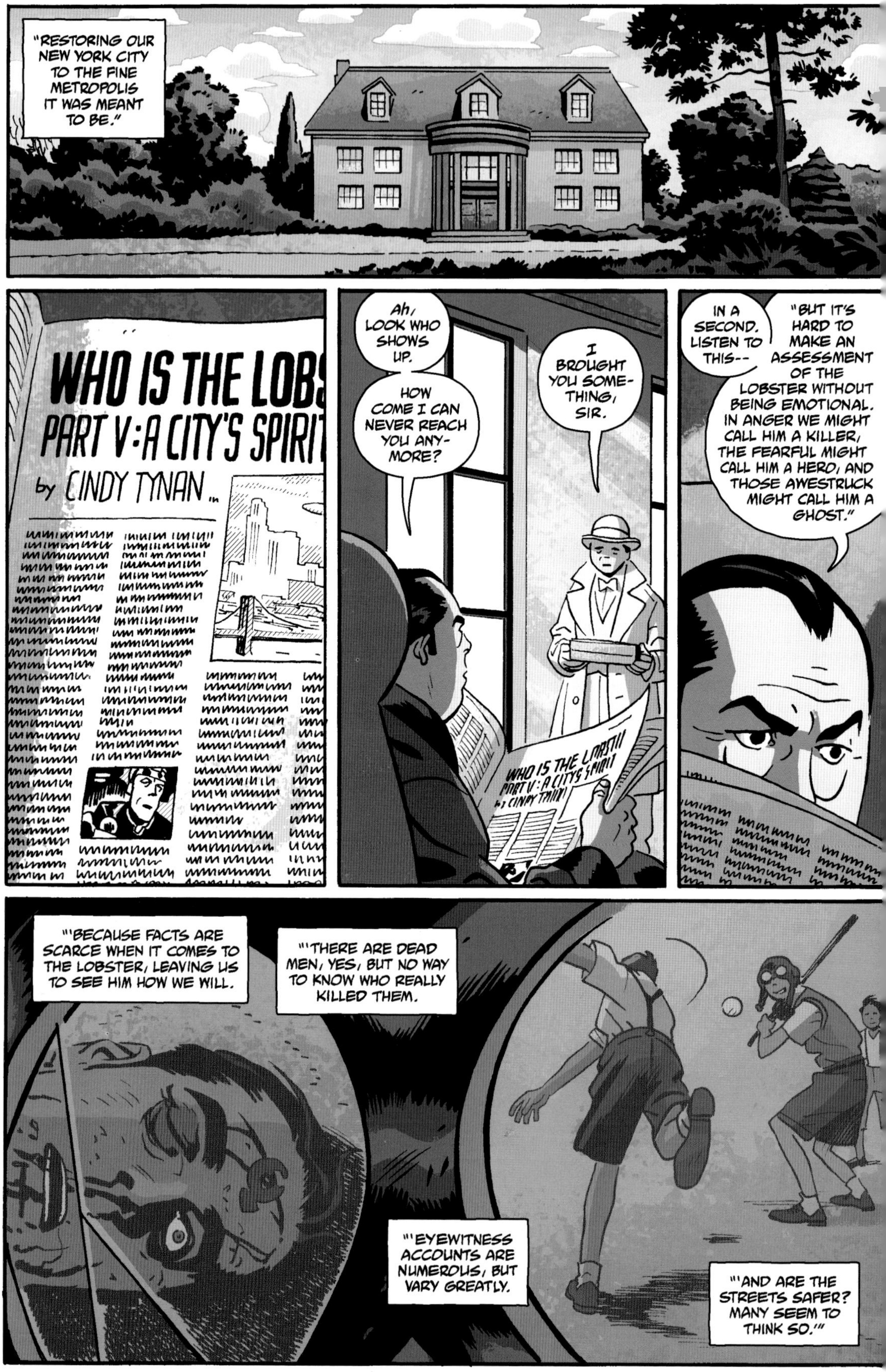
"RESTORING OUR NEW YORK CITY TO THE FINE METROPOLIS IT WAS MEANT TO BE."
WHO IS THE LOBS
PART V: A CITY'S SPIRIT
by CINDY TYNAN
Ah, LOOK WHO SHOWS UP.
HOW COME I CAN NEVER REACH YOU ANYMORE?
I BROUGHT YOU SOMETHING, SIR.
IN A SECOND. LISTEN TO THIS--
"BUT IT'S HARD TO MAKE AN ASSESSMENT OF THE LOBSTER WITHOUT BEING EMOTIONAL. IN ANGER WE MIGHT CALL HIM A KILLER, THE FEARFUL MIGHT CALL HIM A HERO, AND THOSE AWESTRUCK MIGHT CALL HIM A GHOST."
"'BECAUSE FACTS ARE SCARCE WHEN IT COMES TO THE LOBSTER, LEAVING US TO SEE HIM HOW WE WILL.
"'THERE ARE DEAD MEN, YES, BUT NO WAY TO KNOW WHO REALLY KILLED THEM.
"'EYEWITNESS ACCOUNTS ARE NUMEROUS, BUT VARY GREATLY.
"'AND ARE THE STREETS SAFER? MANY SEEM TO THINK SO.'"

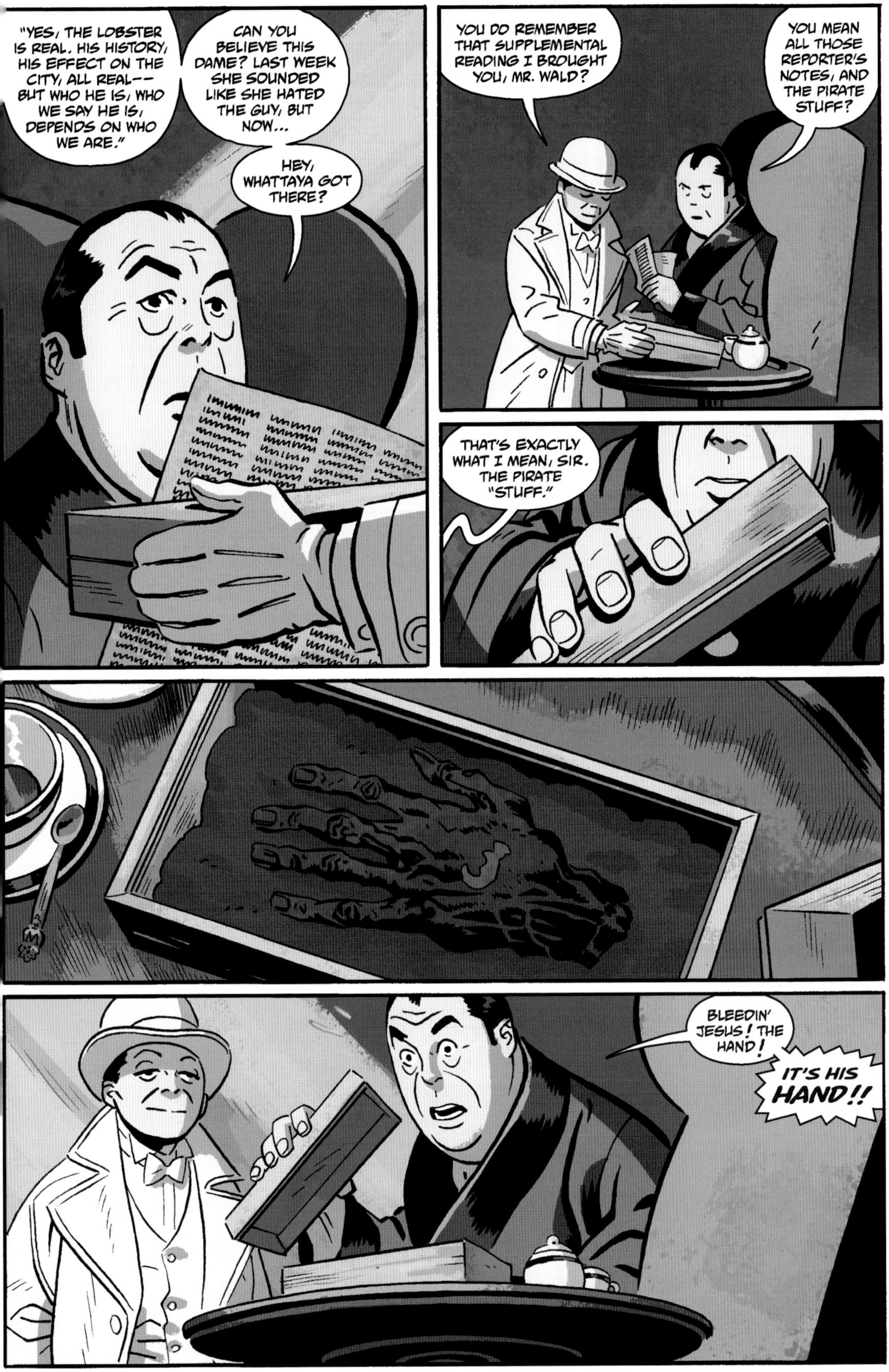
"YES, THE LOBSTER IS REAL. HIS HISTORY, HIS EFFECT ON THE CITY, ALL REAL-- BUT WHO HE IS, WHO WE SAY HE IS, DEPENDS ON WHO WE ARE."
CAN YOU BELIEVE THIS DAME? LAST WEEK SHE SOUNDED LIKE SHE HATED THE GUY, BUT NOW...
HEY, WHATTAYA GOT THERE?
YOU DO REMEMBER THAT SUPPLEMENTAL READING I BROUGHT YOU, MR. WALD?
YOU MEAN ALL THOSE REPORTER'S NOTES, AND THE PIRATE STUFF?
THAT'S EXACTLY WHAT I MEAN, SIR. THE PIRATE "STUFF."
BLEEDIN' JESUS! THE HAND!
IT'S HIS HAND!!

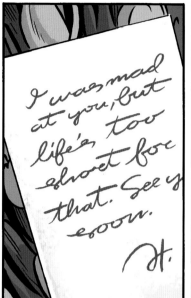

I was mad at you, but life's too short for that. See you soon.

H.

HARRY...

GOOD MORNING, DETECTIVE.

MORNING, AGENT FLYNN. THANKS FOR MEETING ME AWAY FROM THE STATION.

THIS IS EASIER FOR ME ANYWAY. I CAN WALK TO GRAND CENTRAL FROM HERE.

SO TELL ME, DETECTIVE ECKERD--

Herald

--WHY DO YOU WANT TO JOIN THE D.O.I.?

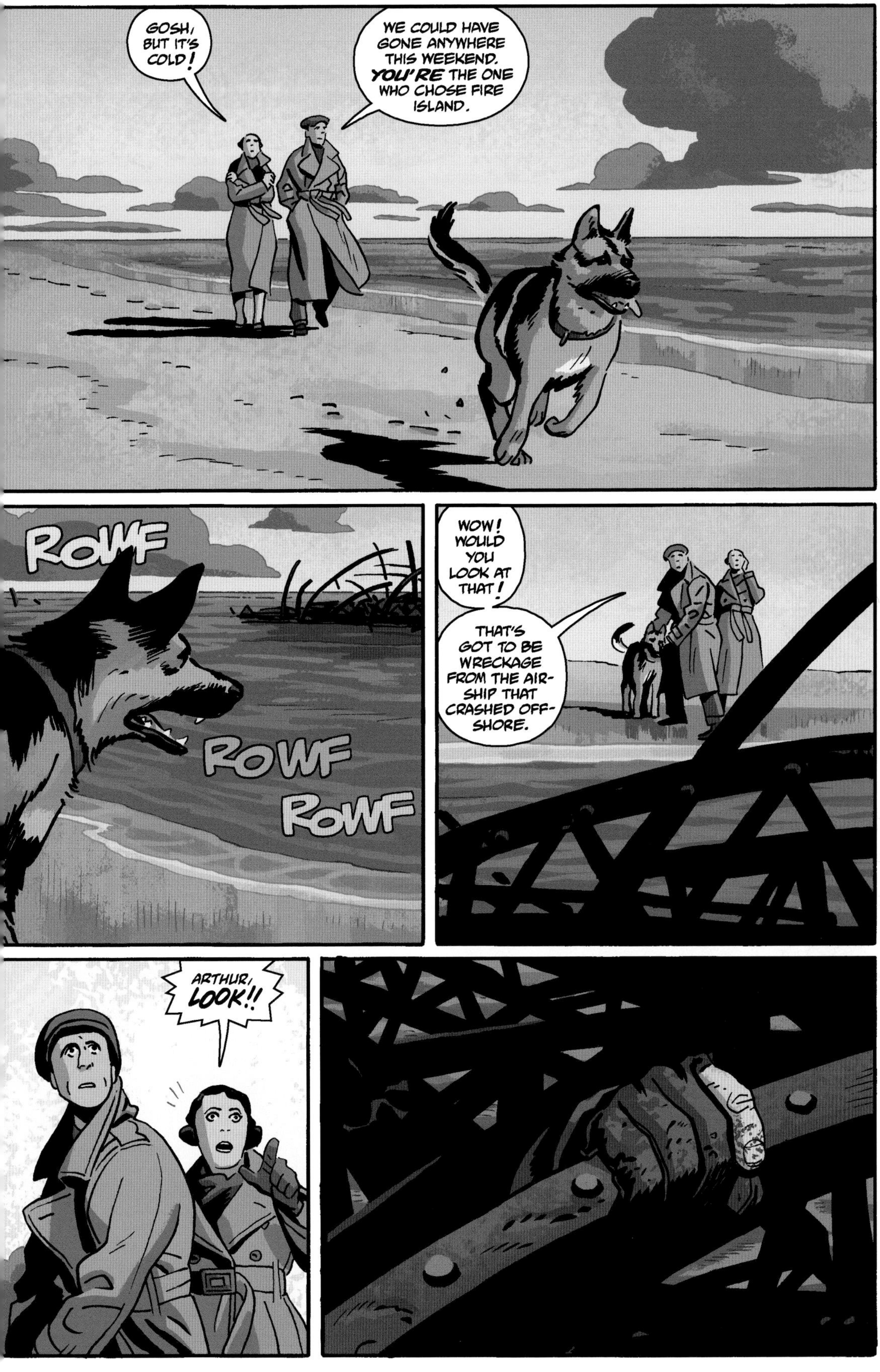
GOSH, BUT IT'S COLD!
WE COULD HAVE GONE ANYWHERE THIS WEEKEND. YOU'RE THE ONE WHO CHOSE FIRE ISLAND.
ROWF
ROWF
ROWF
WOW! WOULD YOU LOOK AT THAT!
THAT'S GOT TO BE WRECKAGE FROM THE AIR-SHIP THAT CRASHED OFF-SHORE.
ARTHUR, LOOK!!

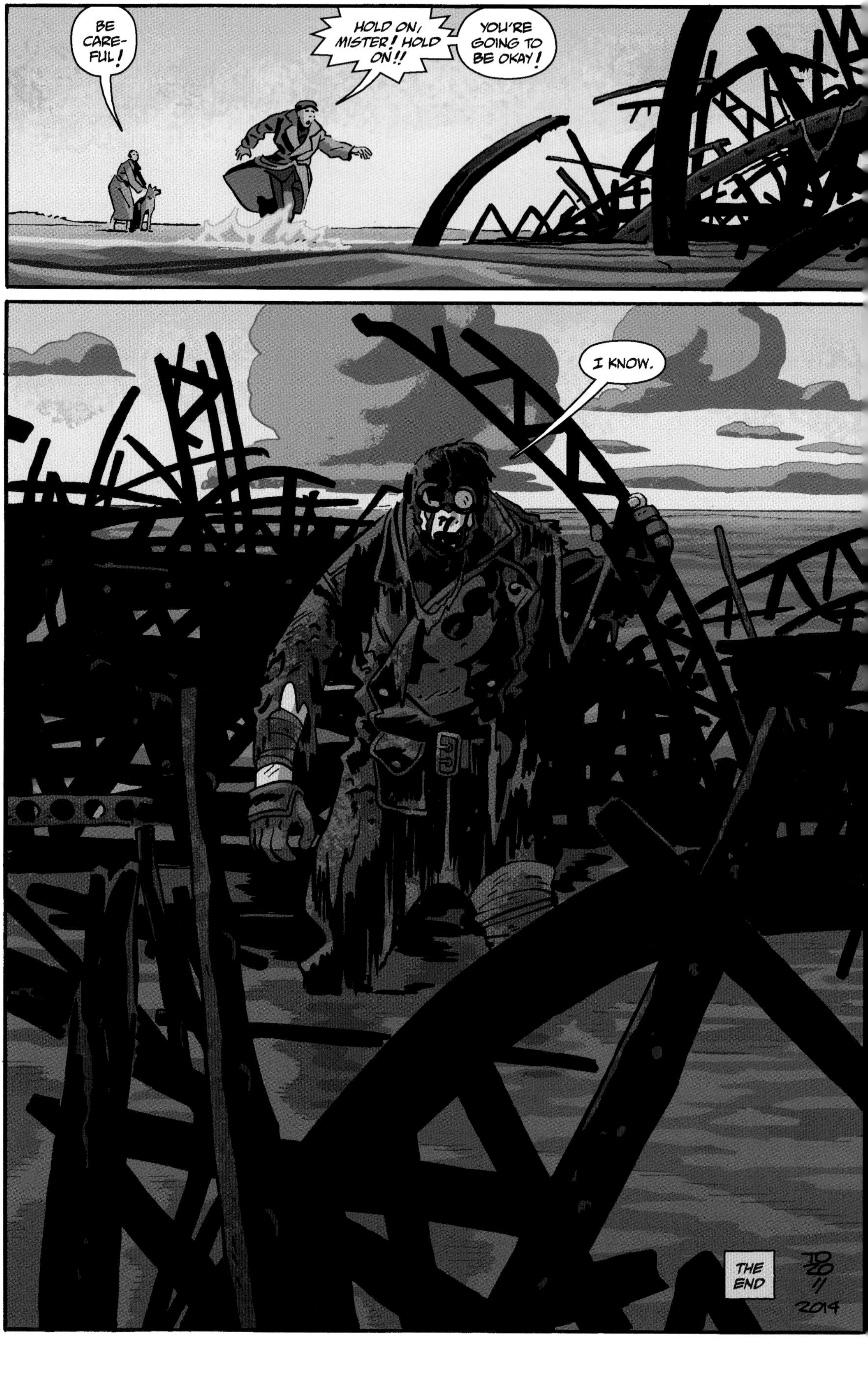
BE CAREFUL!
HOLD ON, MISTER! HOLD ON!!
YOU'RE GOING TO BE OKAY!
I KNOW.
THE END

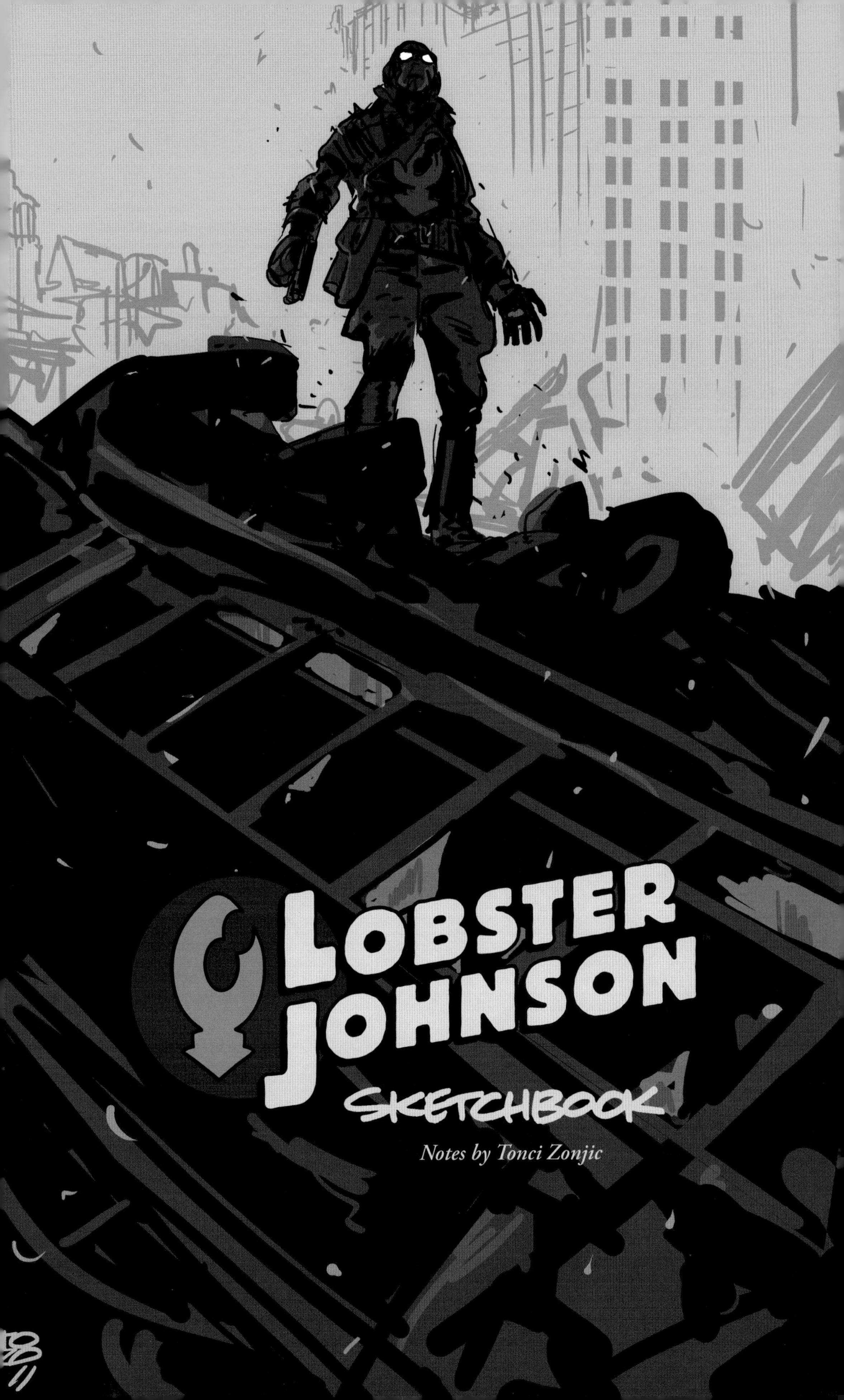
LOBSTER JOHNSON
SKETCHBOOK
Notes by Tonci Zonjic

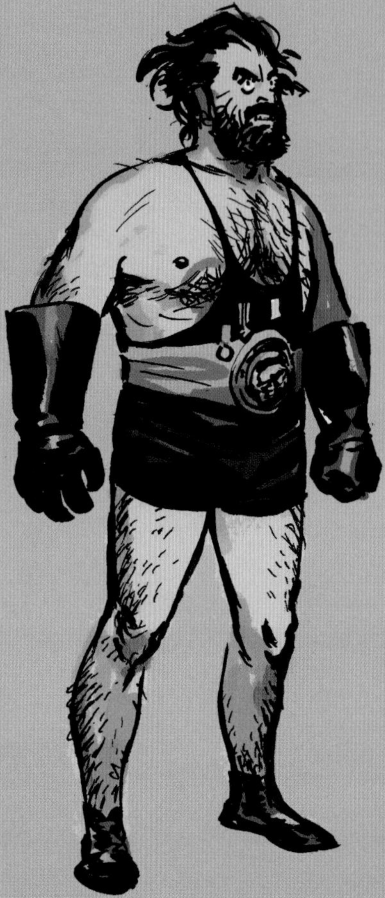

The Bear got much bigger in the comic. He's much more naturalistic in this early sketch. This often happens with characters—they get more cartoony as I go along, partially because I never remember to make model sheets ahead of time, or, if I do, I forget to ever look at them, and end up drawing characters from memory. That way, they get more exaggerated. That doesn't necessarily sound like a bad thing, right?

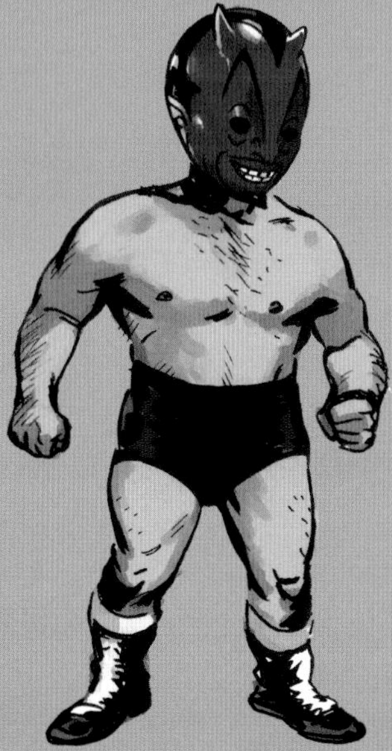

Devil Dwarf was first designed as a Mexican *luchador*, but I needed to show the eyes and the crazy teeth, so ultimately I went for a turn-of-the-century cheap paper mask design, although in a shiny version. The teeth are painted on, but underneath the mask, he has a set exactly like that one! (Try doing that in a movie . . .)

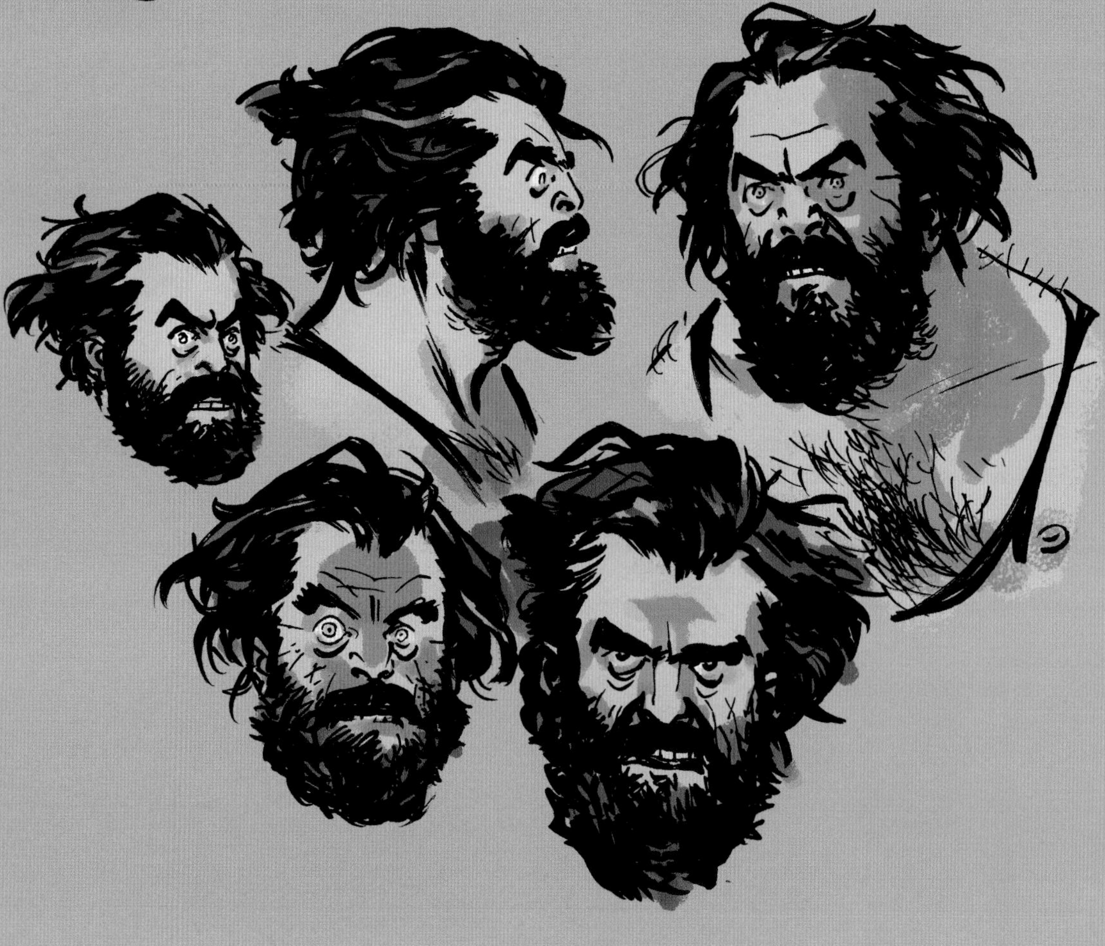

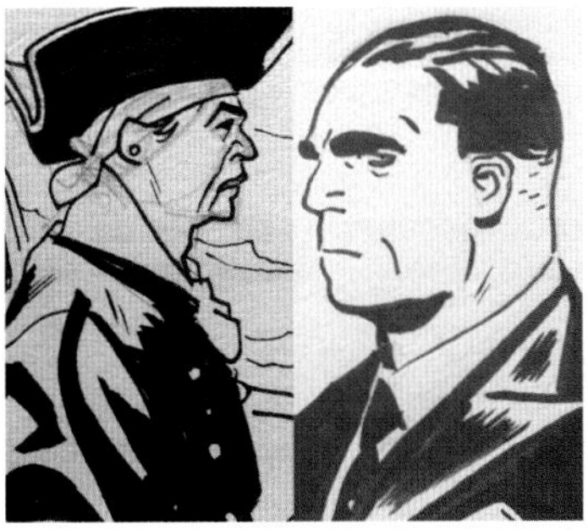

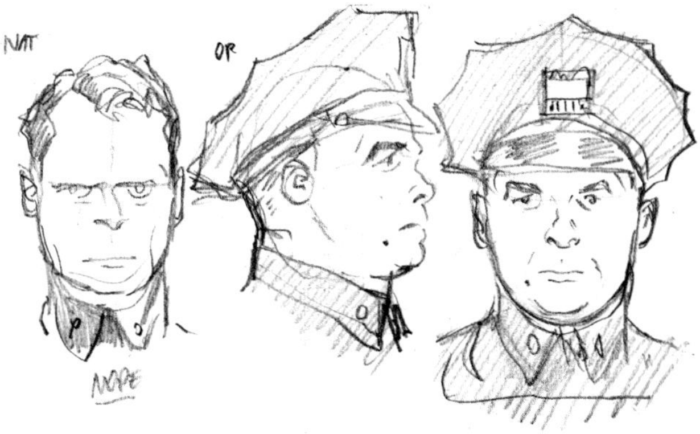
NAT
OR
NOPE

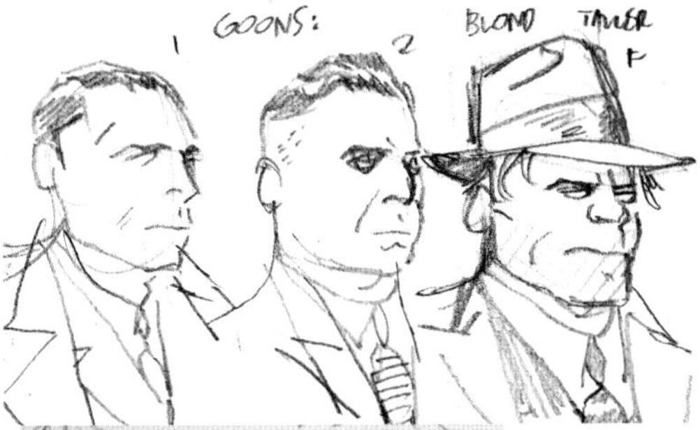
GOONS:
1
2
BLOND

I gave the cops and robbers as many different faces as I could, but purely to avoid confusion. Every single henchman *has* to be specific, so as not to be confused with any of the characters we've seen earlier. "Did we see this guy already . . . ?" That's why the first sketch, for Lt. Nat, has *nope* scrawled underneath. Not immediately identifiable as a new character within the story.

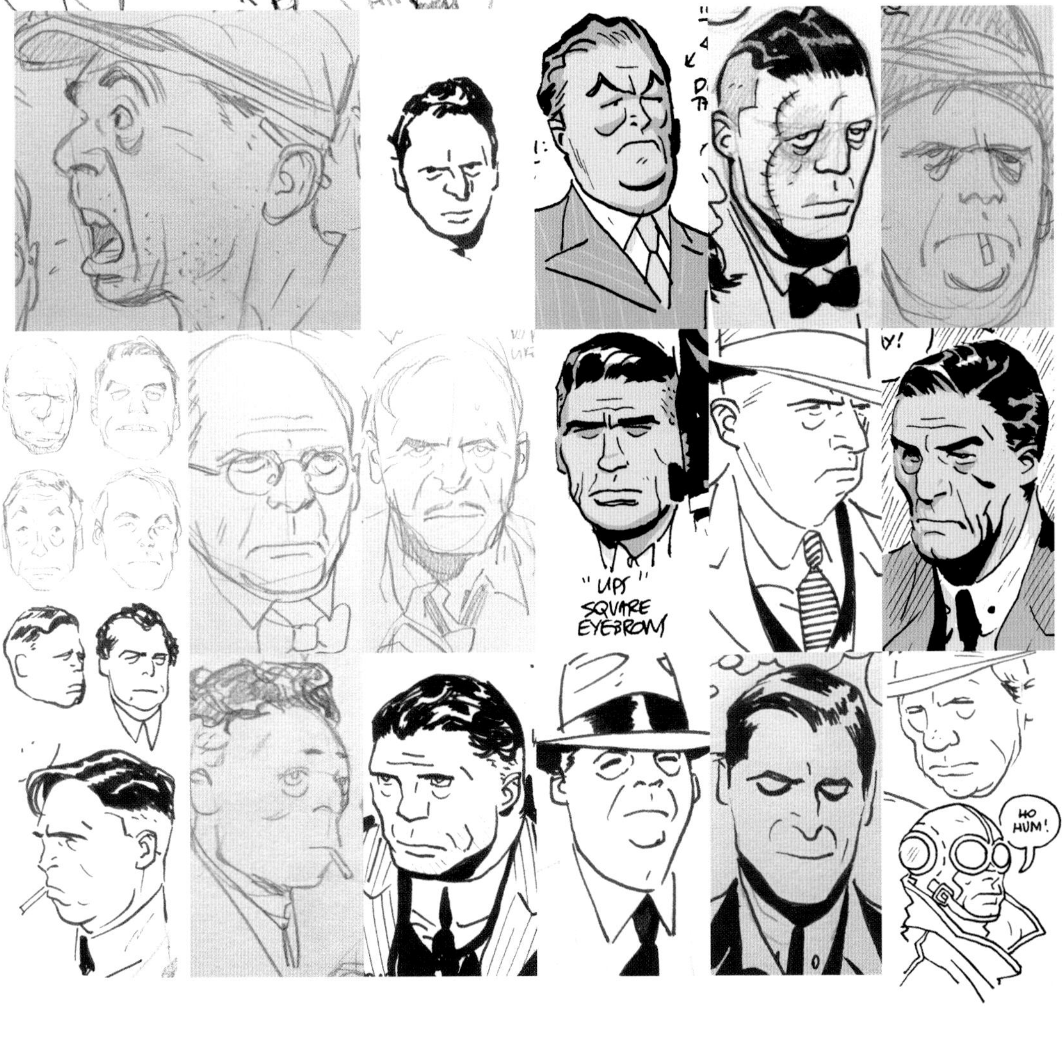
"UPS"
SQUARE
EYEBROW
HO HUM!

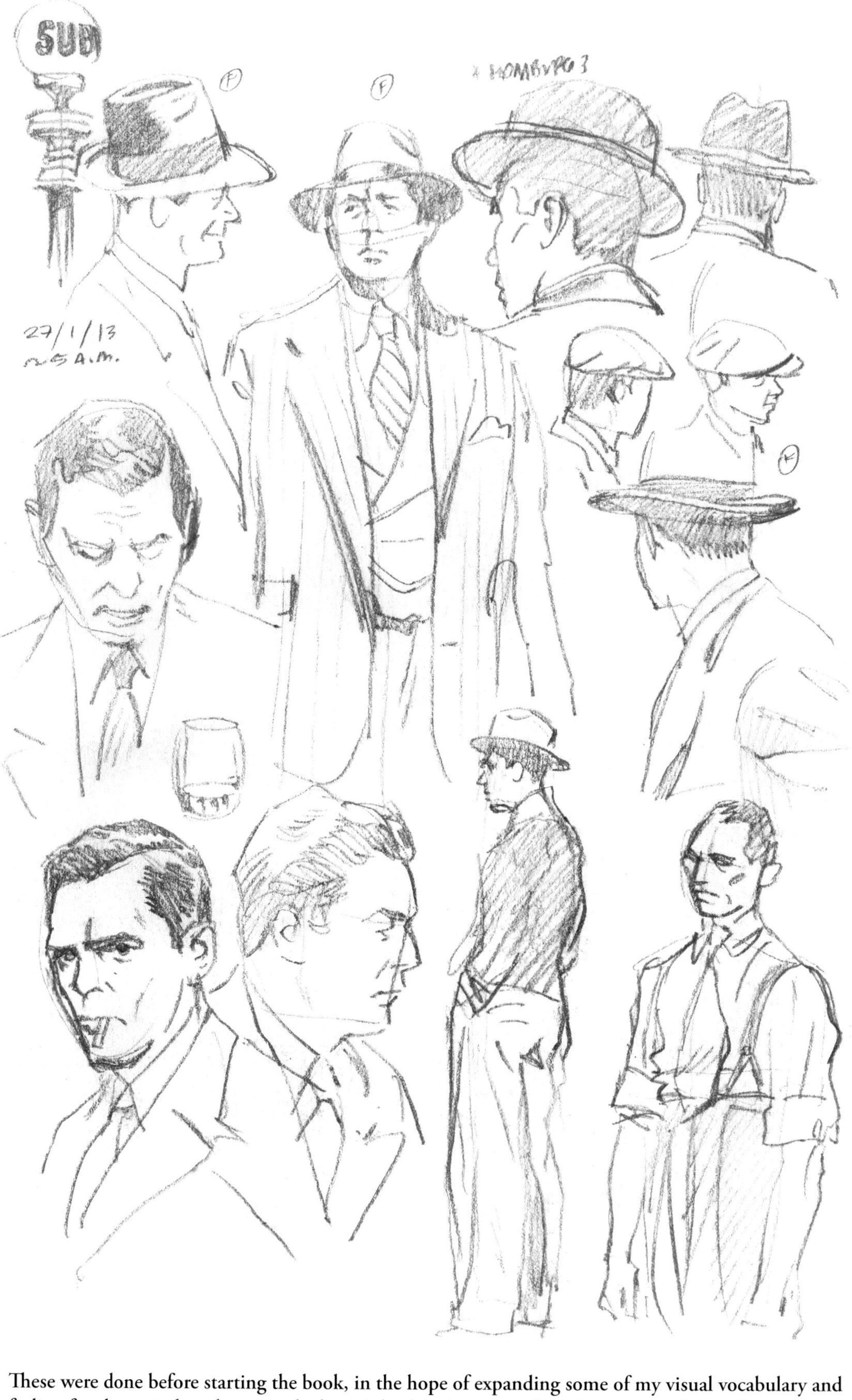
SUB
27/1/13

These were done before starting the book, in the hope of expanding some of my visual vocabulary and feeling for the period, and getting the hats right this time around. Doing them at five in the morning makes me wonder how much of it stuck.

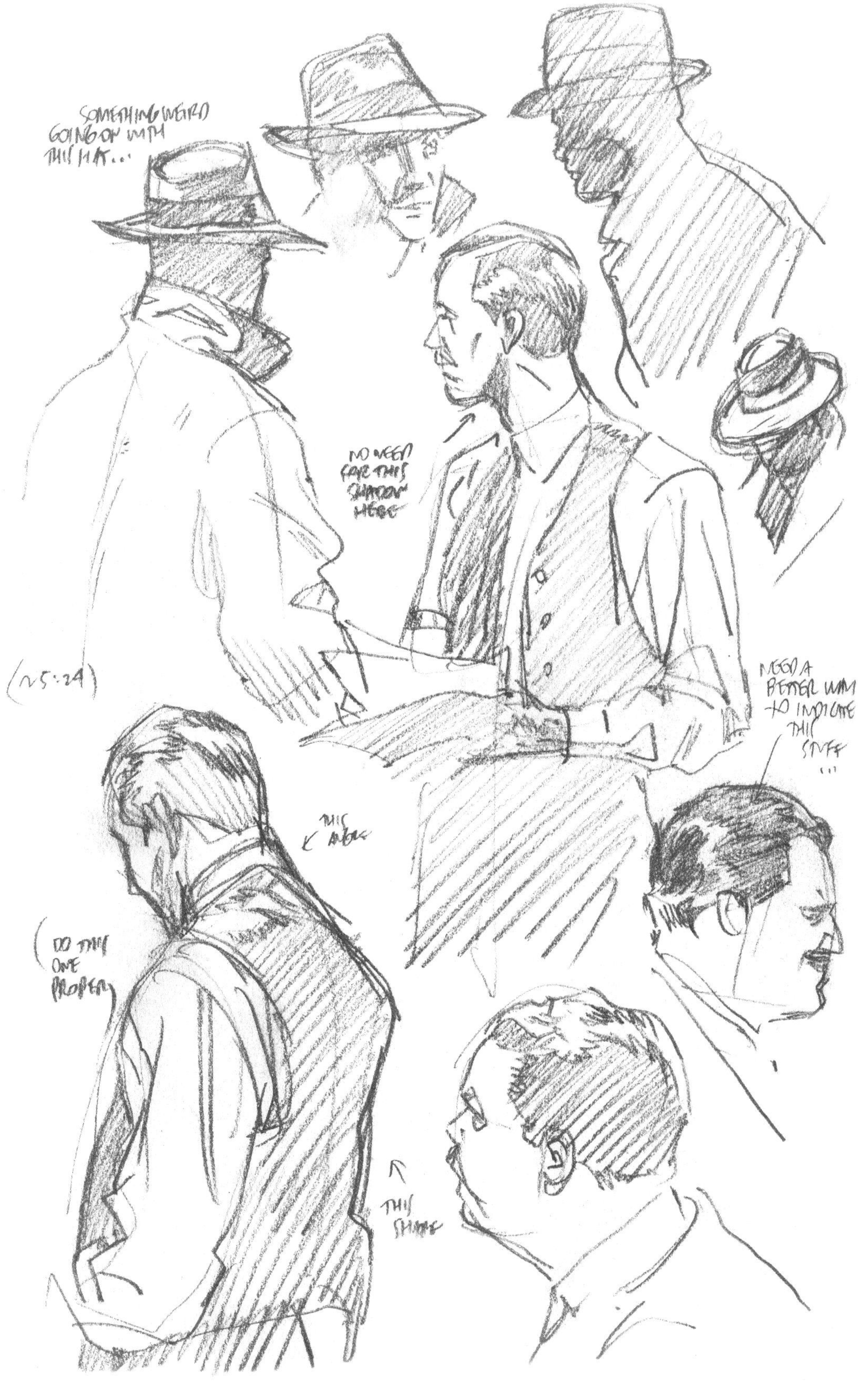
SOMETHING WEIRD GOING ON WITH THIS HAT...
NO NEED FOR THIS SHADOW HERE
(25:24)
NEED A BETTER WAY TO INDICATE THIS STUFF ...
THIS ANGLE
(DO THIS ONE PROPERLY
THIS SHAPE

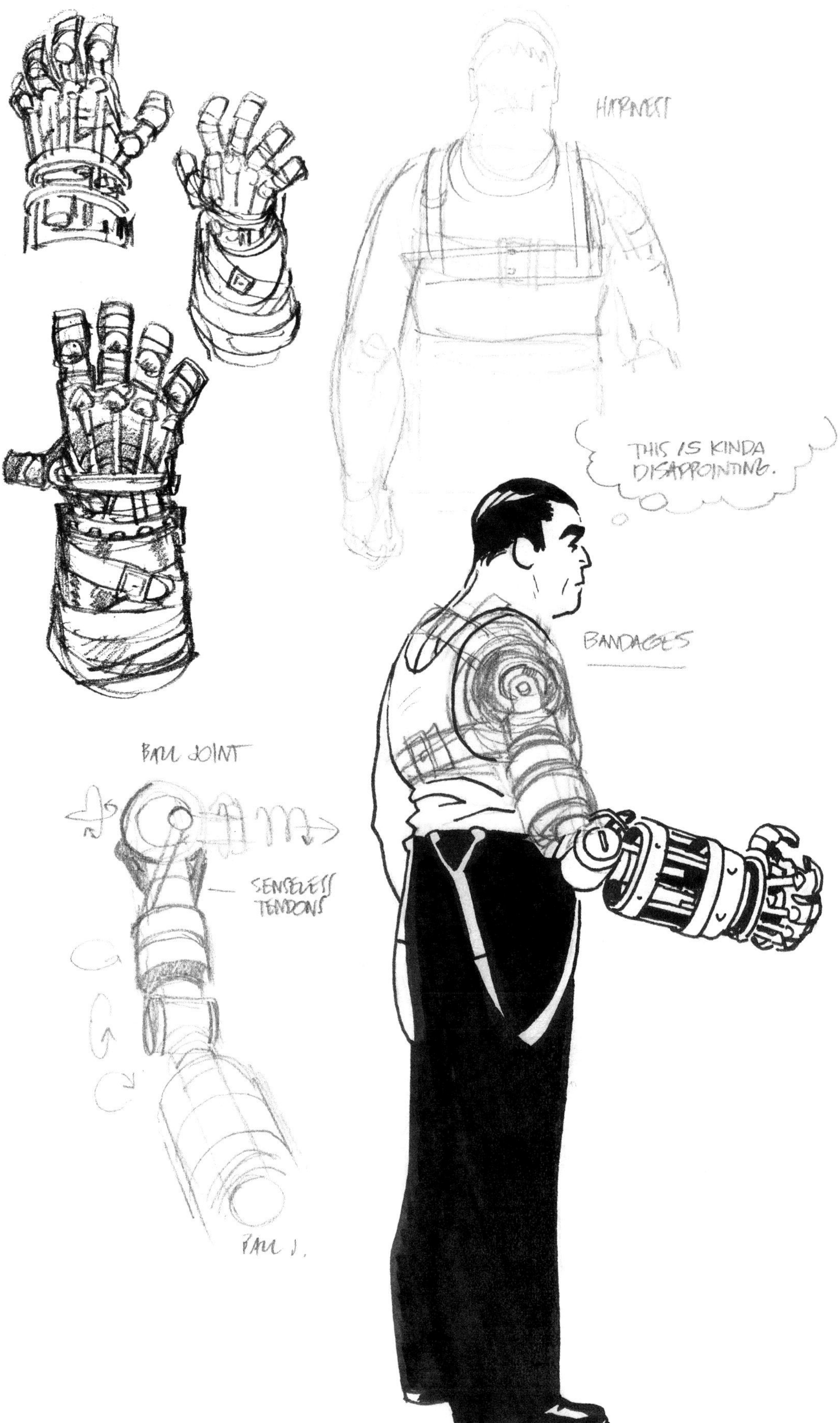
HARNESS
THIS IS KINDA DISAPPOINTING.
BANDAGES
BALL JOINT
SENSELESS TENDONS
BALL J.

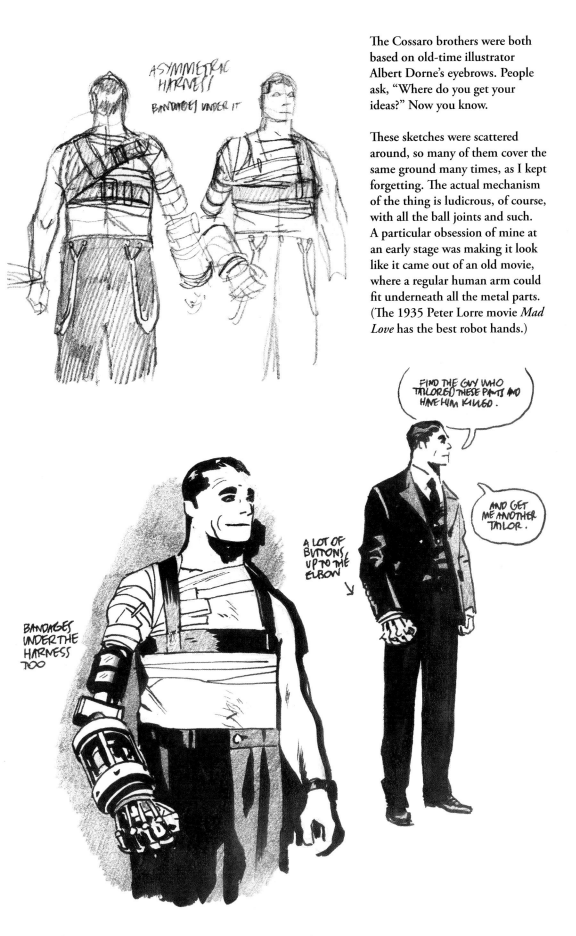

The Cossaro brothers were both based on old-time illustrator Albert Dorne's eyebrows. People ask, "Where do you get your ideas?" Now you know.

These sketches were scattered around, so many of them cover the same ground many times, as I kept forgetting. The actual mechanism of the thing is ludicrous, of course, with all the ball joints and such. A particular obsession of mine at an early stage was making it look like it came out of an old movie, where a regular human arm could fit underneath all the metal parts. (The 1935 Peter Lorre movie *Mad Love* has the best robot hands.)

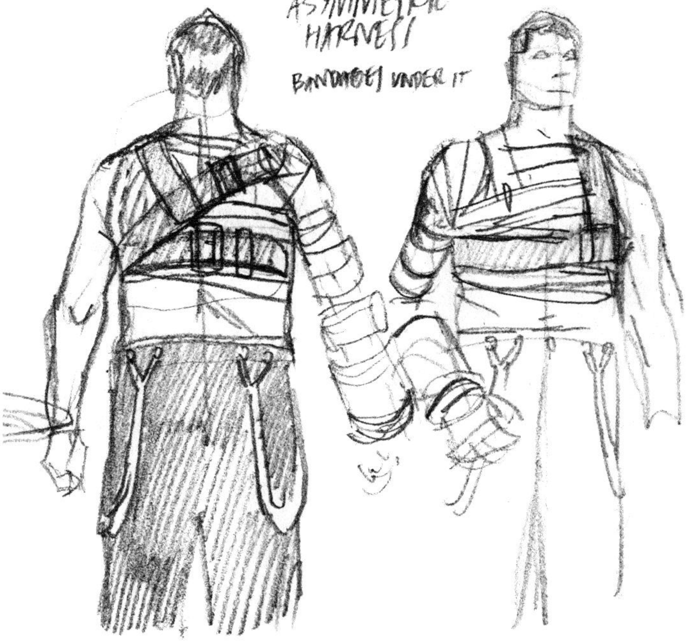

ASYMMETRIC HARNESS
BANDAGES UNDER IT

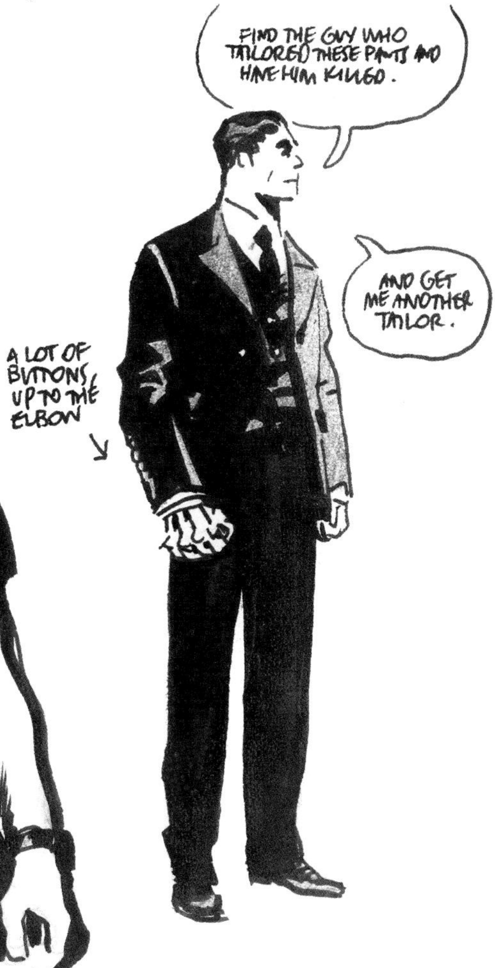

FIND THE GUY WHO TAILORED THESE PANTS AND HAVE HIM KILLED.
AND GET ME ANOTHER TAILOR.
A LOT OF BUTTONS, UP TO THE ELBOW

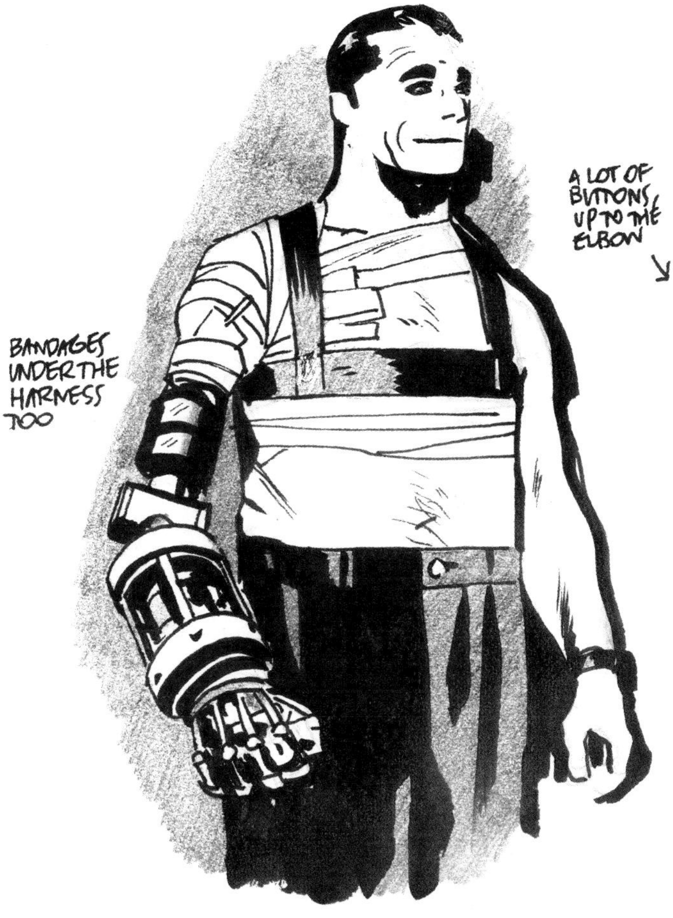

BANDAGES UNDER THE HARNESS TOO

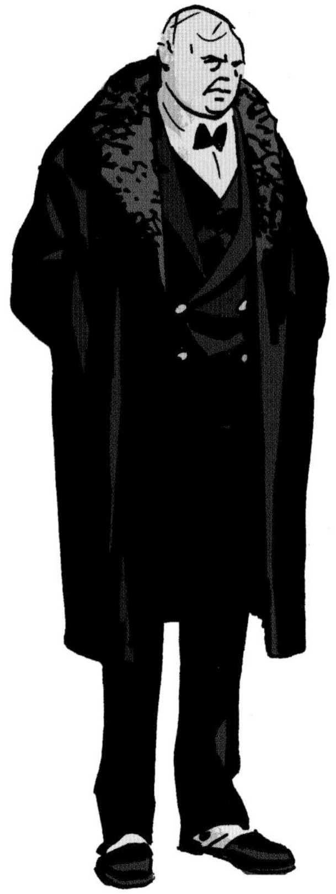

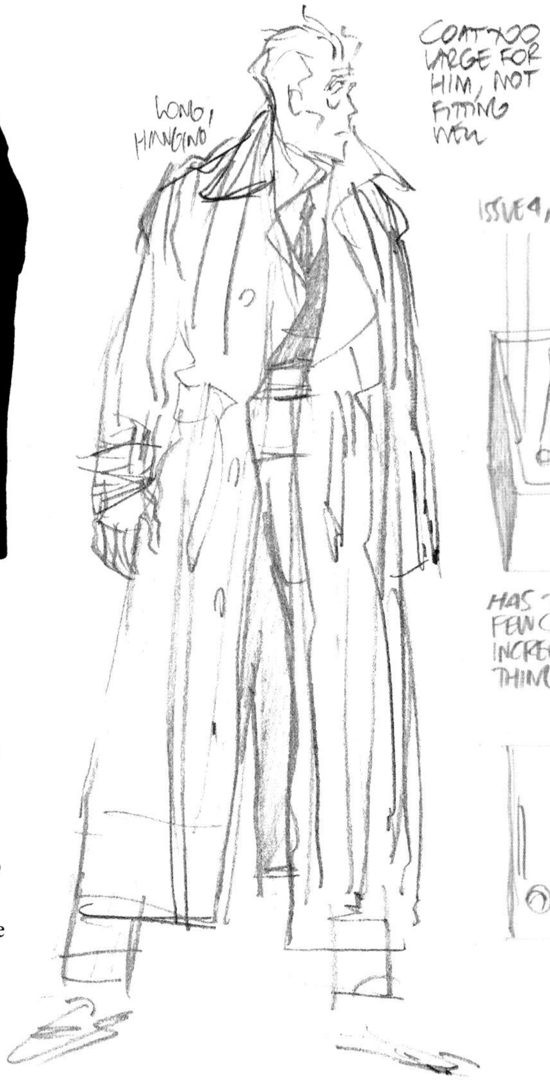
LONG, HANGING
COAT TOO LARGE FOR HIM, NOT FITTING WELL

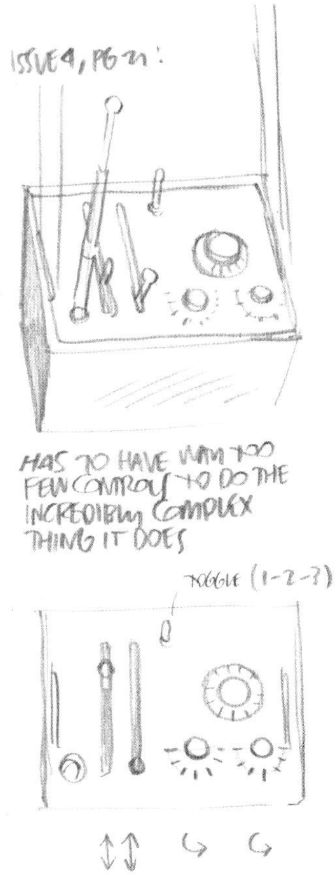
ISSUE 4, PG 21:
HAS TO HAVE WAY TOO FEW CONTROLS TO DO THE INCREDIBLY COMPLEX THING IT DOES
TOGGLE (1-2-3)

The colored Frank Cossaro sketch was the only one done before starting on the book. The rest were done around issue #4, when it was becoming too confusing to look at old pages to remind myself how the characters look.

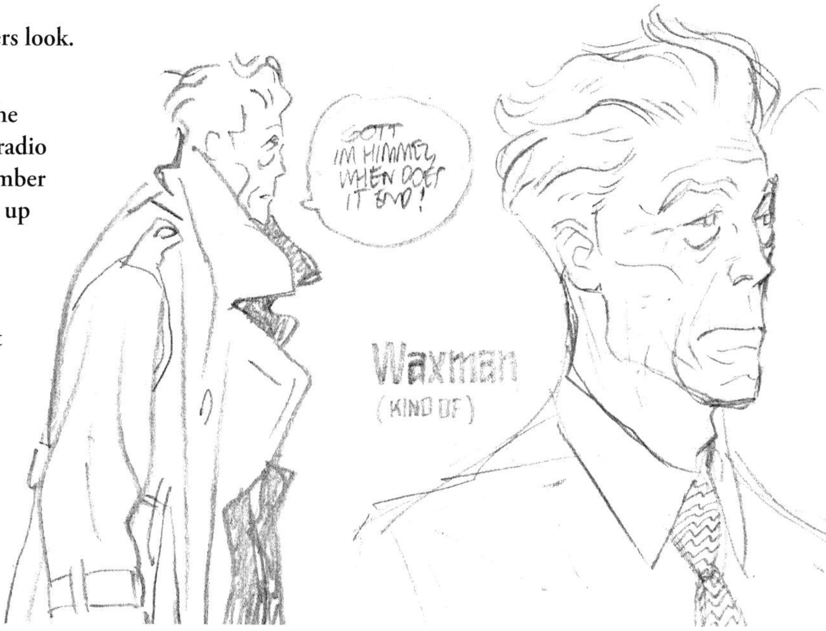
GOTT IM HIMMEL, WHEN DOES IT END!
Waxman
(KIND OF)

In the last issue, I had the challenge of hiding the radio remote control for a number of pages. Luckily, I'd set up Waxman as a kind of a scarecrow already, with ill-fitting clothes, so the too-large overcoat didn't seem too suspicious.

The remote control itself is another impossible device that you can only do in comics, and it makes me really happy.

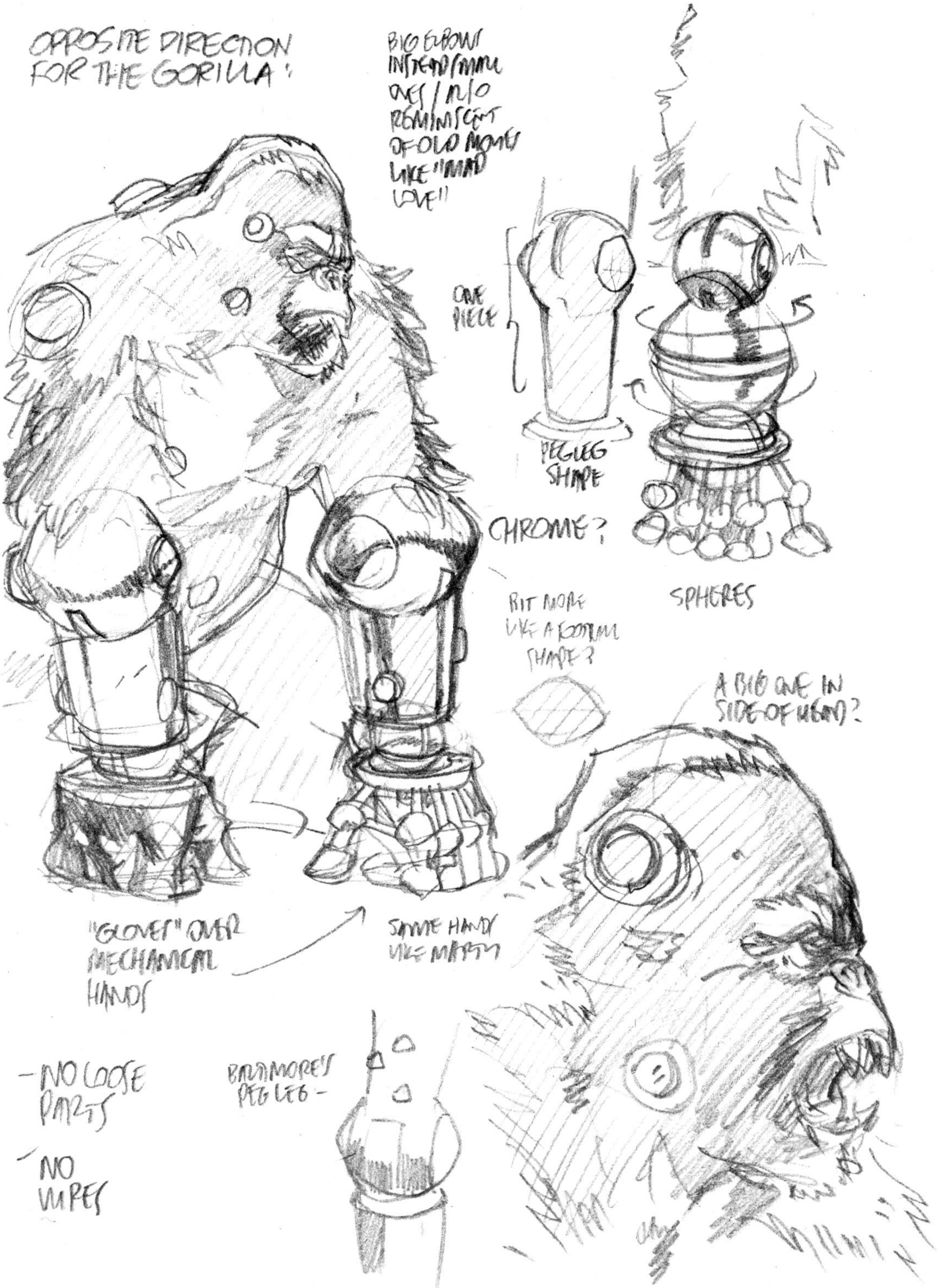
OPPOSITE DIRECTION FOR THE GORILLA:
BIG ELBOWS INSTEAD/SMALL ONES / ALSO REMINISCENT OF OLD MOVIES LIKE "MAD LOVE"
ONE PIECE
PEGLEG SHAPE
CHROME?
SPHERES
BIT MORE LIKE A FOOTBALL SHAPE?
A BIG ONE IN SIDE OF HEAD?
"GLOVES" OVER MECHANICAL HANDS
SAME HANDS LIKE MARTY
BALTIMORE'S PEG LEG -
- NO LOOSE PARTS
- NO WIRES

Sketch for Mukali, after about half a dozen variations that you won't ever see. This one combines elements of Marty Cossaro's mechanical arm, as well as Mike Mignola's designs for the Kriegaffe in *Conqueror Worm*.

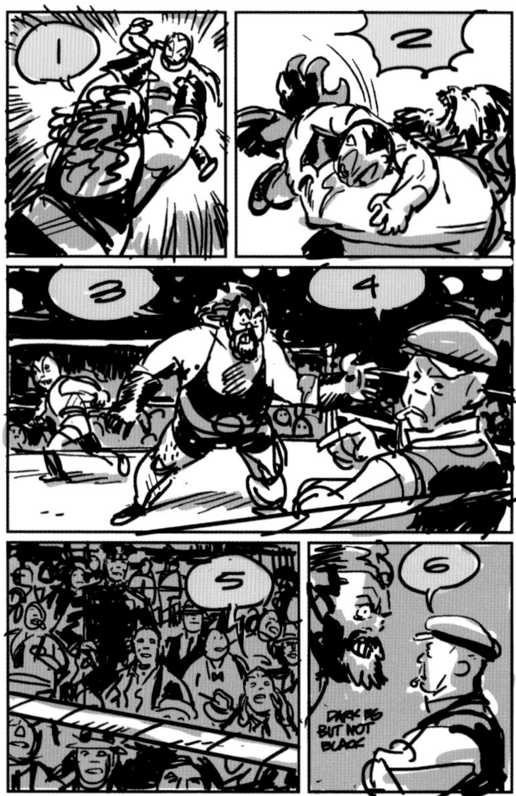

1
2
3
4
5
6
DARK BG BUT NOT BLACK

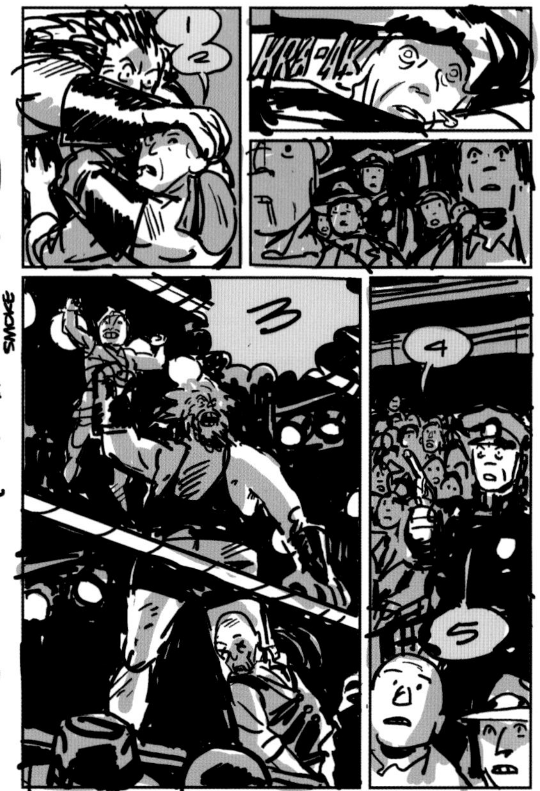

SMOKE
1
2
3
4
5

16

PERFECT PLACE FOR GUEST STARS... ↑

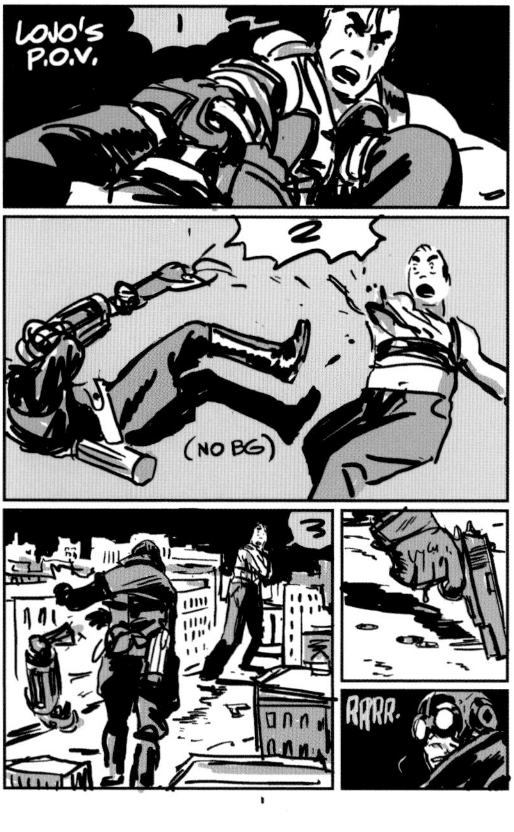

LOVO'S P.O.V.
1
2
(NO BG)
3
RRRR.

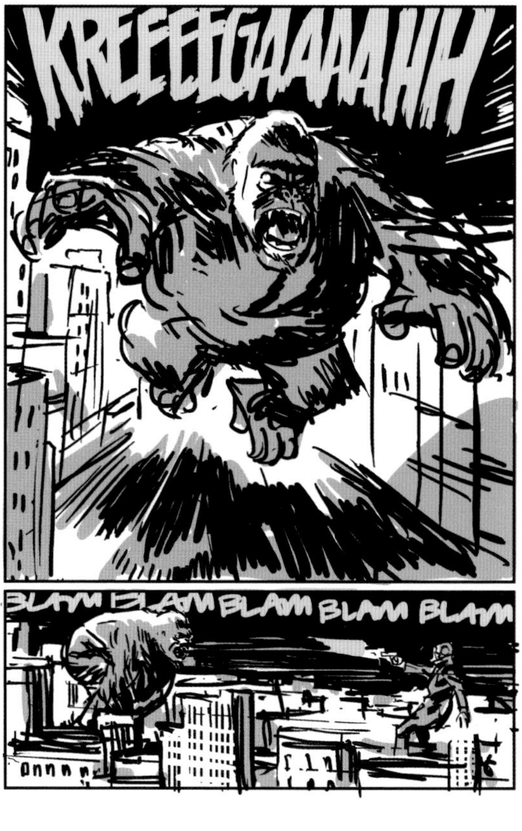

KREEEEGAAAAHH
BLAM BLAM BLAM BLAM BLAM

Opposite: On the *Caput Mortuum* one-shot (see volume 3) I tried doing very loose digital layouts. Here I used them from the get-go, and as always, things got out of hand. The discarded roughs sometimes found their way into other places, like the first drawing of Lobster in this volume, opposite the credits. It was originally a rough for page 18 of the third chapter, the splash page in the middle of the bank robbery.

This page: A rough of a pirate, from a Howard Pyle illustration, and a rough of a trapper uniform, from when I realized I had very little knowledge of North American frontiersman outfits. How did their pants work, exactly? These are the things that shorten the lifespans of comic book artists.

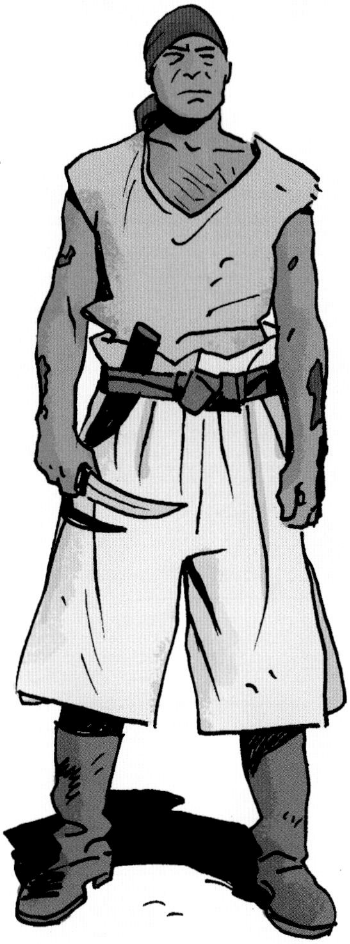

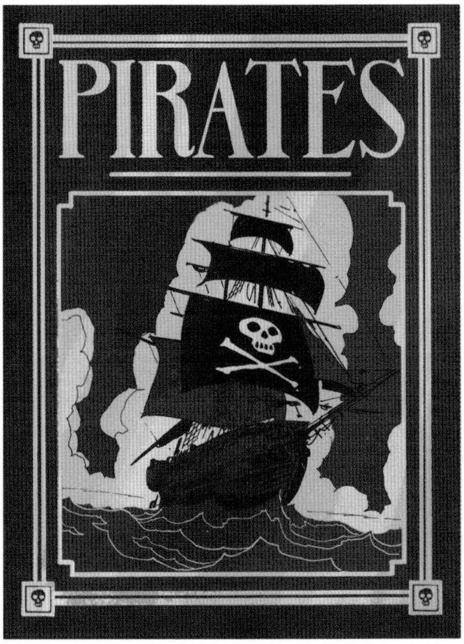
PIRATES

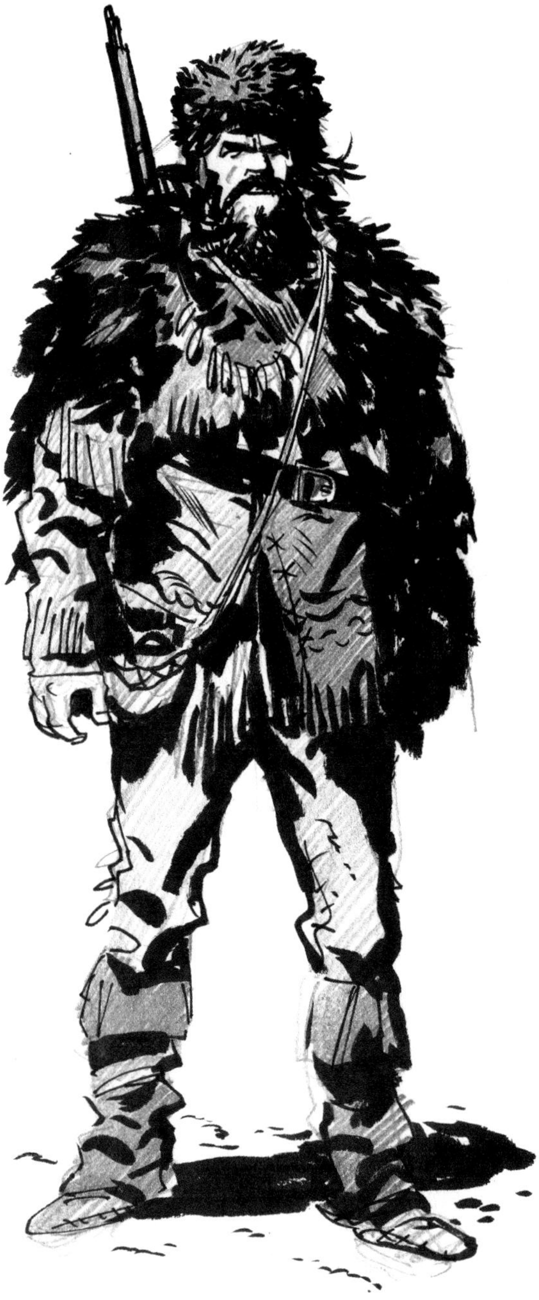

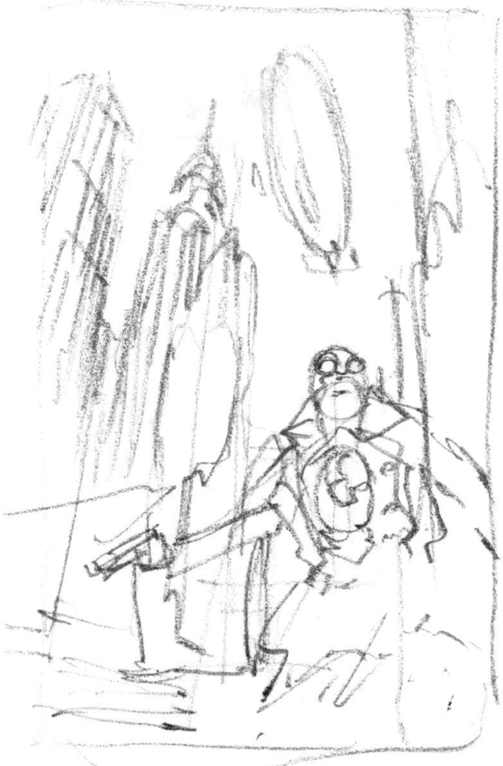
MANHOLE BLOWING UP ALONG AVENUE

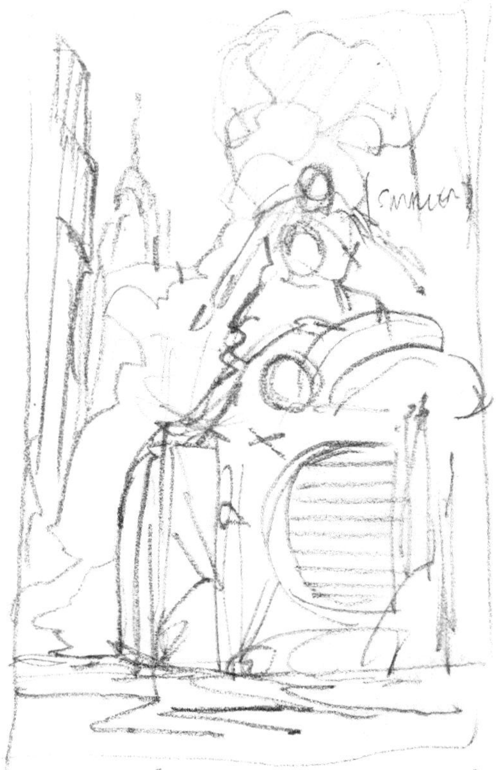
SMALLER
ON FLIPPED CAR
LOBSTER TOO BIG

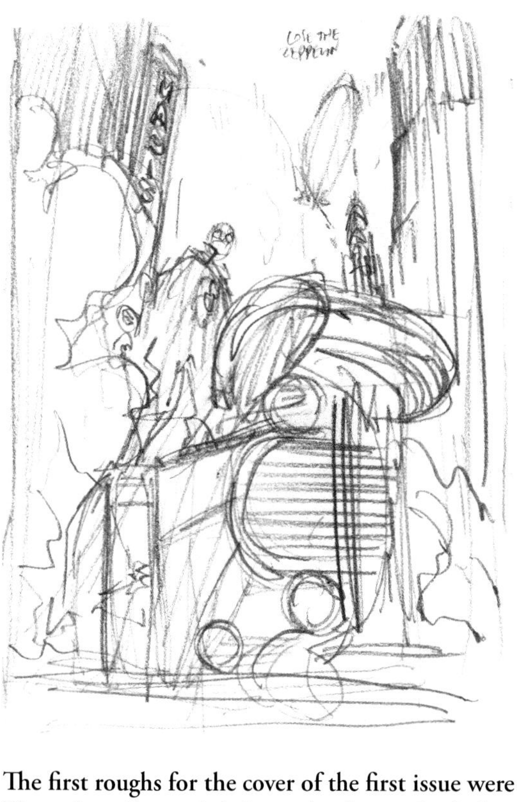
LOSE THE ZEPPELIN

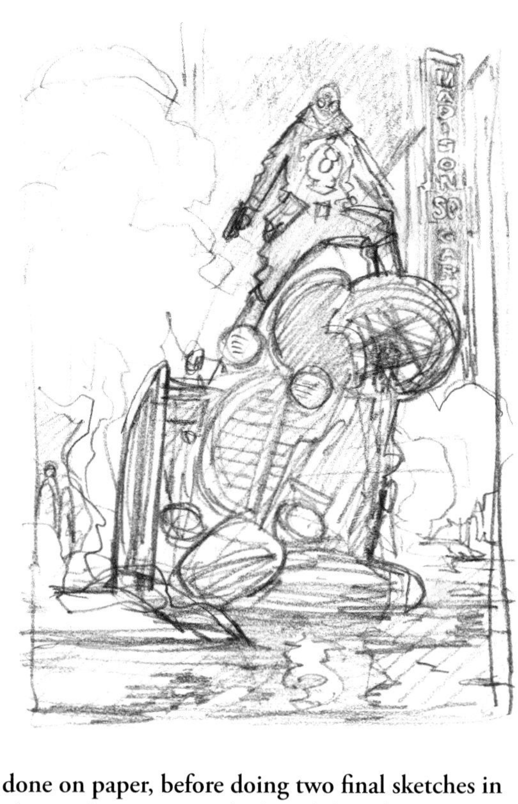

The first roughs for the cover of the first issue were done on paper, before doing two final sketches in Photoshop. For a while I was developing both, but ultimately one was picked, and the other one's on the opposite page in its rough stage. I couldn't get it to work properly back then, but I'd love to make a finished picture out of it someday. I also did the title treatment on these, which was fun.

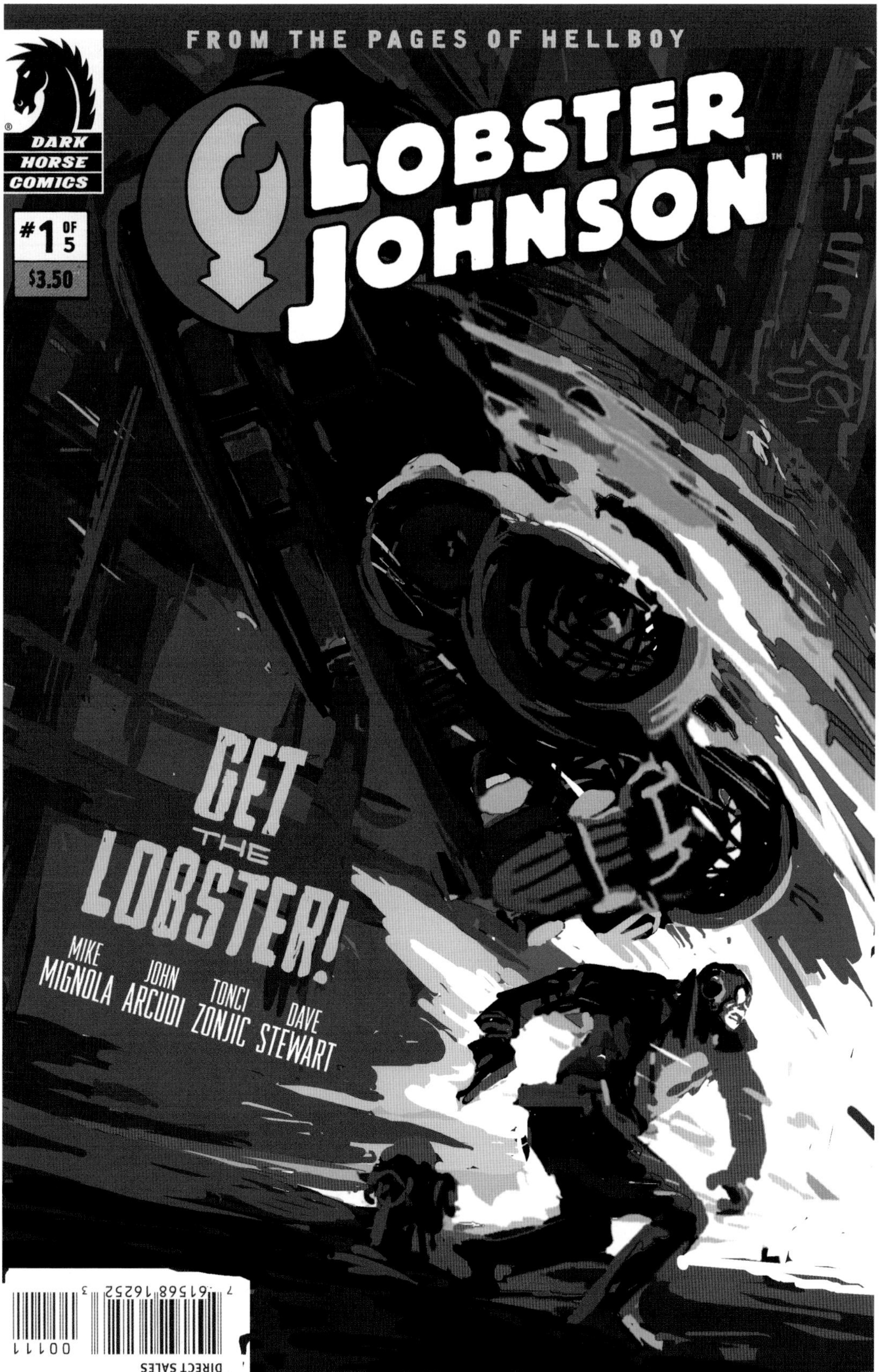

FROM THE PAGES OF HELLBOY
DARK HORSE COMICS
LOBSTER JOHNSON™
#1 OF 5
$3.50
GET THE LOBSTER!
MIKE MIGNOLA
JOHN ARCUDI
TONCI ZONJIC
DAVE STEWART
DIRECT SALES

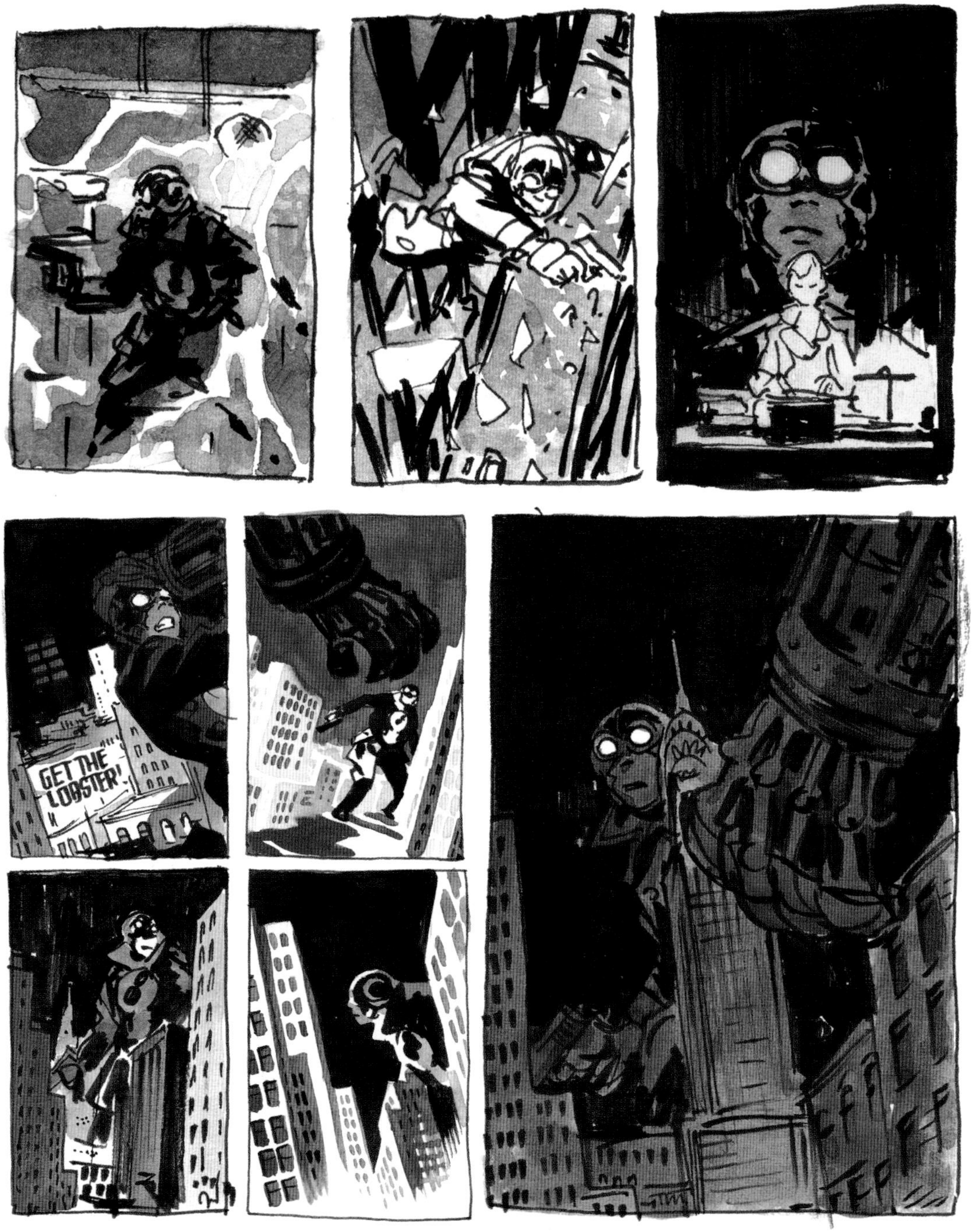
GET THE LOBSTER!

I really like to do cover thumbnails with watercolors. I'm not sure where that came from—most likely I just had a small box of half pans around once when I needed them, and they did the job well. They are perfect for exploring simple, strong color schemes without much detail. Waiting for the washes to dry gives you time to think as well.

Opposite: Unedited page from my sketchbook—trying to come up with the cover of issue #3. You can see me trying out variations and abandoning some midway through. I knew I wanted the vault in there somewhere, but all the compositions looked a lot like the cover of the first issue—Lobster standing against some bright shape. Ultimately I tried reversing it, and making Lobster the *brightest* part of the cover. The very next page of the sketchbook just has that one thumbnail. The final version was tricky and didn't work at all until the very last minute.

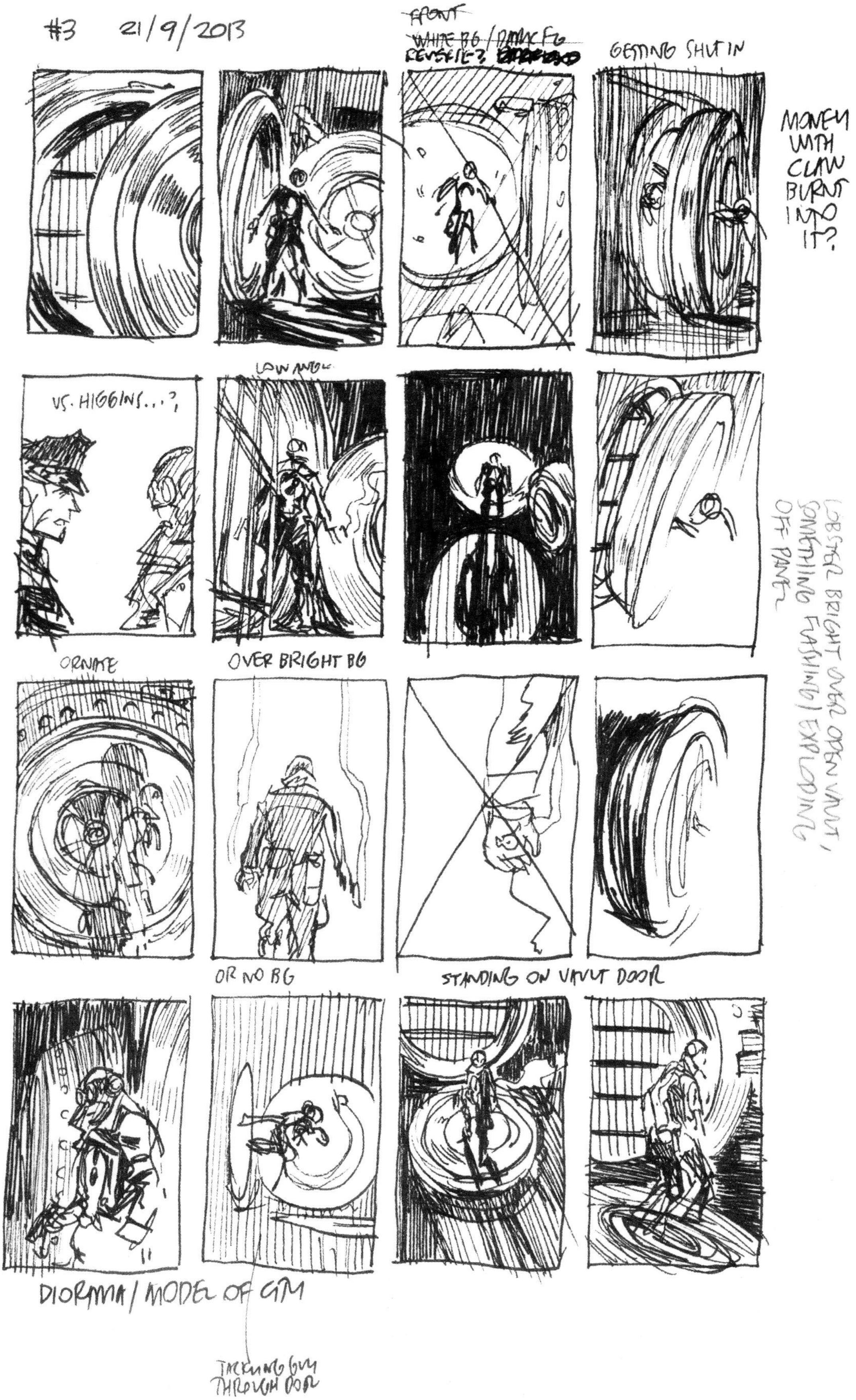

#3 21/9/2013
FRONT
WHITE BG / DARK FG
REVERSE?
GETTING SHUT IN
MONEY WITH CLAW BURNT INTO IT?
LOW ANGLE
VS. HIGGINS...?
LOBSTER BRIGHT OVER OPEN VAULT, SOMETHING FLASHING / EXPLODING OFF PANEL
ORNATE
OVER BRIGHT BG
OR NO BG
STANDING ON VAULT DOOR
DIORAMA / MODEL OF GYM
TACKLING GYM THROUGH DOOR

GET THE LOBSTER!

MIKE MIGNOLA JOHN ARCUDI TONCI ZONJIC DAVE STEWART

16/1/2014

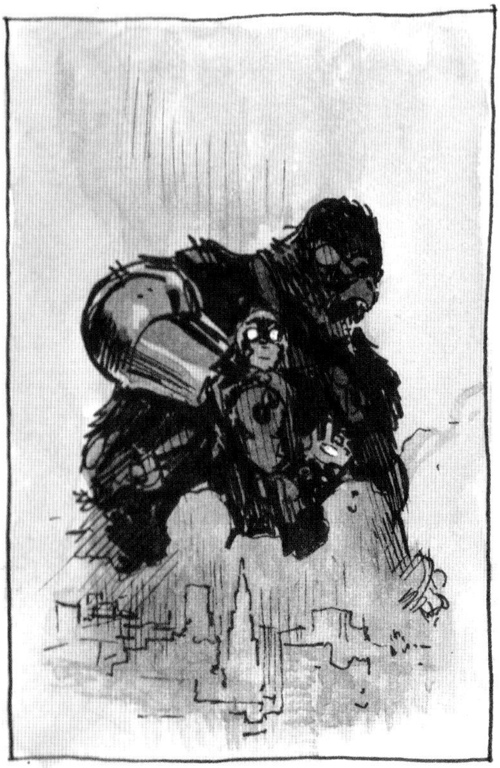

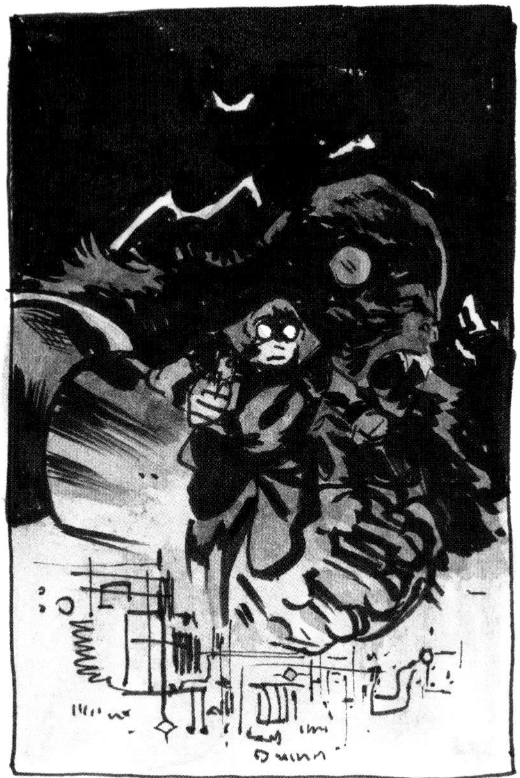

*LESS PANICKED LAJO HERE

(WITH SCHEMATICS FOR RADIO STUFF AT BOTTOM)

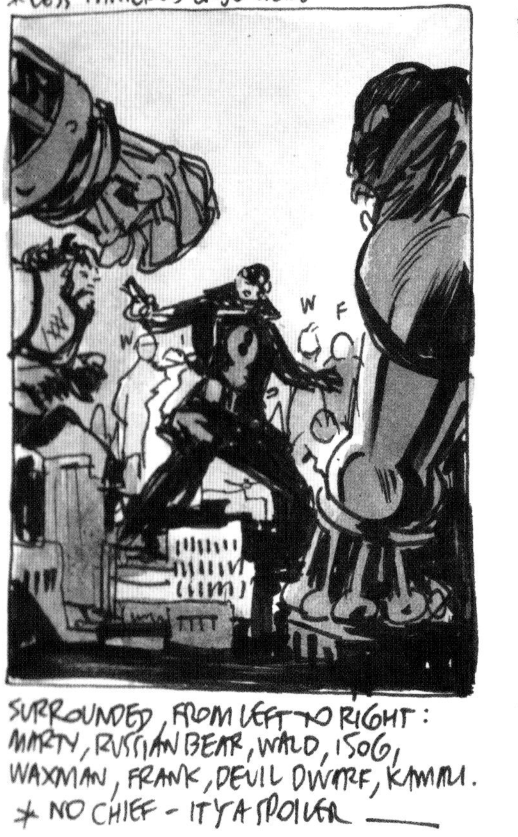

SURROUNDED, FROM LEFT TO RIGHT:
MARTY, RUSSIAN BEAR, WALD, ISOG,
WAXMAN, FRANK, DEVIL DWARF, KAMAL.
* NO CHIEF - IT'S A SPOILER

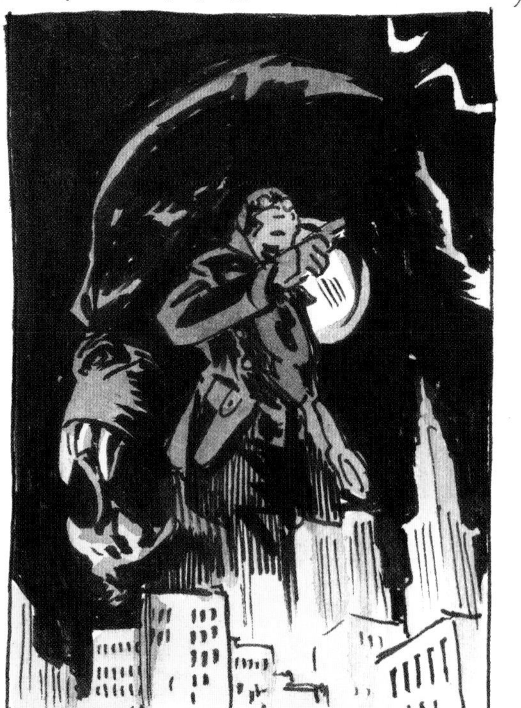

SOME PIRATES?

Sketches for the cover of this book—almost exactly the same size as in my sketchbook. Also done with watercolor. I liked the blue one a lot, but all of them were deemed too gorilla heavy. Ultimately, I went for the numbers, and tried to include as many things from the book as I could. And since I was trying to fill in Mike's very big shoes here, it was nerve racking.

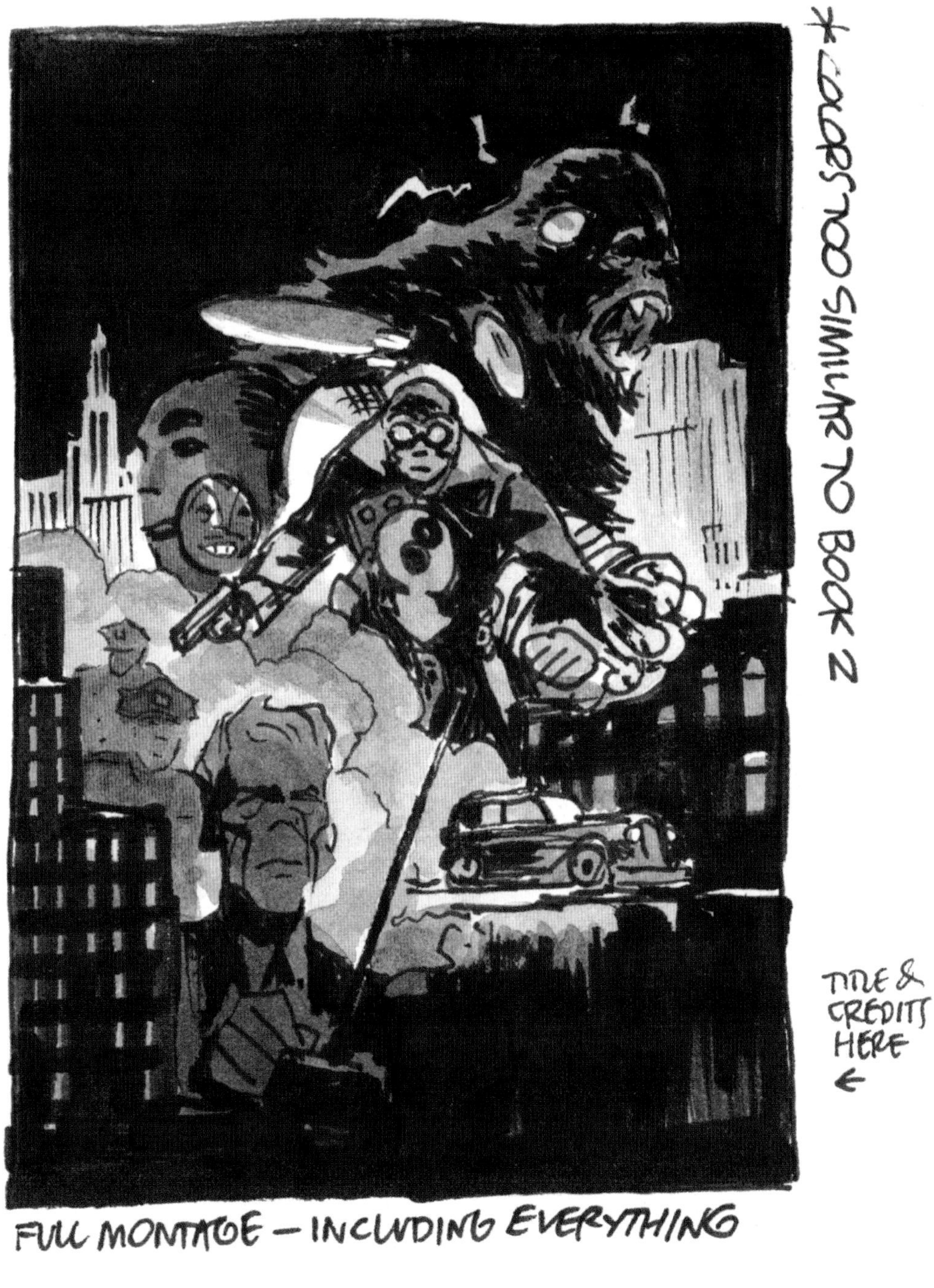
* COLORS TOO SIMILAR TO BOOK 2
TITLE & CREDITS HERE ←
FULL MONTAGE – INCLUDING EVERYTHING

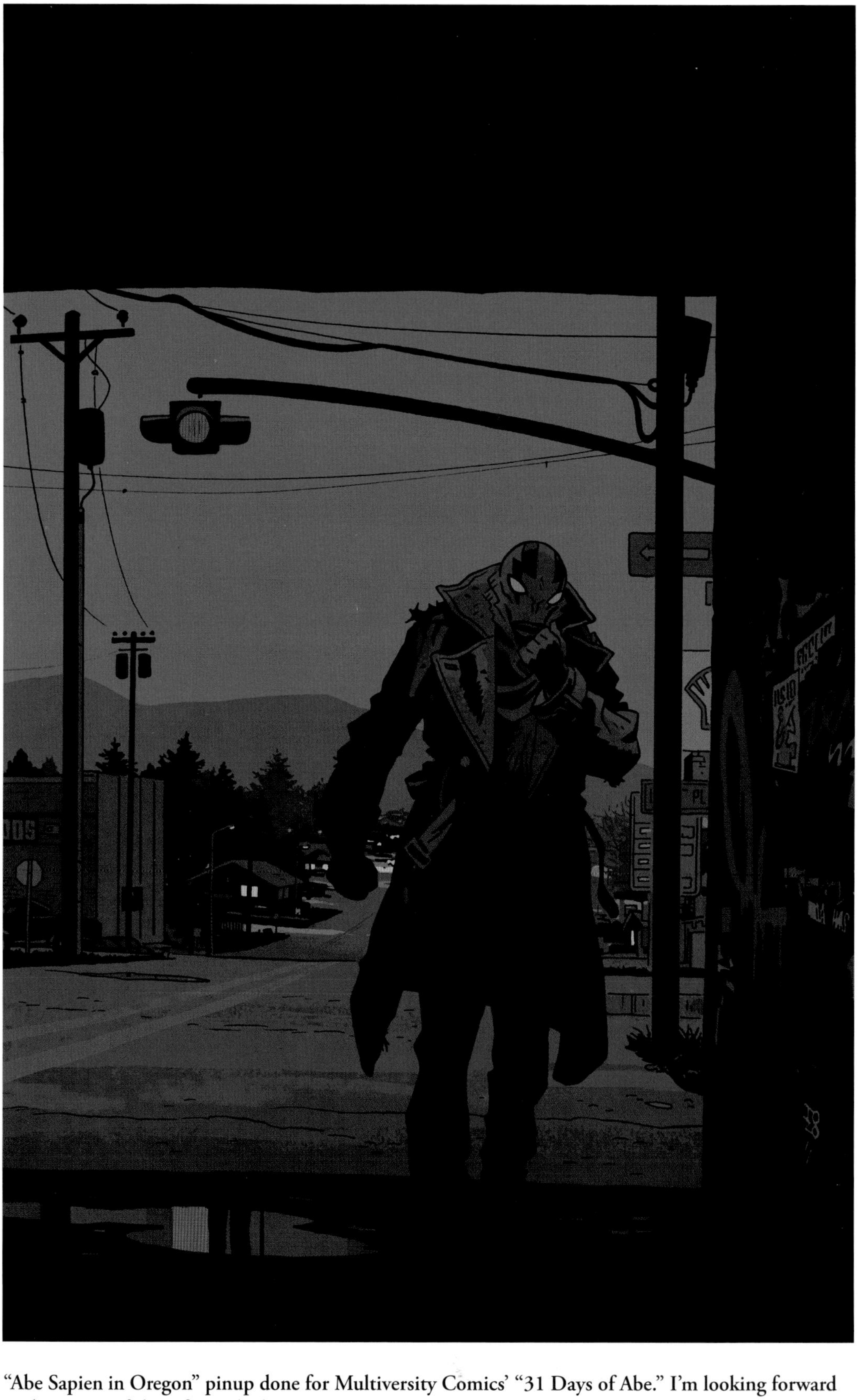

"Abe Sapien in Oregon" pinup done for Multiversity Comics' "31 Days of Abe." I'm looking forward to doing one of these for each character.

Also by MIKE MIGNOLA

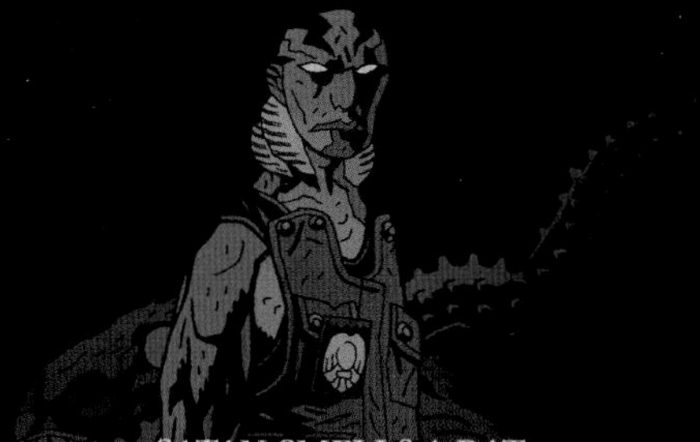

B.P.R.D.

PLAGUE OF FROGS
Volume 1
with Chris Golden, Guy Davis, and others
ISBN 978-1-59582-609-1 | $34.99
Volume 2
with John Arcudi, Davis, and others
ISBN 978-1-59582-672-5 | $34.99
Volume 3
with Arcudi, and Davis
ISBN 978-1-59582-860-6 | $34.99
Volume 4
with Arcudi and Davis
ISBN 978-1-59582-974-0 | $34.99

1946
with Joshua Dysart and Paul Azaceta
ISBN 978-1-59582-191-1 | $17.99

1947
with Dysart, Fábio Moon, and Gabriel Bá
ISBN 978-1-59582-478-3 | $17.99

1948
with Arcudi and Max Fiumara
ISBN 978-1-61655-183-4 | $17.99

BEING HUMAN
with Arcudi, Davis, and others
ISBN 978-1-59582-756-2 | $17.99

VAMPIRE
with Moon and Bá
ISBN 978-1-61655-196-4 | $19.99

B.P.R.D. HELL ON EARTH

NEW WORLD
with Arcudi and Davis
ISBN 978-1-59582-707-4 | $19.99

GODS AND MONSTERS
with Arcudi, Davis, and Crook
ISBN 978-1-59582-822-4 | $19.99

RUSSIA
with Arcudi, Crook, and Duncan Fegredo
ISBN 978-1-59582-946-7 | $19.9

THE DEVIL'S ENGINE AND THE LONG DEATH
with Arcudi, Crook, and James Harren
ISBN 978-1-59582-981-8 | $19.99

THE PICKENS COUNTY HORROR AND OTHERS
with Scott Allie, Jason Latour, Harren, Max Fiumara, and Becky Cloonan
ISBN 978-1-61655-140-7 | $19.99

THE RETURN OF THE MASTER
with Arcudi and Crook
ISBN 978-1-61655-193-3 | $19.99

A COLD DAY IN HELL
with Arcudi, Peter Snejbjerg, and Laurence Campbell
ISBN 978-1-61655-199-5 | $19.99

THE REIGN OF THE BLACK FLAME
with Arcudi and Harren
ISBN 978-1-61655-471-2 | $19.99

ABE SAPIEN

THE DROWNING
with Jason Shawn Alexander
ISBN 978-1-59582-185-0 | $17.99

THE DEVIL DOES NOT JEST AND OTHER STORIES
with Arcudi, Harren, and others
ISBN 978-1-59582-925-2 | $17.99

DARK AND TERRIBLE AND THE NEW RACE OF MAN
with Allie, Arcudi, Sebastián Fiumara, and Max Fiumara
ISBN 978-1-61655-284-8 | $19.99

LOBSTER JOHNSON

THE IRON PROMETHEUS
with Jason Armstrong
ISBN 978-1-59307-975-8 | $17.99

THE BURNING HAND
with Arcudi and Tonci Zonjic
ISBN 978-1-61655-031-8 | $17.99

SATAN SMELLS A RAT
with Arcudi, Fiumara, Joe Querio, Wilfredo Torres, and Kevin Nowlan
ISBN 978-1-61655-203-9 | $18.99

WITCHFINDER

IN THE SERVICE OF ANGELS
with Ben Stenbeck
ISBN 978-1-59582-483-7 | $17.99

LOST AND GONE FOREVER
with Arcudi and John Severin
ISBN 978-1-59582-794-4 | $17.99

THE AMAZING SCREW-ON HEAD AND OTHER CURIOUS OBJECTS

ISBN 978-1-59582-501-8 | $17.99

BALTIMORE

THE PLAGUE SHIPS
with Golden and Stenbeck
ISBN 978-1-59582-677-0 | $24.99

THE CURSE BELLS
with Golden and Stenbeck
ISBN 978-1-59582-674-9 | $24.99

A PASSING STRANGER AND OTHER STORIES
with Golden and Stenbeck
ISBN 978-1-61655-182-7 | $24.99

CHAPEL OF BONES
with Golden and Stenbeck
ISBN 978-1-61655-328-9 | $24.99

NOVELS

LOBSTER JOHNSON: THE SATAN FACTORY
with Thomas E. Sniegoski
ISBN 978-1-59582-203-1 | $12.95

JOE GOLEM AND THE DROWNING CITY
with Golden
ISBN 978-1-59582-971-9 | $99.99

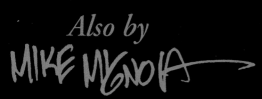

HELLBOY

by MIKE MIGNOLA

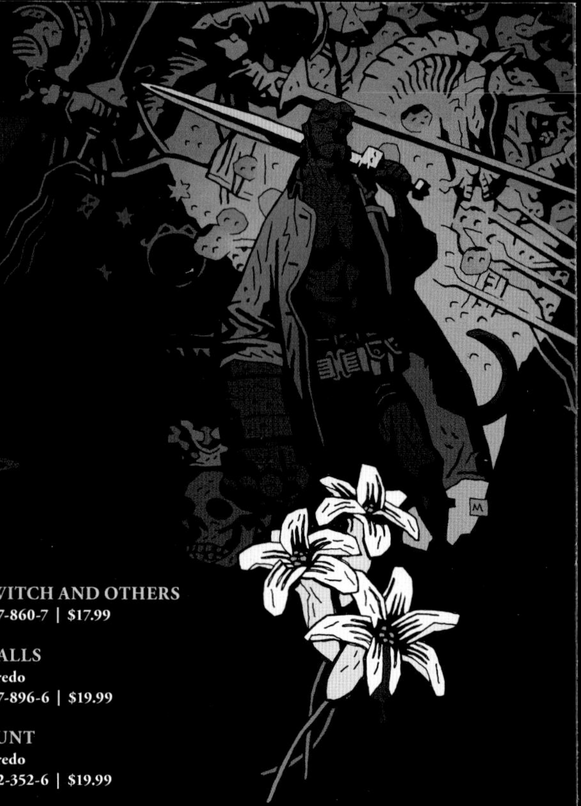

HELLBOY LIBRARY EDITION VOLUME 1:
Seed of Destruction and Wake the Devil
ISBN 978-1-59307-910-9 | $49.99

HELLBOY LIBRARY EDITION VOLUME 2:
The Chained Coffin and The Right Hand of Doom
ISBN 978-1-59307-989-5 | $49.99

HELLBOY LIBRARY EDITION VOLUME 3:
Conqueror Worm and Strange Places
ISBN 978-1-59582-352-6 | $49.99

HELLBOY LIBRARY EDITION VOLUME 4:
The Crooked Man and The Troll Witch
with Richard Corben and others
ISBN 978-1-59582-658-9 | $49.99

HELLBOY LIBRARY EDITION VOLUME 5:
Darkness Calls and the Wild Hunt
with Duncan Fegredo
ISBN 978-1-59582-886-6 | $49.99

HELLBOY LIBRARY EDITION VOLUME 6:
The Storm and the Fury and The Bride of Hell
with Duncan Fegredo, Richard Corben, Kevin Nowlan, and Scott Hampton
ISBN 978-1-61655-133-9 | $49.99

SEED OF DESTRUCTION
with John Byrne
ISBN 978-1-59307-094-6 | $17.99

WAKE THE DEVIL
ISBN 978-1-59307-095-3 | $17.99

THE CHAINED COFFIN AND OTHERS
ISBN 978-1-59307-091-5 | $17.99

THE RIGHT HAND OF DOOM
ISBN 978-1-59307-093-9 | $17.99

CONQUEROR WORM
ISBN 978-1-59307-092-2 | $17.99

STRANGE PLACES
ISBN 978-1-59307-475-3 | $17.99

THE TROLL WITCH AND OTHERS
ISBN 978-1-59307-860-7 | $17.99

DARKNESS CALLS
with Duncan Fegredo
ISBN 978-1-59307-896-6 | $19.99

THE WILD HUNT
with Duncan Fegredo
ISBN 978-1-59582-352-6 | $19.99

THE CROOKED MAN AND OTHERS
with Richard Corben
ISBN 978-1-59582-477-6 | $17.99

THE BRIDE OF HELL AND OTHERS
with Richard Corben, Kevin Nowlan, and Scott Hampton
ISBN 978-1-59582-740-1 | $19.99

HELLBOY IN HELL VOLUME 1: THE DESCENT
ISBN 978-1-61655-444-6 | $17.99

THE STORM AND THE FURY
with Duncan Fegredo
ISBN 978-1-59582-827-9 | $19.99

HOUSE OF THE LIVING DEAD
with Richard Corben
ISBN 978-1-59582-757-9 | $14.99

THE MIDNIGHT CIRCUS
with Duncan Fegredo
ISBN 978-1-61655-238-1 | $14.99

HELLBOY: THE FIRST 20 YEARS
ISBN 978-1-61655-353-1 | $19.99

THE ART OF HELLBOY
ISBN 978-1-59307-089-2 | $29.99

HELLBOY II: THE ART OF THE MOVIE
ISBN 978-1-59307-964-2 | $24.99

HELLBOY: THE COMPANION
ISBN 978-1-59307-655-9 | $14.99

HELLBOY: WEIRD TALES
VOLUME 1
ISBN 978-1-56971-622-9 | $17.99
VOLUME 2
ISBN 978-1-56971-953-4 | $17.99

HELLBOY: MASKS AND MONSTERS
with James Robinson and Scott Benefiel
ISBN 978-1-59582-567-4 | $17.99

NOVELS

HELLBOY: EMERALD HELL
By Tom Piccirilli
ISBN 978-1-59582-141-6 | $12.99

HELLBOY: THE ALL-SEEING EYE
By Mark Morris
ISBN 978-1-59582-141-6 | $12.99

HELLBOY: THE FIRE WOLVES
By Tim Lebbon
ISBN 978-1-59582-204-8 | $12.99

HELLBOY: THE ICE WOLVES
By Mark Chadbourn
ISBN 978-1-59582-205-5 | $12.99

SHORT STORIES

Illustrated by Mike Mignola

HELLBOY: ODD JOBS
By Poppy Z. Brite, Greg Rucka, and others
ISBN 978-1-56971-440-9 | $14.99

HELLBOY: ODDER JOBS
By Frank Darabont, Guillermo del Toro, and others
ISBN 978-1-59307-226-1 | $14.99

HELLBOY: ODDEST JOBS
By Joe R. Lansdale, China Miéville, and others
ISBN 978-1-59307-944-4 | $14.99

DARK HORSE BOOKS

AVAILABLE AT YOUR LOCAL COMICS SHOP OR BOOKSTORE! • To find a comics shop in your area, call 1-888-266-4226.
For more information or to order direct visit DarkHorse.com or call 1-800-862-0052 Mon.–Fri. 9 AM to 5 PM Pacific Time.
Prices and availability subject to change without notice.

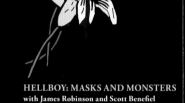